WHITNEY HOUSTON

Contents

WHITNEY HOUSTON

THE UNAUTHORIZED BIOGRAPHY

James Robert Parish

AURUM PRESS

First published in Great Britain 2003 by Aurum Press Ltd
25 Bedford Avenue, London WC1B 3AT

A catalogue record for this book is available from the British Library.

ISBN 1 85410 921 9

1 3 5 7 9 10 8 6 4 2
2003 2005 2007 2006 2004

Designed and typeset by M Rules
Printed and bound in Great Britain
by MPG Books Ltd, Bodmin

For Everyone Who Finds Joy in Singing

Acknowledgments

With appreciation to the following for their kind assistance:

Academy of Motion Picture Arts and Sciences: Margaret Herrick Library, Michael Gene Ankerich, Robert Bentley, Larry Billman (Academy of Dance on Film), Billy Rose Theater Collection of the New York Public Library at Lincoln Center, Lee Borsai, Peter Bowes, Alan Chapman, L. Dannie Chukes, John Cocchi, Stephen Cole, Bobby Cramer, Ernest Cunningham, Bruce Gold, Pierre Guinle, Lynn Kear, Nick Jones (Channel 4 Television), Richard Tyler Jordan, Jane Klain (Museum of Television and Radio—New York), Ann Labbate, Michael Levine, Frederick Levy, Alvin H. Marill, Jim Meyer, Mendham Borough Library (Susan Calantone), Eric Monder, Jay Ogletree, Kathrin Pantzer, Barry Rivadue, David S. Rode, Jonathan Rosenthal, Barry Saltzman, Frank Sanello, Michael Schau, Brad Schreiber, Arleen Schwartz, Nat Segaloff, Tim Sika, Tammie Smalls, André Soares, Les Spindle, Patrick Spreng, J. Randy Taraborrelli, Allan Taylor (copy editor and research associate), and Tom Waldman.

With gratitude to those helpful sources who wish to remain anonymous.

Special thanks to my literary agent, Stuart Bernstein, and to my editor, Karen Ings.

Picture Credits

I

I Will Always Love You

"I married the person I was in love with, the person I was having fun with, the person I could be real with. It wasn't a game. It wasn't based on, 'I need a R&B base, and he needs some pop appeal.' People are so stupid."

WHITNEY HOUSTON, 1999

In 1992, George H. W. Bush was president of the United States. That year, on February 1, Bush and Russian president Boris Yeltsin issued joint statements officially concluding the Cold War. Two months later, in Los Angeles, an all-white jury acquitted four policemen alleged to have savagely beaten African-American Rodney King. The court's decision led to a riot in the City of Angels in which more than fifty people were killed, 2,000 wounded, and over 7,000 arrested.

It was also the year Al Pacino (*Scent of a Woman*) and Emma Thompson (*Howards End*) won Oscars for their acting. *Shiloh* by Phyllis Reynolds Naylor was a best-selling novel, and some of the most popular recordings of that year included "Baby-Baby-Baby" sung by TLC, "Under the Bridge" by the Red Hot Chili Peppers, and "Save the Best for Last" performed by Vanessa Williams.

In mid-1992, on Saturday, July 18, twenty-five-year-old Sharon Belden of Florida would be crowned Miss World U.S.A., Helen Windsor (offspring of the British Duke of Kent) would wed Timothy Taylor, and veteran film critic Roger Ebert would walk down the aisle with Chaz Hammel-Smith.

On that same weekend afternoon, in Morris County, north central New

Jersey, another celebrity wedding was about to take place. The location was scenic Mendham Township, west of Morristown, located forty miles and a hour's drive from midtown Manhattan. First settled in the early eighteenth century, the town had a population of under 5,000 and boasted such historic sites as the First Presbyterian Church (built in 1860) on Hilltop Road and the Iron Horse Inn (in continuous operation since 1742) on Main Street. While some people in the U.S. might be seriously affected by the country's $4.25 per hour minimum wage, the cost of a gallon of milk ($2.14), a loaf of bread ($0.75), a dozen eggs ($1.22), or a gallon of gas ($1.19), such was not the case in semi-rural Mendham, where multi-million-dollar homes on large lots were commonplace.

The focus of the excitement in Mendham was the bride-to-be's 9,000-square-foot home—a circular structure with no square corners amid a lush five-acre spread. (The estate even boasted a special $75,000 canine house especially for its owner's two pet Akita dogs, Lucy and Ethel.) The bride-to-be was beautiful pop diva Whitney Houston, the nearly twenty-nine-year-old singing sensation whose debut movie, *The Bodyguard*, costarring Kevin Costner, was due to be released in the coming months.

By now, the highly successful singer had earned millions of dollars and many industry awards for her hugely best-selling first three albums (*Whitney Houston*, 1985; *Whitney*, 1987; and *I'm Your Baby Tonight*, 1991). As her record label had proudly trumpeted for months before and after her astoundingly successful debut disc (which eventually sold over 13 million copies), she was born into musical royalty: her mother was acclaimed gospel and pop singer Cissy Houston, her cousin was pop legend Dionne Warwick, and her godmother was none other than music's Queen of Soul, Aretha Franklin. The combination of Whitney Houston's pedigree, her gorgeous looks (the five-foot-eight-inch beauty was an ex-fashion model), her classy image, and, especially, her remarkable multi-octave voice with its bell-like clarity and startling volume made her the envy of her peers and the idol of a vast worldwide fan base.

Whitney's soon-to-be husband was handsome, twenty-two-year-old Bobby Brown, a former member of one-time teen-favorite pop group New Edition. Since leaving New Edition in 1986 to go solo, Brown had acquired a heady reputation as the forerunner of New Jack Swing, a musical style which melded hip-hop with rhythm and blues. His breakthrough album was 1988's *Don't Be Cruel*, which produced three major hit singles: the title number, "My Prerogative," and "Every Little Step." The follow-up disc, 1992's *Bobby*, produced the catchy single "Humpin'

Around," which was currently working its way up to number three on the music charts.

Famous (or infamous) for his trademark sexy dance gyrations, Brown's "lewd" onstage choreography had occasionally gotten the singer into legal difficulties with stern-minded local authorities during his concert tours. All the way along his fast track to fame, he'd developed, encouraged, and boasted of his reputation as rock's hard-partying (and, some insisted, substance-abusing) Bad Boy. He had now matured into a fast-spending, high-living dude who could have almost any woman he set his sights on.

On the surface, it seemed that Whitney, known as "the Prom Queen of Soul," and raucous Bobby had far too little in common to make their marriage work. In fact, ever since the couple had become a serious item in 1990–1991, the media had been unrelenting in their shock, disgust, and resistance to the connection between this apparently disparate pair. But they did have at least two things in common: each of these African-American artists had been born in a ghetto—she in Newark, New Jersey, he in Roxbury, Massachusetts—and each had moved remarkably fast from rags to riches within the music industry.

What her devoted fans wanted to know was, what could the stunning Houston possibly want, long-term, with down-and-dirty Brown? After all, he'd already fathered three children (Landon, LaPrincia, and Robert Jr.) by two different women—one of whom was his childhood sweetheart, Kim Ward. He had chosen not to marry either partner. To make matters worse, his third-born (his second child with Ward) had been conceived while he was dating Whitney. His public relations person had attempted to put a positive spin on that sticky situation by rationalizing, "They were only dating casually at that point. Bobby and Kim had a relationship—they [already] had a child together. Bobby and Whitney didn't get serious until after Kim was pregnant."

Some detractors suggested that Houston and Brown were, perhaps, trying to refashion their professional images through this high-profile relationship. It was pointed out that she'd suffered a serious career backlash in the late 1980s when critics and some segments of the public began insisting that she was too "white" a singer: in short, a bland performer of commercially safe pop tunes who had insensitively turned her back on her black roots. In response, her mentor (and Svengali) Clive Davis, the savvy head of her record label Arista, had thereafter redirected her focus towards R&B and hip-hop with her third album (*I'm Your Baby Tonight*). Nevertheless, many in the black community said this belated turnaround was too little, too late. Meanwhile, the white establishment was not particularly captivated by the "new" Whitney. As a result, *I'm Your Baby Tonight* sold "only" 7 million albums. In these circumstances, joining forces with Brown might give Houston a new burst of legitimacy in the African-American community.

Other rumours about Whitney centered on her private life; in particular, on the fact that, although now in her late twenties, she had not yet married. While she had talked to reporters about believing in the traditional institutions of marriage and motherhood ("Getting married and having children. That's old stuff—but it's important to me"), the fact was there was still no Mr. Houston. Regarding this sensitive issue, Whitney explained to *Vanity Fair* magazine, employing her increasingly salty public vernacular: "I just never wanted to be married. I had an independence that didn't include marriage. I always thought men were full of shit. I did. For the most part, they used to talk shit to me all the time. They always had a rap. And I had two brothers, so they all told me what the deal was. They would tell me about the girls they were having and they used to say, 'Do you want to be a whore?' 'Do you want to be a slut?' 'Do you want to get treated like shit?' They made me feel guilty for being a girl."

Nevertheless, Houston had dated movie superstar Eddie Murphy in the late 1980s and early 1990s and was reputed to have had a brief fling with professional football hero Randall Cunningham. However, what truly bothered her non-supporters was her ever-so-special relationship with her female friend Robyn Crawford, two years her senior. Their bond had begun when Whitney was sixteen and the two had been counselors at a New Jersey summer camp. They had quickly become best friends. Houston soon began referring to the striking, athletic Crawford—she of the broad shoulders and mannish garb—as "the sister I never had." Because their bond was so strong, persistent, and exclusive, what had been mere gossip among the camp set and later at Whitney's high school became the province of the tabloids (and thereafter major national publications) once she attained fame as a songstress.

The supermarket newspapers alleged that Whitney "must" be gay and that Crawford "must" be her lover, pointing up that Robyn, an impressive basketball player, had abandoned plans to accept a college sports scholarship in order to become an integral part of Houston's day-to-day life on both a business and personal level. Both women continually denied these allegations. Nevertheless, their constant togetherness—whether sharing an apartment in Woodbridge, New Jersey, in the early 1980s or being soul mates on Whitney's road tours where Robyn was her executive assistant, confidant, and, some said, decision-maker, fueled the ongoing hearsay. Perhaps if the star had chosen to ignore the accusations and let the matter lie, the subject might have eventually lost its appeal for the media. However, Houston was easily baited by reporters, who never lost an opportunity to bring up her association with Crawford and all that it supposedly signified. As would become increasingly common, Whitney would lose her cool and mouth off publicly with a diatribe against her detractors, insisting that she was all woman and, besides, the blankety-blank press should mind their own damn business.

The ongoing speculation about the Houston–Crawford alliance reached a new peak of unpleasant scrutiny when Whitney announced that Robyn would be her maid of honor at her marriage to Bobby Brown. This led naysayers to conjecture wildly about the actual unusual dynamics of this threesome. Although Robyn had recently moved out of Whitney's Mendham Township home into her own place and been replaced on the estate by Bobby, the two of them—so some observers claimed—were still engaged in a fierce battle of wills over Whitney. These spectators scoffed when Brown attempted to cover over the tug-of-war between himself and Crawford by insisting that harmony existed between the two of them: "We're like sister and brother."

Other gossipers insisted that the pending marriage was nothing more than a sham, that Robyn still remained Whitney's true love and that Bobby's role in this unusual ménage was as husband in name only. (Proponents of such rumors didn't seem to care—or know—that Whitney had already become pregnant by Bobby in late 1991, a baby she miscarried in the first months of 1992 while on location for the movie *The Bodyguard*.)

The non-stop rumor mill also pondered what sort of pre-nuptial agreement had been established for this supposedly dubious marriage, since Houston's assets were estimated somewhere between $40 million and $70 million, while Brown only claimed holdings of about $5 million—a sum which was fast evaporating thanks to his lavish lifestyle and lack of careful financial investments.

Some 150 individuals were invited to the 2 P.M. wedding ceremony in Mendham Township, New Jersey, with a total of nearly 800 ("too many,"

insisted Bobby) on the guest list for the gargantuan reception to follow four hours later.

Mindful of the offensive, hysterical media circus that had surrounded such celebrity weddings as that of Sean Penn and Madonna in August 1985, Whitney hoped to avoid a similar situation. As she explained, "I didn't want anybody crashing in—no parachutes out of the sky and stuff like that. So I tried to be kind to the press. We distributed photographs." However, there were forces behind the scenes conspiring against Whitney's plans. For example, according to Kevin Ammons, the then boyfriend of Whitney's publicist Regina Brown, who later wrote *Good Girl, Bad Girl* (1996), "an insider's biography of Whitney Houston," several individuals (including relatives, employees, and friends of the bride) were apparently negotiating with the tabloids in the U.S. and England to sell "exclusive" information and photos of the Houston–Brown marriage, including an actual wedding invitation and minute details of the star-studded ceremony.

For her big day, Whitney, who already had an established entourage of bodyguards to protect her from too much contact with overenthusiastic fans or from the number of stalkers pursuing her, had beefed up her security force to cope with the logistics of so many guests and onlookers descending on her New Jersey estate.

Said one of Whitney's neighbors, who lived across the street in the Oak Knoll development: "It's a bit of a zoo. We're trying to have our own party here and my husband had trouble getting back into the neighborhood. Guards are stopping everybody. They want to know who you are and where you're going." Another neighbor, who resided eight doors away from Whitney's estate, noted that a computer technician had trouble reaching them that day due to the snarled-up traffic: "He said he was stopped at eight different checkpoints."

In actuality, as acknowledged by local deputy mayor Brian Phelan, nearly all of Mendham Township's fifteen police officers were tied up for the blessed event. Nevertheless, he insisted it was "well worth the effort." Phelan reasoned, "This wedding has been the talk of the town for more than a week, and it's important that Mendham put its best foot forward. As for me, I'm just looking forward to meeting Whitney and her family."

In typical fashion for major celebrity nuptials, TV news teams hovered in noisy helicopters over the site, intent on filming the comings and goings of the famous guests. Down on terra firma, the invitees included Mayor Christine Palmer and other Mendham Township dignitaries, as well as ten families from the neighborhood. Most of the VIP guests arrived in limousines with their dark-tinted windows shut, preventing the crowds of onlookers from catching a glimpse of those inside.

Later, it was recorded that attendees that day included showbusiness figures such as Gloria Estefan, Keenen Ivory Wayans, Jackee, Jasmine Guy, Malcolm-Jamal Warner, Dionne Warwick, Patti LaBelle, Blair Underwood, Charles Dutton, Gladys Knight, Valerie Simpson, Phylicia Rashad, Downtown Julie Brown, Aretha Franklin, Heavy D, Dick Clark, Queen Latifah, Natalie Cole, and Leslie Uggams; as well as entrepreneur Donald Trump, former models/actresses Lauren Hutton and Phoebe Cates, and celebrity observer Robin Leach. Guests were requested to forgo buying wedding gifts and instead encouraged to donate to a favorite charity, or, in particular, to the Whitney Houston Foundation for Children, Inc.; as a result, the foundation earned approximately $500,000.

Three elaborate wedding tents had been erected on the estate grounds, including the lavish bridal tent (decorated in Whitney's favorite color, lavender), and the tennis courts were covered by wood flooring for the dancing. A strict believer in privacy, Whitney had planned that the guests for the ceremony and the reception would be ushered directly to the tents, rather than having them parade through the house. However, the weekend was cloudy with intermittent showers, and a few invitees momentarily circumvented the security squad and wandered into Whitney's mansion— muddy shoes and all—which did not sit well with the very in-charge bride-to-be.

Seemingly no expense was spared for the $750,000 festivities (a sum which did not include the cost of Whitney's ten-karat-diamond engagement ring, nor the couple's romantic honeymoon aboard a yacht in the Mediterranean). The future Mrs. Bobby Brown wore a full-length gown of French Lyon lace with iridescent beads, white pearls, and sequins—the lace alone cost more than $4,000. The $40,000 dress was designed by Mark Bouwer, with Diana Johnson of East Orange making thirty-two Houston family wedding dresses. The groom wore a white tuxedo with a silver jewel at the neck. The bridesmaids, including matron of honor Cissy Houston and maid of honor Robyn Crawford, wore lilac-colored gowns.

Inside the main house, as the bridal party prepared for the big occasion, anticipation, excitement, and tension mounted. With all the past and current speculation over Whitney's lifestyle and her relationship to Bobby, one can scarcely imagine the scope of what Whitney, Bobby, and Robyn were mulling over as they dressed in their finery for the imminent ceremony.

What of the bride's family? On hand were her two brothers: Gary (Cissy Houston's eldest child, a product of her first marriage) and Michael (Cissy's first child with her second husband, John Houston). Gary, who had never succeeded in a solo singing career, was a background singer on Whitney's tours and soon to be in the throes of a divorce, while Michael, married to Donna (also on Houston's staff payroll), served as his sister's assistant road manager.

As for Whitney's parents, today was an especially stressful occasion for both of them, and they must have felt the strain of putting on a happy public face for the celebrity gathering. On the one hand, the two of them were united in their strong misgivings about their daughter (whom they usually called by the pet name Nippy) marrying the highly controversial, seemingly uncontrollable Bobby, who already had sired three kids out of wedlock. It was also rumored that their biggest consolation about the nuptials would be that they should serve to end the ongoing media speculation about Whitney's special relationship with Robyn. It was thought that Cissy and John strongly disliked Crawford, in part because of the onslaught of innuendoes her association with their daughter had aroused. Whitney's parents also resented Robyn's powerful influence over their girl's professional and personal life, which left them stranded in secondary positions.

Adding fuel to the fires of contention—and every aspect of Whitney's life seemed increasingly to be filled with complexity, ambiguity, and controversy—John and Cissy Houston were now divorced, having separated in 1977. Although they had lived apart in New Jersey, they had publicly kept a united front and were seen together frequently as a couple acc-ompanying their famous daughter at industry award shows. It was said that strong-willed Cissy harbored the belief that one day she and John, a former truck driver, municipal council employee, and, more recently, full-time talent manager, would have a genuine reconciliation. That hope had been shattered in 1991, when Cissy and the rest of her family had discovered that he was involved romantically with Whitney's maid, Barbara "Peggy" Griffith. The latter was a young woman from Trinidad who had a daughter by a prior relationship. In late 1991, after finally divorcing Cissy, John and the forty-eight-years-younger Peggy had married in Fort Lee, New Jersey. None of John's immediate family attended the small ceremony. Thereafter, John was on sketchy terms with Cissy and their three children. Today, for Nippy's wedding, John and Cissy had pasted on masks of congeniality which might hoodwink some onlookers, but certainly would not fool Whitney or her siblings.

Shortly after 2 P.M., Whitney slipped into her lavish wedding gown. No matter how jittery she may have felt inside or what disparate thoughts were racing through her mind, she seemed, according to one observer, "very calm. The atmosphere in her room was serene." Nevertheless, Houston admitted later that during the entire occasion she "was a nervous wreck," and it was no secret that she cried during the ceremony. After the bridal procession convened, the unharmonious group headed out of the house to the ornate wedding tent, which encompassed a marble and wood gazebo. The lilac-and-white color scheme prevailed everywhere.

The Reverend Marvin Winans had been chosen by Whitney to conduct the ceremony. He was a Baptist minister from Detroit, Michigan, and part of the famed family of gospel singers that included siblings CeCe and BeBe Winans, both good friends of Whitney's. It was this pastor who counseled the couple on their pending marriage. The spiritual tutelage led Houston to alert other couples about the pathway to matrimony: "If you are thinking about getting married, get counseling, because sometimes your love may not be strong enough, but God's love covers it all. I'm a witness." While the statement illustrates Whitney's spiritual fiber, it certainly suggests that her path to the altar had its shares of bumpy obstacles.

As the radiant bride walked down the aisle, a string orchestra played "The Wedding March." Bobby's eldest child, Landon, who had been living in Atlanta, Georgia, with the singer and Bobby's construction-worker father (now separated from the entertainer's school-teacher mother), acted as ring bearer. Bobby's older brother, Tommy, his professional manager, was best man. During the ceremony, Stevie Wonder and Luther Vandross sang for the audience. Said one of the celebrity guests, Charles S. Dutton of TV sitcom *Roc*, "It was great to see how euphoric Whitney was." After exchanging platinum wedding rings and saying their "I do's," the newly-married couple kissed passionately.

The menu for the expensive reception included cold peach soup, exotic fruits, roast beef and Chateaubriand, assorted gourmet side dishes, and a ten-foot-tall wedding cake. To prepare and serve the feast for the huge gathering required the use of twenty stoves and 250 waiters. Napkins, tablecloths, flowers, and so forth were all precisely coordinated to match the lilac-and-white color scheme, even down to the frosting of the towering cake. The carpeted and air-conditioned tent housing the celebration measured 100 by 150 feet.

After hours of wining, dining, toasting, dancing, and well-wishing, the night's merriment was capped by Whitney leading a conga line as she sang "I Want to Thank You, Heavenly Father." When it came time for the guests to depart, each was handed a gift bag. It contained a bottle of champagne, a slice of wedding cake, and a note that read, "Place this cake under your pillow and dream of your own true love."

The playful, festive event seemed, to the unsuspecting, to be truly a dream wedding. However, with so much heavy-duty drama—and unspoken agendas—taking place between key members of the wedding party, it was, to say the least, an emotionally charged occasion. These underlying currents were not lost on some onlookers. For instance, Jamie Foster Brown, publisher of *Sister 2 Sister* magazine and a longtime friend of (but no relation to) Bobby Brown, would say later, "There were bets being made at the wedding as to how long this would last."

One of the people who sighed with great relief when the elaborate celebration came to an end was fifty-eight-year-old Cissy Houston. A very realistic lady who possessed a strong belief in her self-worth and her overall talents as a singer (especially compared to her daughter, who had achieved the showbusiness success she once craved), Cissy would admit in her 1998 autobiography that Whitney's wedding had been a trial for her. "Once again, I would have to see John in public and pretend everything was all right. More important, I wasn't happy about Nippy's wedding. I wasn't concerned so much with who Whitney was marrying as that Whitney was marrying at all. She was . . . certainly old enough to take a husband. But I knew once she was married, I would see her less and less." Such statements only scratched the surface of the complicated professional rivalry and personal relationship between mother and daughter.

As for thirtysomething Robyn Crawford, the third primary member of the wedding triumvirate, it could only be a vast understatement to describe Whitney's special day as highly traumatic for her. Knowing that every attendee was probably speculating on her actual relationship to the bride and how she would fit into the picture with the newlyweds, it must have been a harrowing personal appearance for her. Having already been forced to move out now that Bobby was installed as the new "master" of the house, she must have been well aware that this transition would impinge on every aspect of her own relationship with Whitney.

Already, Crawford had publicly paved the way for these drastic changes in her life in an ambiguously phrased statement to a major magazine: "None of us around her, not her mother nor her father could be to her what a husband can be. In a marriage it seems to me that it is always the woman who has to do more—commit herself more, devote herself more, always be there. I think Whitney is going to be that kind of wife. She's very traditional and Bible-written. And if that means changing anything about her, I think it will mean that she's going to take less shit. She's not high-handed or temperamental or arrogant, but although she walks softly, she carries an invisible stick. If you back her up against a wall, you'll be sorry. In the nicest way, she'll make you feel . . . [small]."

Certainly, as the wedding celebration wore on, Crawford must have been focusing on all the overt and subtle ways that this legal change in Whitney's circumstances would alter her own personal rapport with Whitney, as well as her full-time job as second-in-command in her pal's various industries. As an apparent gesture to appease Crawford, super-rich Whitney arranged to surprise her best friend that special day with an extravagant gift—an expensive black Porsche tied up in a red ribbon. One can only wonder at how Robyn must have felt at receiving this "consolation" prize. Should she regard it as a distraction, or as a payoff, or what?

Yet another individual with a view on this purportedly blissful occasion was twenty-three-year-old Kim Ward, back in Massachusetts. When the media inquired about her reaction to the marriage, the perplexed mother of two of Bobby's children (LaPrincia, age two, and Bobby Jr., age seven months) said, "I'm not ready to talk about it."

Once the wedding festivities were behind them, the newlyweds soon flew off to Europe via Concorde. There, courtesy of Whitney's record label Arista, they were to enjoy a ten-day Mediterranean honeymoon cruise aboard a 140-foot yacht, a craft which boasted a crew of nine, along with a TV, VCR, stereo, and Jacuzzi. To make sure that the Queen of Music and her Prince Consort would not be lonely, the newly-joined couple brought along a few friends to enjoy the luxurious holiday and to amuse their hosts.

By the time Whitney and Bobby returned from their honeymoon at the end of August 1992 and settled into domesticity at her lavish New Jersey quarters, the bride had some big news, which was soon leaked to the press. She was pregnant. On March 4, 1993, a little less than eight months after she became Mrs. Brown, she would become the mother of a baby girl.

So began the unusual union of Whitney and her main man Bobby. Like so much in her intriguing life, their relationship would be built on extremely complex dynamics, crammed full of incongruities, and overlaid with emotional highs and lows. Over the next decade, it would propel Whitney Houston on an incredible roller-coaster ride through personal and professional heaven and hell.

2

From Humble Beginnings

"I am a person who believes in what I am doing, whether in church or in secular music. It's all about the love you feel inside."

CISSY HOUSTON, 1998

Forty years before Whitney Houston's birth in 1963, her maternal grandfather, Nitch Drinkard, had sorrowfully left the small Georgia town of Hilton in Early County. It was certainly not by choice; rather it was dire necessity that forced him to abandon rural life. He had fought hard against making the traumatic relocation, but there were excellent reasons for his migration northward.

In the 1920s—long before Civil Rights legislation and changing attitudes in the U.S. diminished racial discrimination to a certain extent—it was, at best, horrendous for an African American to exist in many parts of the South. It was even more fraught with physical and emotional dangers to be one of those rare land-owning Blacks, when it was so easy to arouse the jealousy of resentful whites. Twenty-seven-year-old Nitch was a third-generation farmer who, by dint of hellish labor and beating the odds stacked against him by unfriendly rivals and unpredictable weather, was scraping by growing cotton on his small spread. Unlike most of the Blacks in this part of the South at the time, he and his family owned their plot of land; they were not tenant farmers.

Through hard times (economic depressions) and worse times (race riots; lynchings; the plundering of black folks' property), Nitch had survived. On a visit to relatives near Pensacola, Florida, he had met and married the decade-younger, shy Delia Mae McCaskill, whom he brought back to share his hardscrabble existence in Hilton. By late 1922, the diligent couple, who were fervently religious and active participants at their local church, had three children: William (born 1918), Lee (1920), and Marie ("Reebie") (1922).

Then, disaster befell the Drinkards. County officials repossessed the family's property for delinquent taxes, which his parents had ignored, or forgotten to tell Nitch about, when they first began receiving legal notifications. Now, with sizable financial penalties attached, there was no way that Nitch could pay the overdue amount. This dutiful son was overwhelmed with tremendous guilt at not being able to do right by his family. It plunged him into a great depression at the idea of losing the precious land he and his forbears had fought so hard to hang on to for all these years.

Nonetheless, in the winter of 1923, a shame-filled Nitch resolved to leave Early County. Like so many Blacks before him, he chose to head north, where it was said that there were greater opportunities for African Americans to make a living and racial discrimination was less prevalent. He already had relatives and friends in Newark, New Jersey, so he decided to make that his destination. Joined by his parents, wife, and three children, Nitch Drinkard boarded a train and traveled north. They were a sad lot, these impoverished railroad passengers, dejected by their bad luck and fearful of the uncertain future that lay ahead of them in a strange land.

The port city of Newark on the banks of the Passaic River had been founded in 1666 by forty Puritan families who had fled Connecticut to live a religious life as they so chose. By the end of the seventeenth century, the settlement had grown, its population swollen with other refugees from Connecticut, and had become celebrated for its fine apple cider. Within another hundred years, the spiritual community had transformed into a secular manufacturing site, specializing in the production of hats and shoes. By the 1830s, with the building of the Morris Canal and the expansion of the railroads, Newark was developing rapidly into a major industrialized city, especially noted for the making of jewelry, leather goods, and carriages. In the 1840s, several breweries arose in the metropolis, joining financial services and insurance firms as key components of the city's growing economy; the breweries were to disappear in the 1980s.

By the 1920s, burgeoning Newark, in Essex County, was a densely populated city—in fact, the biggest in the state. But in spite of its economic virtues and the vistas of its imposing civic buildings, the metropolis already suffered from urban blight and an increasing sense of apathy among its citizens in the face of fast-declining living conditions. As if to distract from the mushrooming economic disparity between its social classes, the city harbored a horde of clubs serving bootlegged booze. In addition, Newark boasted over sixty theaters catering to tastes for drama, vaudeville, and burlesque, as well as several movie theaters and quite a few bawdy houses.

By now, Blacks comprised about 10 percent of Newark's population and, although their treatment was far better than in the South of the day, this ethnic minority was still discriminated against in terms of available work, decent living quarters, and fair treatment from the white majority. This was the urban jungle that Nitch and his family reached in February 1923 when they disembarked at the railroad station. They quickly realized they had *not* reached the "promised" land, but there was no turning back.

Newark had been settled centuries earlier, around the spot that would become the intersection of Market and Broad Streets. It was not far from there that Drinkard and his clan moved into a dilapidated three-story tenement building. It was located at 199 Court Street (at the corner of Broome Street) in the midst of the city's ramshackle black ghetto, which had been inhabited earlier by waves of German and Jewish immigrants. If a bewildered Nitch could find no solace in Newark's noisy environment, nor the rundown home where he and his family shared outdoor plumbing facilities on the back porch, nor in his manual labor at the foundry of the Singer sewing-machine factory, at least St. Luke's AME Church was nearby, on Charlton Street. There he and his family found a sanctuary, and they attended services with great dedication and fervor.

Between 1924 and 1933, Nitch and Delia had five more children, beginning with Hansom ("Hank") in 1924 and ending with Emily ("Cissy") in 1933. On the September day the latter was born, Nitch's beloved mother passed away.

As his offspring grew up in the city's infamous Third Ward, the highly spiritual, very strict Nitch tried to keep a tight rein over his children, insisting that they stay far away from the nearby Barbary Coast district, which was filled with speakeasies, theaters, brothels, and gangsters' headquarters. As if to compensate for the bewildering turns of fate that had brought him and his loved ones to Newark, Drinkard became even more immersed in religion. When not at St. Luke's communing with God and finding great emotional release singing out in his booming voice, he was at home praying. As Cissy would later describe her father: "He was not a complaining man. He did everything through prayer. He prayed all the time . . . He knew what it was to pray without ceasing. He praised God all the time; for everything—the good and the bad. My father was really a minister without being ordained."

Although Nitch was a very godly man, he was not afraid to be outspoken, as when he talked back to his hard-nosed foundry superiors over their callous treatment of his fellow black workers. Nitch, who later left the sweltering foundry to open a small neighborhood grocery store (which eventually failed), also had a tough time with his eldest son. William was just full of himself and was in constant conflict with his parents. The reckless teenager was drawn to gambling and other aspects of the sporting life and inevitably got into trouble with the law. By the time the police came looking for him at the Drinkards' modest home, the boy had run off.

The Drinkards struggled to bring up their remaining seven children during the Great Depression. With Nitch usually earning no more than eighteen dollars a week—especially when there were no jobs to be had and he had to shamefully accept welfare relief—sometimes the family meal consisted only of milk and corn bread. But somehow they endured and, in the process, remained steadfast in their religious faith. Despite the already overcrowded household, Delia became pregnant twice more after Emily's birth. Both times she was pregnant with twins and each time she lost them just after their birth.

By 1938, Delia's constitution was failing badly. It was little wonder, considering the physical and emotional strain of her recent difficult pregnancies and the pressure of caring for and feeding a large household, and on top of all this she was coping with other severe stresses. There was the sudden reappearance of her unfeeling mother (who had abandoned her years before but had recently moved to Newark, close to the Drinkards) and the nagging concerns about her vanished son William. That same year, when Cissy was nearly five years old, her mother, then only in her mid-thirties, suffered a stroke. As a result, Nitch, engaged in back-breaking manual labor repairing Newark city streets, had to assume more of the burden of raising his children. To make matters even worse, a fire swept through the tenement building where the Drinkards lived. They had to abandon their destroyed home to relocate to 38 Hillside Place, with financial assistance from a city welfare agency.

On the night of the devastating fire, as the Drinkards stood aghast in the street watching their life literally go up in smoke, they were comforted by two missionaries from the Church of God in Christ. The duo (Elder Wyatt and Mother Gillespie) had recently moved into this section of town to open a storefront place of worship. A friendship grew between Nitch and the two proselytizers. Before long, the godly Mr. Drinkard agreed to Elder Wyatt's request that the seven children attend his newly formed Sunday school before they went to worship at St Luke's.

Part of the Sunday-school experience at the storefront sanctuary was a religious revival meeting, and the rest of the service was filled with African-American worship music. The Drinkard children quickly became captivated by singing, especially when they discovered during an impromptu home singsong that they could create near perfect harmony together. When their father heard the glorious sounds coming forth from his youngsters, he was transfixed. Soon, besides singing at the Church of God in Christ, the Drinkard brood was harmonizing at St Luke's, as well as often performing at home for visiting relatives and family friends. Nitch demanded that his children practice constantly to perfect their God-given talents.

Since William had vanished, Lee and Reebie were the eldest children in the household and they dutifully became the leaders of the singing group. However, self-willed Cissy, not yet six years old, was not enthralled with the new regimen in her young life: "I wanted to keep playing like a normal kid—hopscotch . . . jump rope. Eventually, when threatened with corporal punishment, I relented and joined my brother and sisters." As the future gospel star admitted later, "The discipline of rehearsing, learning new songs was good for me. . . . I might have pouted and stuck my lip out a mile long, but I couldn't deny my daddy anything. Not when I saw how happy our singing made him."

As Nitch watched his youngsters practice and perform—with different members taking turns to assume lead vocals—a dream began to form in which he envisioned his progeny becoming the renowned Drinkard Singers. Not only would his personal flock spread the word of God, but they would also be a sterling example to others in the neighborhood and elsewhere of what talent and hard work could achieve. Pretty soon, the core Drinkard Quartet was established, made up of Anne, Larry, Nicky, and Cissy, with Reebie (and sometimes Lee) serving as their coaches.

As the children began to form into a defined singing group, Delia Drinkard suffered a second, severe stroke, which left her with a limp left arm and leg. Nevertheless, she valiantly continued doing household chores, and those she could no longer perform she taught her elder youngsters how to accomplish. So, between attending school, doing the daily chores, and pursuing their religious education, the Drinkard offspring had a busy schedule. And, of course, there was church attendance on Sundays at the Mercer Street storefront and, later in the morning, at St. Luke's. That was not the end of the routine, however, for often on Sundays the Drinkard Quartet would perform at other churches and then, if not preoccupied with schoolwork, they would attend evening services.

Over the next few years, the Drinkards perfected their ensemble singing and became noted in the neighborhood and surrounding areas for their fervent harmonizing on gospel songs. Meanwhile, Cissy's oldest sister, Lee, fell in love with Mansel Warrick Jr., the son of the reverend at St. Luke's. In January 1940, the young couple married and that December they became parents of a baby girl, Dionne, followed in 1942 by another daughter, Dee Dee.

In April 1942, as America was engulfed in World War II, Delia Drinkard suffered a cerebral hemorrhage and died, at the age of thirty-nine. Being the youngest, Cissy was especially inconsolable over her mother's death. She earnestly prayed to God to bring her beloved parent back to life, promising to become a good little girl who *always* obeyed, *always* rehearsed, *always* was religiously devout. But her prayers did not bring about the desired miracle, and soon a dejected Cissy turned to her older sisters, Lee and Reebie, for maternal comfort and guidance.

As for grief-stricken Nitch, then forty-six, he did his best to supervise his children who still remained at home, but the effort strained all his resources and those of his kin. As Cissy has recalled, "If it wasn't for singing, I don't know what would have happened to us. Singing, rehearsing, kept us together. We were never lonely for somebody to play with, that's what saved me. We were still a singing quartet at that time. Later on, when Nicky started playing piano, we graduated to gospel." Before long, the enlarged group was performing on local radio gospel programs. During this period, Lee became the performers' manager, and, after joining a Quartet Association, they traveled to assorted member churches to sing God's words. Their avocation even led to the Drinkards visiting the resort town of Atlantic City, where the Association's yearly convention was held.

In 1948, when Cissy was nearly fifteen, Mr. Drinkard, now in his mid-fifties, became romantically involved with Viola Jewel, a woman ten years his junior. When he married Viola, adolescent Cissy felt even more abandoned. This feeling was accentuated when, in the same period, her sister Reebie wed her longtime boyfriend. Feeling very much adrift, Cissy became involved in her first serious romantic relationship, something she kept hidden from her strict father and her conservative older siblings.

After Nitch and Viola were married, it became apparent that the coolness between Viola and her stepchildren would never disappear. As a result, Mr. Drinkard moved away from Hillside Place to Viola's home on Livingston Street, a distance of several blocks. Intent on not abandoning his youngest-born, he insisted that Cissy must come to live with them. She did so reluctantly.

Despite, or because of, the fractured family's living arrangements, the Thursday-night gospel rehearsals became more important for each of the Drinkard offspring. Thanks to helpful counseling from the reverend at church, Cissy soon made an emotional turnabout. She was now able to accept her father's new domestic situation and being made to live with Nitch and Viola. The adjustment brought her new emotional peace and fresh religious fervor. Years later, looking back, Cissy would describe her feelings: "Now that I knew what and *Who* I was singing about, I enjoyed singing. There was a wonderful feeling when I sang now . . . I couldn't wait to take my solo, close my eyes and praise Him. . . . Everything was different; the words meant something to me, meant something personal to me now."

Before too long, Cissy graduated from high school. Afterwards, she found a day job (at a drycleaners, where her job was to remove the paper from hangers), while continuing with her gospel rehearsals and performing in the evenings and on weekends. Through their on-again, off-again professional manager, Ronnie Williams, the Drinkards increased their bookings on the gospel concert circuit. Often they were performing with such well-known artists as the Davis Sisters and the Dixie Hummingbirds. Through such appearances, the Drinkards came to the attention of Joe Bostic, a famous gospel disc jockey in the New York City area, who predicted they could have a great professional career encompassing recordings, radio and TV appearances, and concert tours. However, because the young performers were so attuned to performing only for the glory of God, they thought it sacrilegious to abandon their ministry by turning to crass commercial assignments. Meanwhile, in 1950, the Drinkards encountered twelve-year-old Judy Clay, a girl from the South who was staying with a New York relative and performing in church choirs. When Lee Warrick learned that Judy was being molested by a male relative, she immediately removed the youngster from that unsavory environment and adopted her into her own home. Possessing a fine singing voice, Judy became an active member of the Drinkard Singers.

Blossoming Cissy occasionally strayed from the spiritual into the secular world to experience the excitement of attending a local club gig or a theater offering. However, her strong religious background and her father's (and Lee's) constant supervision usually kept the young woman reined in tight.

In October 1951, encouraged by Joe Bostic, the Drinkards performed at Carnegie Hall in a gospel festival headlined by the noted Mahalia Jackson. The evening was a great success, but the next day Cissy and her siblings were back at their day jobs. In May 1952, Nitch, who was already suffering from a progressive ulcer condition, was operated on for cancer. It was discovered the disease had spread throughout his lungs. He died soon afterwards.

After this new loss, Cissy began spending more time with her sister Annie and her brothers. Together they partied at nearby clubs in the evenings after group rehearsals, but she never stayed out long enough to miss work the following morning. (Already she had found a new day job at the RCA factory in Harrison, New Jersey, where she worked on the production line assembling cathode-ray tubes for TVs.) By now, Reverend Warrick had left St. Luke's and the Drinkards felt uncomfortable in that congregation without his familiar leadership. They transferred their allegiance across town to Newark's New Hope Baptist Church on Sussex Avenue. As at St. Luke's, Cissy became heavily involved in directing the church's choirs, even establishing a special group for young adults.

Now in her early twenties, Cissy felt it was time to marry. Through a cousin she met a construction worker named Freddy Garland and they dated for several months. When he proposed matrimony, she eventually accepted. She reasoned, "I thought marriage would cure my restlessness, that unsettled feeling I had." The couple were united at a big ceremony held at New Hope Baptist Church and settled into domesticity in their Newark home. Years later, Cissy would remember: "Freddy was a good provider and treated me wonderfully. . . . He respected me, he didn't beat me . . ." However, Cissy soon realized she didn't love Freddy romantically. Her friends encouraged her to remain with this good man; her sisters insisted it would be wrong to abandon her marriage vows. Thus persuaded, the bride remained with her groom for two years. Then, in January 1957, she left him. Financially she could support herself, because she'd kept her RCA factory job. However, now she did not have only herself to worry about, for she was pregnant.

Throughout all the recent changes in their lives, the Drinkards continued to perform. In the summer of 1957, Joe Bostic booked them into the Newport Jazz Festival on the same program with Mahalia Jackson and Clara Ward. It was an innovation for gospel to be presented to white audiences on such a large scale. The event proved to be a huge success.

On October 12, 1957, Cissy gave birth to a baby boy, and she named him Gary. By the next year, the Drinkard Sisters had recorded an album (*Make a Joyful Noise*) of gospel songs for RCA Victor. The album made a great impression on another label mate: Elvis Presley. He wanted the Drinkards to record and tour with him, but Lee refused to let the group accept a purely secular offer.

Meanwhile, so that she could keep her day job, Cissy was forced to board baby Gary out during the working week. It was a painful but practical decision that the young mother had to make. During this challenging period, when Cissy could have used the comfort of friends in whom to confide, she stayed aloof and remained emotionally contained within herself. She feared that her private problems would somehow be circulated within the community and cause her shame. Furthermore, because of her responsibilities directing choirs at New Hope Baptist Church, she believed that she must remain in the role of teacher/advisor and not friend/confider to fellow church members.

In the spring of 1958, the Drinkard Singers made their TV debut on a local gospel show airing from Newark's Symphony Hall. Watching one of these Saturday-morning sessions, a member of the home viewership was quite smitten by the youngest member of the group. He asked a musician pal to introduce him to the attractive, fervent young singer. The enthusiastic man with a penchant for gospel performances and performers was John Russell Houston.

At the time, John was thirty-seven—thirteen years older than Cissy. He was born in September 1920 in the First Ward section of Newark. His father (a black man whose own father was part Lenni Lanape Native American) was an electrical engineer and his mother, who had earned a master's degree, was a Manhattan school teacher. John was brought up a Catholic, educated at Seton Hall Prep in West Orange, New Jersey, and later served in the military, seeing armed service in Europe during World War II. Thereafter, he married Elsie Hamilton. They had a child (John Russell Hamilton III), but the couple had later divorced.

After being discharged from wartime duty, John had taken a job at Newark City Hall. However, this appointment did not last long, as he found the red tape and paperwork too bothersome. While waiting for the right job to turn up, he became a taxi driver at night and sometimes drove eighteen-wheel trucks on the run from New Jersey to Chicago and back to collect truckloads of beef from the Windy City.

Despite the warnings of her sisters that John was too much older than her and that he was not settled properly into a steady livelihood, Cissy was drawn to this tall, handsome, light-skinned man who had such a passion for gospel music. What probably bonded the couple most of all was that John took a liking to little Gary. Taking this as the sign she needed, strong-willed Cissy ignored the advice of her sisters and friends. On May 24, 1959, the couple were married in a small local ceremony, and they moved into an apartment on the top level of a three-story tenement on Newark's Eighth Street. Cissy continued to work at the RCA assembly plant, while John drove a cab at night. By the following year, the new Mrs. Houston was pregnant, and, in August 1961, their son Michael was born. Before long, both Gary and Michael were being boarded out during the week so their parents could be free to support the household.

As time wore on, John, a lapsed Catholic, became increasingly immersed in gospel music and the world of its high-charged performers. Repeatedly he suggested to the Drinkards that he could expand their circuit of venues to include more prestigious and glamorous sites, but Lee, still in charge of the group, refused his requests.

If that avenue was shut to John, another professional opportunity opened up for him. Lee's children, Dionne and Dee Dee, now young adults, had formed a group called the Gospelaires. The group consisted of Dionne, Dee Dee and three other young women from the Young People's Choir at New Hope Baptist. They permitted Houston to shepherd them to their church and gospel concert engagements.

Later, through a chance meeting with a trumpet-player backstage at the Apollo Theater, John maneuvered the Gospelaires into a recording session to provide background vocals. It quickly led to other such secular assignments and, before long, the Gospelaires were in constant demand for studio sessions in New York City. John was the one who would escort the five girls into New York to these recording jobs, where the group spent long evenings in front of the studio microphones. Houston thrived on the atmosphere and made friends with the producers, engineers, and label big shots with whom he negotiated.

As time progressed and Dionne and the others become increasingly entrenched in the world of popular music, John begged Cissy to spread her singing wings into this new forum. With her deeply ingrained religious background, she felt it was the wrong path for her to follow. She therefore constantly refused his suggestions, although the work would have brought much-needed extra revenue into their household. Somehow, while Cissy and her sisters, especially Lee, could countenance Dionne and Dee Dee—the new generation—"abandoning" the church by giving up gospel, they felt it was not right for the older generation to do the same. That was just the way it was.

Things changed in mid-September 1961. Dionne had been called upon to contribute background vocals for the Shirelles and was unavailable to join the Gospelaires for a promised session for producer Henry Glover. Deeply concerned about breaking his word and getting a bad reputation in the industry, Houston begged his wife to make an exception. Would she please fill in for Dionne at this important engagement? Realizing the urgency of the situation, Cissy went against her instincts and agreed to go into Manhattan that evening. She left both her youngsters with her new friend Ellen White ("Aunt Bae"), who had moved in across the hall from the Houstons. A mother of four whose husband had abandoned her, Ellen was fast becoming a mainstay in Cissy's life and would remain so well into the future.

At the session at Roulette Records for Ronnie Hawkins and the Hawks, the producer reluctantly allowed Cissy to fill in for the missing Dionne. The work was grueling, lasting until 6 A.M. Cissy returned over three subsequent evenings to complete the task. When it was over, she was most happy to return to her daytime job at the RCA factory and the world of gospel music. Nevertheless, thereafter she was occasionally persuaded by John to attend further recording sessions in Manhattan. She even convinced her sister Annie to go along with her on a few occasions. Annie, however, was even more guilt-ridden over accepting this kind of non-sacred work, not to mention her own need to find last-minute babysitters to care for her children. As a result, Annie soon permanently retired from participating in these secular recording sessions with the more outgoing Cissy.

As might have been anticipated, John continued to ask Cissy to accept more of these New York gigs. Although still conflicted spiritually about such assignments, she was now less resistant about accepting. Soon, Cissy was joining Dionne and Dee Dee in frequent background-vocal sessions for popular recording artists. The trio began working a great deal for the rising songwriting team of Jerry Leiber and Mike Stoller, including doing harmonies at Atlantic Records on cuts by the Drifters.

By now, Dionne, as a solo artist, had graduated from doing demo tapes for the writing team of Burt Bacharach and Hal David to recording her first single, "Don't Make Me Over." Due to a typo, her name was listed on the Scepter single as Dionne Warwick, and she adopted it as her professional surname. Before long, Cissy herself became a fixture as a well-regarded, much-in-demand background singer at Scepter, and she embraced this role with increasing enthusiasm. Part of her change of heart was due to her growing sense of her own self and her need to share her vocal talents with a wider audience. But there was also a practical reason. She and John needed the extra money such assignments provided, for she was pregnant again and was expecting her third child in August 1963.

3

Greatest Love of All

"Let me tell you about my mother, Cissy Houston. She is a very suspicious lady. . . . The day I was born, she thought my father was playing a very cruel joke on her, telling her that she'd just had a beautiful baby girl."

WHITNEY HOUSTON, 1998

When Cissy Houston became pregnant again in December 1962, she quickly made up her mind that this would be her third and final child. Having already had two boys, she hoped that this time it would be a girl.

Meanwhile, there were constant bills to be paid. Cissy continued with her recording sessions, working largely for Atlantic Records in New York City and providing her background-vocal magic for the likes of Solomon Burke, Gene Pitney, Dionne Warwick, and Wilson Pickett. Another lead artist with whom Cissy collaborated was a rising performer from Detroit whose father was a well-known minister there; his sermons could often be heard on the radio. The young woman's name was Aretha Franklin, and, thanks to her fine, soulful vocals, she was quickly gaining a strong reputation within the music business. First at Columbia Records and later in the 1960s at the Atlantic label, Aretha came to rely heavily on the expert harmonizing of the decade-older Cissy.

With so much natural aptitude and experience, Cissy was increasingly being called upon to supply the background harmonies that gave tracks that extra special quality. Having an intuitive ability to lead others, Cissy was now expected to step in automatically and direct the background singers in arrangements she devised—often on the spur of the moment—for these recording sessions.

By early August 1963, Cissy's baby was overdue; she was experiencing false labor pains and was having a difficult time, especially in the intense summer heat. Nevertheless, she continued to commute into New York for recording sessions, although she looked and felt miserable. Tom Dowd, the sound engineer usually at the Atlantic studio console, had by now become good friends with Cissy. He was extremely concerned about her physical condition and asked repeatedly, "Are you okay? Are you all right?" She would grumble polite reassurances, insisting she was "fine, come on, roll the tape." With that, the very pregnant artist would return to her work, carrying on no matter how uncomfortable the deep breathing required for her energetic vocalizing made her feel. Years later, Cissy would recall proudly, "I was singing like a mockingbird when I was pregnant."

Late one night in the second week of August, Cissy awoke from a deep sleep. Her waters had broken—and in fact had spilled over John as she reached over in the bed to shake him awake. Once Cissy was cleaned up, he rushed her to the local Newark hospital. There was a long waiting period before the baby decided to make its first appearance in the world. In the meantime, to distract herself, the mother-to-be half-heartedly watched TV. One program in particular caught her attention. It was *Hazel*, a popular sitcom starring Shirley Booth as a garrulous, bossy maid. What really made an impression on Cissy was the actress playing the genteel wife in the household where Booth's character worked: Whitney Blake. Cissy decided Whitney was an elegant name.

Cissy recalls, "After I did all that pushing and the baby's head was out, they gave me some anesthesia and knocked me out." When she awoke after the delivery, John informed her that their new baby was a girl. At first, Cissy refused to believe that was true, as she was certain she had given birth to a third boy. When the nurse finally brought the infant to her, the new mother was finally convinced that her deepest wish had been granted—she had her girl. The baby was soon named Whitney Elizabeth Houston. (The child's first name derived from the TV actress, while her middle name was that of John's mother.)

With three children in the household, the cramped apartment on Eighth Street was now crowded to bursting point. A cash-strapped John had to borrow $500 from a music-arranger friend to tide them over. Soon the family of five relocated to Newark's Wainwright Street, near Lyons Avenue in what were known as the Baxter Terrace Projects. To make their new (at least to them) small home more complete—and to add a degree of security in this somewhat dangerous neighborhood—the Houstons purchased a German Shepherd dog they called Thor. The children, and especially the baby, quickly came to love their new mascot.

As for Whitney, she soon acquired a nickname, Nippy, that would stick with her forever. It came about courtesy of her dad. According to Cissy's account: "[John] would put her in the carriage, put a blanket over her and wheel her out to the porch. She was so feisty that despite the cold she would kick the blankets off and keep John running back and forth, trying to keep her covered and warm. She reminded him of a comic strip character from the old *Journal-American*, a character that was forever getting into trouble. 'Nippy—seldom right,' the slogan went."

While John was still trying to gain a real foothold in the music business, he drove cabs at night and at weekends he occasionally undertook fast-turnaround delivery hauls in big rigs—anything to help make ends meet. As Cissy was in such demand for sessions in New York City, she had no choice but to abandon hopes of being a full-time mother and return to the recording studios. Since the children, especially infant Whitney, required constant supervision and attention, John agreed that he would remain at home during the day to tend their needs. Thus, long before it became a common trend in America, John Houston became the hands-on parent at the Wainwright Street home, cooking meals, cleaning up the house, and so forth. It was he who generally changed Nippy's diapers, played with her, and kept her out of too much mischief while Cissy was away working.

On the other hand, it was Cissy—far more direct and no-nonsense than her husband—who gained the distinction in their Newark neighborhood as the one to be feared in the Houston family. In particular, this reputation stemmed from an incident that occurred one day when Cissy was around to pick up Gary, her seven-year-old first-born, from school. When she arrived, she found him in the playground being bullied by another youngster. The aggressive youth was taunting the taller Gary, who merely stood there, quietly accepting being bested by his opponent. Observing the one-sided confrontation, an angry Mrs. Houston rushed into the schoolyard. Furiously, she pushed past the boy threatening her son and ordered Gary, "Hit him back." When her child continued to stand there frozen, looking intently at the ground, she shouted at her offspring, "Look at me, look at me!" To emphasize her point, she threatened, "If you don't hit him, you're gonna get whupped twice: once from him and another one from me!" Still Gary refused to heed his agitated mom.

To make her message sink in, she began slapping him hard on the backside. He was so embarrassed by being humiliated in front of his classmates that he turned in anger on his attacker and soon won their skirmish. Word of this playground encounter soon spread throughout the neighborhood. Thereafter, not only was Gary treated with new-found respect by his peers, but Cissy became known as the person in the vicinity not to *ever* upset. Such was the fiber of Mrs. Houston where and when her children were concerned.

By now, after eleven years of working on the cathode-tube production line at the RCA factory, Cissy quit her steady job. It was clear to her what her direction would and must be. The math made it easy: she could earn in two days of music session work what she was being paid for an entire week at the plant. So it was no longer an option to honor her father's memory by avoiding the more frequent job opportunities for doing background singing on secular tunes. Any lingering sense of guilt or shame she had at "abandoning" her gospel background was pushed aside in favor of economics.

With John still unable to break through the barriers of racial discrimination to make a real name for himself in the music industry and earn a solid income in his preferred field, Cissy embraced her role as the family's key provider. As she and her background singers (who now hardly ever included the too-busy Dionne or Dee Dee Warwick) performed on records with Aretha Franklin, Van Morrison, and many others, Cissy put aside her past resistance to singing "everything, from blues to country." At least she could take solace in the fact that "our church background is what made us unique."

Cissy's career decision proved to be a good one in many ways. By 1964, Dionne Warwick was a fully-fledged solo artist who gained international acclaim when she appeared that year in concert in Paris. There, at the Olympia Theater, the legendary Marlene Dietrich introduced her on stage to a responsive audience. With her array of song hits ("Walk on By," "A House Is Not a Home," and later other pop tunes such as "Alfie"), mostly penned by Burt Bacharach and Hal David, the star had by now outgrown any sort of management that John Houston could provide for her. She moved on to more prominent artistic representation. Having lost Dionne as a major client, Houston turned to his wife to fill the gap.

Cissy was fully prepared to take on the task. Already she had formed a fresh nucleus of black female singers (Estelle Brown, Sylvia Shemwell, and Myrna Smith) from her church choir who worked with her steadily. So constant a presence was this talented, hard-working group at the recording studios about Manhattan and elsewhere that they quickly became known as Cissy's Girls. As the months passed, their résumé filled to bursting point with harmony work they'd supplied for the likes of Aretha Franklin, Solomon Burke, and (before his untimely death at the end of 1964 in a shooting mishap) Sam Cooke. Recalling his wife's career transition, John Houston would reflect, "People thought the group would fold when Dionne left, but with Cissy in the act it was a whole different sound. They began to wipe out all the other background singers."

Constantly praised for her professionalism, her inspired input at sessions, and for the beautiful, distinctive sounds she and the girls contributed to the many tracks they recorded, it was easy to understand why Cissy increasingly felt she was destined for great things in the music world. If it ever occurred to her that her extreme loyalty to John as her manager was, perhaps, holding back her career potential, she kept such uneasy thoughts to herself. Instead, she buried herself in work and kept constantly busy. Sometimes she and her group traveled to Memphis, Tennessee or to Muscle Shoals, Alabama to record with soul and rhythm and blues (R&B) artists in the Deep South.

While strong-minded Cissy proved to be flexible as to the type of music she would now sing, she remained firm in other areas. For example, when she and the Girls were hired for concert engagements on the road, she quickly made it a rule that she would *not* travel with other artists on the bill. She'd already had the bad experience of being confined in a car on more than one occasion for long jaunts between gigs and having to endure the other passengers puffing away on marijuana and other such things. With her strict religious beliefs, she recoiled at such activity. Besides, reasoned Cissy, "I couldn't stand the smell. I'm afraid of drugs period. I've never wanted anything or anybody to control me." Because she was so much in demand, Cissy could confidently make "requests" to be given private transportation when she and the Girls were taken on tour.

Far more so than when she had a day job at the not-distant RCA plant, Cissy was away from home a great deal during these years. Whitney was still too young to be fully aware of her mother's lengthy absences, while Gary was rapidly developing his own independence. However, Michael, now three years old and very aware of everything going on around him, felt the day-to-day loss of his mom the most. He would often burst into tears when she announced she was going on the road yet again.

Whatever her pain over "neglecting" her children, the sharply focused Cissy stayed firmly on track. She was motivated not only by her family's monetary needs, but also by the hope that one day the Houstons might reside in a better neighborhood, in a much nicer home. In addition, this veteran performer was propelled onward by the constant compliments she received from fellow artists, record producers, sound engineers, and others, who marveled at her musical acumen, her vocal prowess, and her determination to stay the course in an industry that repeatedly saw talents burn out and disappear from the music scene.

As Cissy became increasingly well known in the recording business, one might expect that she would have found occasion to network with industry executives. However, she was extremely conscious of the still-prevalent racial lines that separated her (and to a lesser extent, her light-skinned, Catholic-born, prep-school-educated husband) from the largely white (and frequently Jewish) contingent of owners, producers, technicians, and songwriters who dominated the music business at the time. In fact, while Cissy could comfortably interact with the white majority at work, she felt uncomfortable—even disloyal—doing so away from the microphones. To ensure her ties to the black community continued unbroken, she made doubly sure never to neglect or treat lightly her activities as choirmaster at New Hope Baptist Church. As in her bumpy childhood, her place of worship remained her rock.

In these years, one of Cissy's favorite artists to work with was Aretha Franklin. Together they recorded such memorable cuts as "Ain't No Way" and "Natural Woman." Explaining their professional rapport and close friendship (which led to Aretha becoming Whitney's godmother), Franklin has explained, "Cissy and myself, we groove together so good because we come from the same places—different churches, but the same place. Whenever we got together, we knew that we were going to sing, that we were going to do some good singing here today, wherever 'here' was."

Sometimes, Aretha and Cissy's Girls would perform together on the road, and on such occasions the joy the participants had in singing together spilled over after a concert. Frequently they would continue to harmonize together after hours at the site where they had just put on an energetic, exhausting show. But these post-show jam sessions were different. Here they could really relax, kick back, and have even more fun singing together.

Meanwhile, in the studio, Aretha, with the background support of Cissy's Girls, turned out a deluge of memorable recordings such as "I Never Loved a Man," "Respect," and "Baby, I Love You," all of which proved to be crowd-pleasers.

Throughout this professionally productive period, Cissy continued to gain respect in the industry. Her distinctive strong, high voice became well known to the listening public, whether it was executing gospel, soul, R&B, or even, heaven help her, pop tracks.

Cissy found herself again questioning her secular activities thanks to Jerry Wexler, a top executive, songwriter, and producer at Atlantic Records. Increasingly fearful that Cissy and her Girls might stray too far from the label's fold, he signed them to a recording contract in 1967. Now known as the Sweet Inspirations, the group made their debut on the Atlantic label with a self-titled album later in the year. It would produce one top-twenty chart hit, "Sweet Inspiration."

In the process of Cissy and her Girls becoming a lead group under contract to a major label, Houston wondered anew if now she really had drifted too far away and too permanently from her deeply ingrained church teachings. But her strong practical side exerted itself and she soon put the crossover situation into perspective: "Making the decision to sing pop was traumatic. . . . As far as I knew, the only right way to sing was to sing for the Lord. But I had three children to raise. I had to think about that and what was best for my family. So when I saw the opportunity, I decided it was brought forth by God. Rock and roll, rhythm and blues, and gospel, it's the same thing, let's face it. It's all about love. . . . I loved my God, I loved my husband, and I loved my children. And I just wanted to sing out that love for all the world, straight from my heart. I knew what I could do, how I sounded, how I could sell records if I had the chance." Cinching her argument, she told herself: "I knew I was wronging my children by not taking advantage of the opportunity God had laid at my feet. . . . So when I decided to sign that contract with Atlantic, the Sweet Inspirations were born with God's blessings. I believed in my decision. And the magic of believing gave me peace with that decision."

As the 1960s progressed, John and Cissy Houston followed with great enthusiasm and optimism the activist work of the charismatic Reverend

Martin Luther King Jr. On August 28, 1963, Cissy had been at her Newark home nursing her infant Nippy as she watched the TV coverage of King's landmark "I Have a Dream" speech, orated to a crowd of over 200,000 during the March on Washington demonstration. Even with their complex family and career obligations, Houston and her husband avidly followed the anti-racists' efforts to smash segregation in Southern schools and how authorities in the South continually defied federal laws on such matters. Like millions of others, Cissy and John wondered how the November 1963 assassination of President John F. Kennedy would affect the process of integrating Blacks with the white majority.

When Martin Luther King Jr. won the 1964 Nobel Peace Prize, it brought joy and pride to his people, but racial strife began to erupt in different parts of the United States. The black masses were fast tiring of well-intentioned speeches and peaceful means that brought no substantial end to racial bigotry, whether it be the overt discrimination in the South or the more subtle brands in the rest of the country. Regarding the latter, the Houstons could well relate to the unspoken but actual separation of the races that existed in Newark, where African Americans were relegated to a ghetto. While neither John nor Cissy was a militant activist, they certainly supported the cause of their beleaguered brothers and sisters. This was especially true of Cissy, who felt a direct connection to the pains of her people. After all, she had experienced instances of racial prejudice close to home, having heard so much family history of her father and his kin suffering constant injustices back in Georgia.

In early July 1964, President Lyndon B. Johnson approved a Civil Rights Act that pledged to "eliminate the last vestiges of injustice in America." The chief executive implored the country to "close the springs of racial poison." While Johnson's words sounded admirable in theory, in actuality the bitterness of 22 million black Americans began to explode dramatically. That same July, there were racial outbursts in Harlem, and later that month rioting broke out in Rochester in upstate New York. The following February, in Selma, Alabama, Martin Luther King Jr. and 770 supporters were arrested for picketing a county courthouse; their aim had been to force the abandonment of discriminatory voting requirements. Weeks later, there was a fifty-mile Freedom Walk from Selma, Alabama, to the state capitol in Montgomery. Amid tremendous tension and under the monitoring of federal troops, King and his 25,000 followers reached their destination relatively unscathed. There he impassionedly informed the crowd, "We are on the move and no wave of racism will stop us."

As the strife continued its violent course, it vied with the unpopular war in Vietnam as the major focus of the American public. In mid-August 1965, race riots tore apart the Watts district of Los Angeles, where it required over 20,000 National Guardsmen to restore a degree of order. The end results were approximately thirty dead, over 2,000 arrested, and millions of dollars' worth of damage to property.

It took nearly another two years for a major ethnic clash to erupt close to the Houston household, but erupt it did. In mid-July 1967, racial unrest exploded in Newark. During four days of pandemonium of fighting, looting, and destruction, the death toll reached twenty-six. Over 1,500 were injured and 1,000 arrested before the National Guard troops and local police restored a truce of sorts.

During the mayhem, the aghast Houstons and their badly frightened children remained barricaded in their house, watching in horror and pain as TV coverage recorded the devastation that rained on their city and within their neighborhood. By the time quasi-peace was restored, a very shaken John and Cissy had come to a firm decision. No matter what, they must leave Newark for a safer environment in which to raise their children.

Cissy hated the thought of abandoning her community and especially her beloved New Hope Baptist Church and the congregation she had come to know so well over the years. However, the safety and future of her children came first. If this would require her to work even harder (if that was possible) at her career than before, then so be it. There was no other viable option. The Houstons, along with their offspring, would abandon the town in which they had grown up.

4

Finding Her Voice

"By taking me to church, my mother gave me two wonderful gifts: my foundation in gospel music and a godly heritage."

WHITNEY HOUSTON, 1998

Gambling that Cissy's career would continue to move forward and provide much-needed income, the Houstons used their meager savings, plus a bank loan, to acquire new living quarters, this time in East Orange, New Jersey.

Propelled by the horrors of the Newark riots and their chaotic aftermath, John Houston immediately scouted neighboring towns and quickly found a real-estate bargain of sorts. While the potential new dwelling—a small, Cape Cod-style house—was located only six miles and approximately fifteen minutes' drive away from their modest home in the Newark projects, East Orange was a more upscale community than the troubled one they were leaving behind. What was especially exciting about the spacious, two-story home that John found was that it happened to have its very own swimming pool in the back yard.

Examining their new haven on East Orange's tree-shaded Dodd Street, the Houstons felt their past hard work was now really paying practical dividends. But their joy was tempered by the realization that to meet the monthly mortgage payments and other living expenses, Cissy must accept even more singing engagements than before. For her, it would mean more time on the road—and more time away from the children. But she and John agreed that the sacrifice was worth it so that their children could live in a better, safer neighborhood.

Occasionally, when Cissy and the Sweet Inspirations accepted out-of-town gigs, John, still a part-time cab driver, would accompany the quartet. In such instances, the Houstons' friend Phyllis Hardaway would stay with the three kids, or sometimes the children would bunk out with family acquaintances at nearby housing projects. These brief returns to such bleak, low-income environments would make the Houston offspring much more appreciative of their new home when they returned to East Orange.

Like most performers on road tours, the Sweet Inspirations were subject to the whims of often-crooked promoters, who frequently tried to take financial advantage of vulnerable singers visiting an unfamiliar part of the country. On one such occasion, however, the Sweet Inspirations turned the tables. John, who was learning the ropes of talent management through trial and error, had a hunch that the wheeler-dealer supervising their current tour was intending to cheat the group. He therefore insisted that the act be paid before they go on stage that night. When the promoter called their bluff, John had his clients walk out of the venue *before* the show began. Showing his growing flair for survival in a tough business, John left the club carrying one of the act's garment bags over his arm, with his hand crooked in such a position that it suggested he was carrying a gun. Adding to the impact of the situation, the singing quartet had already broken apart a chair in their dressing room. Each of them was now brandishing a chair leg in her hand and ready to use it! This scared the promoter into paying up and the act went on as planned that evening.

As a little girl, Nippy was overly pampered by the trio of people who spent the most time with her: her dad and her two adoring brothers. The Houstons required that their little girl stay close to home, wanting her to be safe and not distracted by bad influences. When no-nonsense Cissy—the family's rock—returned from her commutes to the recording studios or from her latest road trip, it was left to her to discipline Nippy.

Very rarely did John discipline daddy's girl. In later life, Whitney would recollect, "My father spanked me once and slapped me once. I was running off at the mouth. I should have stopped while I was ahead, but I didn't." As such, most of the future diva's memories of John during this period would be rosy and nostalgic, leading her to tell columnist Liz Smith in a 1997 *Good Housekeeping* interview: "I have a great dad. My father stuck by my mother and was a good friend to her. If my mother had a recording session, he would stay home, dress me, and do my hair. He would put a beautiful dress on me with tube socks—like sweat socks. And my hair would look kind of crooked, but it was cute. He was a very affectionate and loving dad."

☆

Like her seven-year-old brother Michael, who still became visibly upset whenever Cissy departed on out-of-town singing engagements, young Whitney hated those days when it was time for her mother to vanish yet again from the household. She now understood that these goodbyes usually meant her strict but beloved parent would be away for several days or even for weeks at a time. Once, in the middle of one such emotional farewell, Nippy insisted to Cissy, "I'm gonna make a lotta money one day Mommy so you won't have to go away and work." Such sentiments left Mrs. Houston dumbstruck with guilt, but at the same time made her proud of her child, who was growing up fast.

On one tour engagement with Aretha Franklin, Cissy and the Sweet Inspirations found themselves performing and staying in California. As Cissy has remembered, "Something kept gnawing at me. I woke up in the middle of the night, crying, like something was wrong at home. I called my husband. I said, 'What's wrong with my baby?' and he said, 'Nothing's wrong, nothing's wrong.' But then he told me what happened."

Whitney had been "roughhousing" with her brothers when she fell down, and the stick or the handle of a wire hanger she had been playing with was pushed into her mouth. As the foreign object was jammed back into her throat, it nearly severed her palate. A horrified John rushed his badly bleeding baby to the nearest hospital emergency room. There he held the frightened little girl as the attending physicians did their best to stitch up the bad tear. The damage from the accident was so severe that even after sewing her up, the concerned doctors warned Mr. Houston that Whitney could possibly lose her voice forever.

Learning all of this bad news on the phone, a distraught Cissy wanted to rush home, but she could not in good conscience abandon the Sweet Inspirations, nor leave Aretha in the lurch. As such, Cissy dutifully completed the tour. By the time she arrived back in East Orange, New Jersey, Whitney's stitches were ready to be removed. Thankfully, no permanent damage had been done. In Mrs. Houston's mind, it was another sign from above that the Lord had special plans in store for this beautiful little child.

☆

Having waited so long for a daughter, Cissy found it hard not to indulge some of the fantasies left unfulfilled by her own deprived childhood. She would insist that her youngster be dressed in frilly dresses, that her hair be braided just right, and that her good shoes not get scuffed. This regimen satisfied something deep within Cissy, but it bothered her young daughter. Even before she could articulate her unease, Whitney sensed that this special treatment regarding her outfits, her hairstyles, and her carefully taught manners was setting her too far apart from the other little girls in the neighborhood. Already a tomboy at heart, she began to rebel inwardly against her mother's stringent supervision of her wardrobe, appearance, and manners. But, for now, mama was not to be opposed, and so Whitney dutifully accepted her guidance—and the fancy attire.

Once young Nippy began attending the nearby Franklin Elementary School in East Orange, her intuition about being different from her peers proved to be correct. She was indeed dissimilar in many obvious ways. For one thing, in this emerging era of Black Pride, she was far more light-skinned than the other youngsters. This certainly set her apart from the others. For another, Cissy had taught Whitney to talk in a refined way and to behave politely—which also contrasted greatly with the majority of her more rambunctious peers. But the most obvious difference (and the worst from Nippy's point of view) was in how she dressed. The other grade-school girls typically wore T-shirts, jeans, and sneakers. In comparison, Whitney was sent to school in frilly frocks and dressy footwear. While many of the other girls wore the increasingly trendy Afro-style frizzy hairdo, Whitney's hair was meticulously combed, groomed, and braided.

Feeling so set apart from other children of her age, the once-so-talkative Whitney became shy and withdrawn. At school her classmates began picking on her and she increasingly shrank back into her shell, becoming frequently moody. When her parents inquired about her growing apathy about school, she would be uncommunicative or, occasionally, dare to question her mother's sartorial judgment. Timidly, she would suggest that she wanted to change her appearance so as to be more like the others. Nevertheless, Cissy stood firm in her vision of how her cherished daughter should and must look, act, and talk. At the end of such discussions about values, individuality, and so forth, the mother frequently instructed her offspring, "Sometimes, you just have to be your own best friend." Such advice may have worked for Cissy in her life, but it didn't satisfy or help Whitney. It became the start of a running argument between parent and child that would escalate as the years passed.

Sometimes, Whitney took a different approach to avoiding the dreaded classroom. For example, on one occasion, she arrived home from school and informed Cissy that she had done so well in class that her teacher had said she never had to return . . . ever again. This announcement quickly aroused the mother's suspicions and she finally extracted from her child the real reasons why she wanted to avoid school. Thereafter, an angry Mrs. Houston spoke with the school principal, asking, then demanding, that the bullying be stopped or else she'd deal with it herself. The principal promised he would look into the matter but cautioned there was only so much he could do in such situations. Even Whitney's brother Michael got into the act, wanting to seek revenge on the girls who were badgering his sister. However, Cissy told him it was not right for a boy to beat up girls.

With so many social problems at school, Whitney was always relieved when classes were over for the day and she had outrun her bullying classmates who would chase her on the way home. Upon reaching Dodd Street and the safety of her house, she would remain within the confines of her sanctuary. She turned to her brothers as her companions. However, as they grew older—especially Gary, who was six years her senior—they naturally wanted to be with friends their own age and often left Whitney to entertain herself.

As the months of being a loner turned into an established pattern, Whitney adjusted to the strange social situation. She recalled decades later, "I finally faced the fact that it isn't a crime not having friends. Being alone means you have fewer problems. . . . [Years later] when I decided to be a singer my mother warned me I'd be alone a lot. Basically we all are. Loneliness comes with life."

Not so long ago, as an adult looking back on this "misfit" period, Whitney voiced additional insights into her me-against-the-world situation as a youth. For one thing, both her parents lived in the same home, something not so common in many households within the lower economic classes of the black community. Furthermore, as she reasoned from the perspective of time, "My mother and father worked very hard so that we would be self-contained, we wouldn't have to go out in the streets to find or do anything. That was difficult for neighborhood kids who didn't have the same things or the kind of parents that sacrificed. My parents worked very hard. I think that's what people missed. They saw our lives as something that was almost like a fairy tale, instead of something that was really worked for."

Despite her growing sense of being a loner—even a misfit—among her unsympathetic peers, Whitney found an occasional comfort zone in her weekly routine. For example, there were the religious services at the New Hope Baptist Church. Once she had become accustomed to the ritual of attending these sessions, she felt safe and protected there. She was especially pleased to attend services on those Sundays when her mother was not away on tour and she could proudly watch mama expertly leading the gospel choir. As time passed, Whitney felt a great connection with the congregation, who in many ways became her extended family. Here were people who, unlike her antagonistic classmates, treated her with consideration and interest, and showed her deference because of their great respect for choirmaster Cissy Houston.

For another thing, there were visits from, and with, her beloved Aunt Dionne (Warwick), whom she had come to regard as a second mother. Dionne was especially fond of Nippy: "the little girl I never had." Sometimes, the singer, who had two boys of her own, would indulge cousin Cissy's kids in the summertime when school was out of session. Dionne would arrange for them to fly with her to attend a concert engagement somewhere in the United States. If Nippy's two brothers were especially awed at being privileged passengers in a chartered jet, little Whitney would return to her parents' home full of excitement about different matters. She was particularly excited about being backstage, watching her famous aunt perform and receive adoration from audiences. These events gave the child a refreshing glimpse of what life could be like. They instilled hope in her of an existence where people would approve of her—unlike her classmates and young neighbors. She realized there was a chance for her to be appreciated for being different, rather than scorned.

Another occasion on which Whitney felt at ease was when she accompanied her mother into Manhattan to attend the recording studios. She would sit outside the glass enclosures as her mama and the Sweet Inspirations made glorious music hour after hour. The youngster especially enjoyed those times when Cissy was recording with "Aunt Ree." She gloried in Aretha Franklin's soulful singing. Even watching from a distance, Nippy observed how her mother was respected and appreciated for shaping the background harmonies that brought out the best in the lead talent. It was a very comforting, creative atmosphere for the budding young artist.

In retrospect, Whitney remembers of those times: "I had no idea then that Aretha Franklin was famous—just that I liked to hear her sing, too! I just remember being in an atmosphere of total creativity. When I heard Aretha, I could feel her emotional delivery so clearly. It came from deep down within." It made the youngster think: "That's what I want to do."

Years later, Aretha could also recall these occasions: "Cissy would bring Whitney to those sessions. She must have been about five years old. And she was always there, in my face. I loved her. She wanted to sing. I knew that even then. She was always watching closely, whispering to her mother. She had great spirit. She sang in the corner, always humming to herself, trying to duplicate the sounds she was hearing. She would say, I want to be a Sweet Inspiration, too."

One thing that Cissy insisted upon when Whitney tagged along to these recording sessions was that the child must *never* interrupt her mother while she was working and she must stay out of the others' way. Usually the youngster was mindful of her authoritative mom, thrilled to be allowed to hear her mother's impassioned, powerful singing. However, one day she couldn't help herself—she broke her mother's rule. That was the occasion when Cissy had made an exception and said that, for once, rather than remaining on the other side of the glass, Whitney might come into the actual recording room itself. However, she was cautioned repeatedly that she must remain absolutely quiet—she must not even hum to herself (as she often did while listening outside the room to her mother and the others at work).

Nippy agreed to the stringent conditions and sat quietly on the floor in a corner inside the studio. Cissy and the others began their number. The tape was already recording the session when the little girl burst out with an enthusiastic "Ooooh, that sounds good, Mama!" While the others were amused, a horrified Cissy gave her daughter a very severe look. By now, the music had stopped and there was a stony silence as everyone looked back and forth between Cissy and Nippy. As a deeply embarrassed Cissy led her daughter outside the enclosure, the others heard the child saying, "But, Mommy, that just sounded so *good*, I couldn't help myself." After chastising Whitney, Cissy returned to the inner sanctum and promised that such a thing would *never* occur again. And it didn't.

Sometimes, as a school vacation treat, especially if there was no trusty babysitter available to help out, Cissy would take her daughter on brief road tours with her. The girl thrived on these exciting excursions. She felt the same way in May 1968, when she attended the Atlantic label's annual revue (starring Ben E. King) held at the legendary Apollo Theater in Harlem, uptown Manhattan. While Cissy and the Sweet Inspirations performed on stage, young Whitney stood agog in the wings, chaperoned by an aunt. Seeing such an array of inspiring African-American performers that evening made a marked impression on the girl.

As might be expected, young Whitney already had vague dreams of being a singer herself. Sometimes, when she thought no one was home, she would head down to the basement playroom and put on a stack of records. Using a broom as her make-believe microphone, she would sing along with Aretha, the Sweet Inspirations, Anita Baker and others. One time, when her parents had gone out for an early-evening appointment, Nippy went to her basement haunt and began singing in "harmony" with the records on the player. As she got into the groove of her singing session, she became so engrossed that she was soon shouting out the lyrics at the top of her voice. She was so caught up with her performance that she didn't hear her parents return home. When her number finished, she suddenly heard a round of applause and was greeted with their beaming faces.

After this initial show of approval, Whitney became more fervent and open about her singing sessions. It quickly reached the point where John Houston would beg Cissy, "Can't you do something to make her stop that noise? I need some peace and quiet. She's worrying my nerves." Mrs. Houston would do her best to smooth things over.

As a little girl, Whitney, who loved children and animals, had wavered between one day becoming a school teacher or a veterinarian. But now, as she matured to a degree, she became increasingly convinced she wanted professional singing to be her life's goal. As time went on, she became more focused on this decision.

While Cissy was flattered that her daughter wanted to follow in her footsteps, she had already experienced too many ups and downs in her own showbusiness career, and seen too much within the profession, to want her daughter to be caught in its enticing web. For one thing, Cissy was increasingly concerned about where her own performing career was heading. She knew—and she was definitely not shy about letting anyone know—that she was a top-flight singer. In fact, in her mind she could easily match any of the competition with her beautiful multi-octave vocal range. This was emphasized when Cissy, in particular, received rave reviews from the audience and critics alike after she and the Sweet Inspirations had joined Aretha for a concert at Philharmonic Hall at New York's Lincoln Center in October 1968.

Part of Cissy appreciated that being an experienced background singer who could perform easily in a wide variety of genres made her a much-in-demand commodity that would never go out of fashion. While soloists might fly quickly to the top of the charts with hit numbers and become the singer of the moment, too many had just as suddenly lost favor with the fickle public and rapidly descended into obscurity. This realization had made Cissy more inclined to take the middle road professionally by pushing her career as part of the Sweet Inspirations rather than going solo herself. However, after the group's debut album in 1967, their follow-up discs (including *Songs of Faith and Inspiration*, *What the World Needs Now*, and *Sweets For My Sweet*) had neither brought the Sweet Inspirations the degree of popularity nor the high income they or their record label had optimistically anticipated. Cissy did not want her daughter to suffer the whims of such a tough business, in which the chances of real success were so miniscule and so fleeting.

Meanwhile, in summer 1969, when Elvis Presley made his showbusiness comeback at the International Hotel in Las Vegas, he convinced Cissy, whom he had admired professionally for years, to come to the gaming capital. He wanted her and the Sweet Inspirations to be the background singers for this crucial concert. It was too important an offer for Cissy to turn down. Thus, she (along with John) and the Sweet Inspirations spent several weeks in Las Vegas as part of the lineup for the King's landmark return to prominence.

Exciting as the gig was, Cissy still hated being away from Whitney; it had been a difficult decision for her to go to Nevada. Afterwards, when Aretha Franklin was embarking on concert appearances in Paris that would be recorded for a live album, she planned for the Sweet Inspirations to be part of the proceedings. However, at that time Nippy was suffering from a severe case of flu, and Cissy put her foot down. Neither she nor the others in the group would go to Europe. It was out of the question. As for Aretha, she had professional commitments to fulfill and found substitute background singers to take over the harmonies.

The three other Inspirations (Estelle Brown, Sylvia Shemwell, and Myrna Smith) were very upset by this change of plan. It was a sign of the growing fracture between the older, more conservative, more home-oriented Cissy and themselves. Another issue of contention was that the three others wanted the Sweet Inspirations to develop a flashier, sexier stage image by making their wardrobe more youthful and enticing. They also suggested moving away from the rhythm-and-blues numbers that were not winning them the big audiences they needed.

Morally conservative, firm-minded Cissy continued to disagree with her band mates, and after one more Atlantic album together (1970's *Sweet Sweet Soul*), the quartet broke apart. Estelle, Sylvia, and Myrna went their own way as a "new" group, first adding a new member (Ann Williams) and then, after they left Atlantic Records in 1970, becoming a trio again.

Part of Cissy's motivation to pull away from the singing group was to have more time at home. In particular, she had always regretted that concert appearances in Italy with the Sweet Inspirations had prevented her from being on hand when five-year-old Whitney had been in a school play. The girl had sobbed loud and long when her mother could not attend the performance. Torn between being there for her children (especially her daughter) and being on the road to fulfill career obligations, Cissy felt constantly in conflict.

Adding to the complexity of her professional situation was her ongoing uncertainty about venturing away from background singing to lead vocalizing. Now, with this exit from the Sweet Inspirations, she was at a career crossroads—one that she had partially engineered, at least on a subconscious level. Eventually, she decided that becoming a solo act would be her main thrust and that her background singing would be merely fallback, bread-and-butter work. She reasoned that this would provide her with more control over her time and how often she had to travel away from home. As she wrote in her 1998 autobiography *How Sweet the Sound: My Life with God and Gospel*: "I was missing the most important years of my children's lives and no kind of money was worth that."

Having now lost the Sweet Inspirations as a management client, John Houston obligingly devoted his energies to helping Cissy move into a solo singing career. What other choice did he have? However, just as his lack of true industry clout or sophisticated music business know-how had held back the career of the Sweet Inspirations, he was still not in a strong enough position to help Cissy land a major recording contract. The situation was not helped by Cissy herself being so inflexible about what she would or would not sing, how she would dress on stage, and so forth.

Thus it was that, in 1970, she joined forces with Commonwealth United Records, who released her debut solo album (*Presenting Cissy Houston*). While this sterling mix of soul, rock and pop tunes (including "I'll Be There" and "Be My Baby") didn't make much of a dent in the charts, a single released on the Janus label (who had acquired her Commonwealth contract) the following year *almost* changed the tide for her. It was a restructured variation of Jim Weatherly's "The Midnight Plane to Houston," revamped with the songwriter's permission into "The Midnight Train to Georgia." The disc received favorable airplay from radio stations, but it lacked the necessary promotional campaign to turn it into a commercial hit with the record-buying public. It seemed that Janus would not (or could not) spend the $5,000 or so required to hype the single. Rubbing the proverbial salt into the wound, a few years later Gladys Knight and the Pips recorded a cover version of "The Midnight Train to Georgia" and it became a million-seller for them. This cruel twist of fate remained a sore point with Cissy and John for years to come.

Such bitter music-industry lessons were not lost on Cissy or John Houston, nor even on their eight-year-old daughter. But despite everything she'd seen her mother experience, Whitney remained convinced that she wanted to become some sort of a singer—no matter what the odds were, nor how much hard work it required.

5

Deciding on the Future

"By the age of ten or eleven, when I opened my mouth and said, 'Oh, God, what's this?' I kind of knew teaching and being a veterinarian were gonna have to wait. What's in your soul is in your soul."

WHITNEY HOUSTON, 1993

As Whitney Houston progressed through the fifth and sixth grades at Franklin School between the fall of 1973 and the spring of 1975, the situation between the girl and her unfriendly classmates remained tense. Because of her mother's dictates, Whitney still dressed in the dreaded plaids and pigtails. As she reflected later, "That getup didn't play well in East Orange, New Jersey." Nor did the girl's refined manners—courtesy of Cissy's how-to-be-a-little-lady training—sit well with her less sophisticated equals.

Branded an outsider, the unhappy student often hid in the school building at recess and lunchtime, hoping no one would find her and begin harassing her yet again. However, when her tormentors did find her, they would often tear her pretty clothes and yank the ribbons from her hair. The distraught child would then run home, both upset by the uncalled-for treatment from her persecutors and fearful of what her mother would undoubtedly say about her disheveled clothing and scratched knees. Usually Cissy took a hard line by forcing Whitney to return to school, telling her: "If you don't stand up for yourself and show them you're not afraid, they'll never leave you alone."

Understandably, it was difficult for the ostracized youngster to appreciate her mother's unwavering attitudes towards dress code and conduct. Given the degree of scorn and abuse she was receiving from her peers, it was bitter medicine to hear her mother's decree: "Until the time when you can say 'I'm grown, I can take care of myself,' you do what I say, and you understand that one day it is going to be best and you will thank me. I know you're going to hate me now, but you are going to love me one day."

Then came the day when even Mrs. Houston had had enough of her daughter being victimized. A group of the tougher girls had once again chased Whitney home. This time, Mrs. Houston happened to be in the house, and she overheard the taunting going on outside. She mentally flashed back to the situation with her son Michael and his persecutor in the school playground a few years earlier. She decided to take action and, hopefully, put an end to this new harassment.

Cissy positioned herself at the front door of her house with a belt in her hand and firmly ordered her daughter to climb the stoop steps and turn around to face the gang. Mrs. Houston then said, "I want the baddest one of you to come [over] here because Whitney is going to fight you today." The sassiest one of the group came forward. Egged into action by her dynamic mother, Whitney unleashed the fury of years of pent-up frustration and took on her opponent. She acquitted herself well and, thereafter, while the other girls were never particularly friendly to her, some of their aggressiveness towards her diminished. Years later, when Whitney had become a famous star, she observed with a note of irony, "Now, when I see those girls in my old neighborhood, they all act like they were my best friends."

What made these ongoing difficulties with her peers even harder to understand or accept was that, when she accompanied her mother on recording sessions or short road tours, everyone would make a fuss over Cissy's girl, extolling her prettiness, fine manners, and nice clothes. Mrs. Houston said of these occasions: "She loved it because she was treated like a little queen; she heard all these amazing voices, and if that doesn't inspire you, I don't know what will."

While Whitney was progressing—unhappily—through elementary school, she was receiving another type of education. Her mother enrolled her in the Youth Choir at New Hope Baptist Church. Cissy had decided that if her daughter loved so much to sing in the basement along with the recordings of her favorite stars, she might better use her energy for the glory of the Lord. She still prayed that Whitney, who loved to dress up in Cissy's wigs and high heels as she sang in front of her pretend microphone in the basement, would eventually choose a more secure future profession than showbusiness.

The choir had both good and bad aspects for young Whitney. For example, on the positive side, it gave the youngster an opportunity to mingle with more spiritually minded individuals her own age who wanted to express their love of God through music: "The choir was like my family, my second home, where I could express myself. It kept me out of trouble and off the street. The church was a safe haven."

On the other hand, the choir was another situation in which Whitney was under the strict guidance of her no-nonsense mother. As at home with her three children, Cissy (the church's minister of music) brooked no disrespect or unruliness from her sixty-plus charges. Whether at the group's frequent rehearsals or when they gathered in the basement of New Hope Baptist Church to march upstairs to perform at the Sunday service, she would remind them firmly in a loud, commanding voice: "Don't be talking, chewing gum or acting crazy!" and then launch into a mini-lecture. It was a variation on the discipline and tough love that Whitney experienced all the time at home. As she concisely summed up her mother's approach: "She don't take no mess." About Cissy's insistence on musical professionalism from her flock, Whitney observed, "She could embarrass you so badly, you'd feel like you just wanted to slide under the chair and crawl away. She's real good at that."

Such matters aside, Nippy thrived on her choir practice: "Gospel taught me a wide range of things: how to sing fast, how to sing slow, how to sing when the tempo changes in the middle of a song, how to sing four-part harmony without thinking about it. And how to sing without music, in terms of your voice being the instrument, your feet being the drum, your hands being the tambourine."

As Whitney progressed at choir, Cissy discerned that her child had a special aptitude for music which, like her maturing voice, seemed to her to be a gift inherited from God. With the passing months, Mrs. Houston decided it was fitting that her daughter should perform a solo at a future Sunday service. Cissy had set a psalm to music and determined that "Guide Me, O Thou Great Jehovah" was the right song for her girl's debut. Whitney continually practiced the number, wanting to be letter perfect and make her mother proud.

As the appointed Sunday approached for the twelve-year-old to step out from the chorus ranks to sing this song for the Almighty, Cissy learned that she must be out of town for a concert appearance, one the family could not afford for her to miss. Reluctantly, she told her daughter she could not be at the joyous occasion, but that on this special Sunday her father would definitely be in attendance.

The auspicious day came, and John dutifully accompanied Whitney and the other children to church. Wearing a blue sailor dress with white pleats, the adolescent nervously stepped forward from the rest of the choir at the appointed time. What followed is indelibly stamped into Houston's memory. "I was scared to death [and] aware of people staring at me. No one moved. They seemed almost in a trance. I just stared at the clock in the center of the church." Then, trying to remember everything that her mother had taught her, she closed her eyes and "just began to sing. When I opened my eyes, it was like the Holy Spirit had come to the church. People were just shouting and happy and praising God."

It was a religious experience for the youngster to hear and feel the heartfelt reaction of the much-moved congregation: "From then on, I knew God had blessed me." To celebrate her success, she did a gospel encore for her appreciative audience. "I knew then and there that if this is what I can do with what God gave me with this gift, my voice, then this is what I will do. It was a done deal. . . . I knew I had to sing."

Of all those in attendance at New Hope Baptist Church that day, John Houston was the most pleased and most surprised by Whitney's stellar vocal performance. As he recalled proudly years later, "What I heard that day was the voice of a young woman coming from the throat of a twelve-year-old-child." When Cissy returned to town, she heard all about the wonderful reception her daughter had received at church, and she was heartened that her faith and instinct about her daughter had been confirmed so powerfully. To judge for herself—and to belatedly share in her daughter's solo debut—she had Whitney perform the song again at church. The response was just as impressive as before.

By now, Mrs. Houston was convinced that if Whitney truly wanted to pursue her singing—in whatever forum she chose—she would support her daughter's decision. "I had a peace with her choosing this as her life's work," was how Mrs. Houston phrased it. While Cissy had a reservoir of wisdom from her years as a vocalist and choirmaster that she could share with the fledgling singer, the mother was the first to admit, "There was something in her voice that no one, not even I, could teach her."

Now, whether at church choir practice, at home, or on those increasing occasions when Whitney accompanied her mother to recording sessions, concerts, and so forth, Cissy made every effort to carefully point out to her pupil the do's and don't's of the art of singing. Among Mrs. Houston's words of wisdom were, "You don't start loud because then you have no place to go. . . . that songs tell a story, and you don't blare out a story, control is the basis for singing: up, down, soft sweet and diction was very important."

Whitney quickly got caught up in her musical education and absorbed everything she could about her craft from the masters close at hand: "My mother always said to me, 'If you don't feel it, then don't mess with it, because it's a waste of time.' When I used to watch my mother sing, which was usually in church, that feeling, that soul, that thing—it's like electricity rolling through you. If you have ever been in a Baptist church or a Pentecostal church, when the Holy Spirit starts to roll and people start to really feel what they're doing, it's . . . it's incredible. That's what I wanted. When I watched Aretha [Franklin] sing, the way she sang and the way she closed her eyes, and that riveting thing just came out. People just . . . ooooh, it could stop you in your tracks. . . . So my mother was my first example that I looked at and said, 'Wow, that voice right there.'"

Whitney's participation in the Youth Choir at New Hope Baptist Church was giving her a degree of social confidence. Nevertheless, her parents worried about her academic wellbeing. She was a naturally bright child. In fact, on several occasions the school administrators had suggested that the student should jump ahead a class. However, Cissy felt that her daughter was already too sheltered and shy and that to be associating with classmates a year or more older would not be in Whitney's best interests.

In fact, after further consideration, the Houstons concluded that Whitney should not continue in the local education system at Hart Middle School. Instead, they enrolled her at Mount Saint Dominic Academy in Caldwell, New Jersey, about six miles and a fifteen-minute drive from East Orange. The all-girls institution had been founded in 1892 by the Dominican Sisters, who, as detailed on the school's website, were mandated to "bring their Catholic and Dominican tradition of education to Essex County and the surrounding area. Here are laid the foundations for a spiritual, cultural, physically vigorous, and self-directing adult life."

In retrospect, it might seem a strange choice to send an African-American girl reared in the Baptist church to a Catholic institution predominantly filled with Caucasians. But Cissy, as always, had her reasons. "Whitney was a very delicate kind of child, and I thought she needed a certain kind of environment. I thought she could get more education there. I know it can be regimented, but that wasn't my main reason. . . . Besides, I didn't need anyone to enforce my rules. Early dating, cruising around—she's wasn't going to do that anyhow. She wasn't going to wear stockings until I said okay, even if her friends did. No makeup, no lipstick, no high heels. And no discussion. . . . She didn't like it. She hated it. Sometimes she would go to her father—her brothers would, too—because they thought he was a little more lenient. But they didn't get around what I told them." As the mother explained on another occasion: "One of the reasons I had strict rules was just so the kids wouldn't become adults too fast."

So, in September 1975, as Whitney's older brother Gary was preparing to embark on his college career—thanks to a basketball scholarship—at DePaul University in Chicago, the youngest Houston transferred to Mount Saint Dominic (courtesy of her parents' financial sacrifices and economic assistance from the school itself).

The parochial academy was certainly a strange environment for the youngster, not only because her classmates were now all girls, but also because her instructors here were all nuns, and strict and demanding in their regimen. The newcomer was initially intrigued by Catholicism, which permeated every aspect of her daily school life. As she explored the unfamiliar religion, she decided, "Catholicism is a trip. I was serving a God of love, a God who has compassion and is kind and loves His children unconditionally, who sent His son here to die for our sins so we wouldn't be accountable for them. And these people are talking about damnation and purgatory and hell, and if you're good and you don't have any abortions and you don't take any birth-control pills, you're going to heaven."

Whitney remembers of her brief spiritual investigation: "I went to confession one time in seventh grade; it totally turned me off. I sat behind the curtain and said, 'Listen, I'm just here because I want to know what this is all about.' The priest said, 'Well, do you have any sins to confess?' I said, 'I don't, but God already knows what I've done. Why do I have to sit here and talk to you?' He said, 'Really, you don't.' We had a deep conversation within a couple of minutes. He was kicking it and I was kicking it back with him. At the end of the conversation, I said, 'Well, I guess there's no need for me to be here.' He said, "I guess not. I hope that you have found what you wanted to see.' I said, 'Yes, I did, and I won't be back.'"

If her teachers' spiritual background and the school's religious atmosphere differed from her public-school education, one thing remained the same: Whitney was once again *not* liked by her classmates. At her mother's continued insistence, she dressed differently from her fellow students, and her demeanor made her seem more refined than most of them. While she may have had a radiant, winning smile, it did not compensate for her shyness, which she tried to hide beneath an increasingly distant air. As she quickly discovered, she was still an outsider.

While her status with classmates had not changed significantly, the budding teenager had grown somewhat wiser in the ways of dealing with such unsettling situations. And if this meant skirting around her mother's dictates, she reasoned it could not be helped. As such, she had the bright idea of sneaking less formal outfits out of her wardrobe at home and bringing them to school each day. Thus she might arrive at Mount Saint Dominic wearing what her mother deemed to be appropriate attire, but, once there, she made a beeline for the ladies' room and quickly changed into Levi's, a casual top, and sneakers. As she admitted later in life: "Blue jeans saved my ass a lot of the time." At the end of the bothersome school day, Whitney would reverse the routine so that, hopefully, her observant parent would not catch on to her deception.

In these formative years, Whitney found herself caught uncomfortably between different worlds. Because she attended school in another town, she was considered even more of an alien by the neighborhood crowd in East Orange—they wanted little to do with the fancy miss who was too good to go to public school with them and attended a private Catholic institution instead. Conversely, the girls at Mount Saint Dominic didn't know what to make of the shy newcomer in their midst. She might be following their academic and physical education curriculum, but she did not share in their Catholic religion, nor did she seem like most of the other girls their age, the majority of whom were Caucasians.

During this difficult transitional period, Whitney continued to feel isolated from her peers and from life in general. This was the 1970s, when pop culture was still heavily weighted in favor of the white majority. As such, there were relatively few ethnic role models for Whitney to emulate. This was true even when she watched TV or went to the movies. "I loved musicals," Whitney said later, "but for a young African-American there wasn't much to look at except for Diahann Carroll and Sammy [Davis Jr.], who I loved. But I loved them as people—not really for what they did but what they stood for. I loved [old] Ginger Rogers and Fred Astaire musicals because to me they were really what Hollywood was all about."

In fact, looking back on her formative years and remembering what her favorite movies were then, she realized anew how little was being offered to black moviegoers, who wanted personalities and stories on screen to which they could really relate. The pickings were indeed slim. "I loved *Sparkle* [1976] and *Cooley High* [1975], and then there were *Superfly* [1972] and *Shaft* [1971]. But you'd go see that and say, 'Ahhhright, Superfly lives down the street—why I had to pay to see that?'"

Reacting to all this alienation in her social and academic lives, she turned to her siblings, whenever they were on home turf and allowed her to join in their activities. Because they were more mature, male, and supposedly able to handle themselves better, they were far less closely supervised by their parents than Whitney. When the brothers hung out on the streets of East Orange, she occasionally managed to accompany them. What she observed and experienced, at first mostly from afar, appealed to her. Doubtless part of the attraction was that such a down-and-raw lifestyle was vastly different from the relatively sheltered, purified existence that her parents, especially Cissy, imposed upon her most of the time.

In later life, the former tomboy-at-heart would make veiled references in an almost bragging fashion to the escapades she got into with brothers Gary and Michael, and sometimes with other acquaintances she acquired over time on her East Orange turf. These exploits, whether exaggerated or not, offer a brief glimpse into the growing dichotomy between the contrasting aspects of Whitney's personality. In later years, these alternate facets of the "real" Whitney would lead her into attitudes, situations, and activities that would confuse, disappoint, and upset multitudes of her fans and others.

As Whitney continued with her church gospel work and special vocal coaching from Cissy, she followed the course dictated by her demanding teacher. The curriculum required her to sing every Sunday in the church choir (with the teenager now promoted to the adult group) and take her musical training very seriously. Before long, she had advanced to such a degree that she could help Cissy in guiding other choir members. But this promotion did not mean, by any stretch of the imagination, that she was exempt from her mother's intense scrutiny—at church or at home—regarding her vocal exercises and her personal decorum. There were many nights when the duo returned to their Dodd Street home still embroiled in heated discussion over the proper interpretation of a particular piece of music they had been practicing at their Newark church.

Months passed, and it reached the point where Whitney felt a strong need to have a heart-to-heart talk with her mother. She wanted her to fully understand that, although she might still be considered a child in her parents' eyes, she had definitely made up her mind that she wanted to be a singer with a capital "S." The discussion gave Cissy pause, for she understood how determined Whitney had become on the subject of her vocation. She asked her daughter a very pointed question: "Do you want to sing or do you want to be in the business?"

"What's the difference?" Whitney inquired.

It was then that Cissy spoke to her daughter woman to woman, adult to adult. She carefully outlined the hard work, heartache, and whims of fate that characterized a full-time career in showbusiness. She bluntly explained how many unscrupulous individuals were in the business just waiting to take advantage of naïve newcomers, how tough life could be on the road, and the difficult odds of achieving any real degree of success—let alone success that lasted. In what must have been a painful self-examination and brutal re-evaluation of her own uneven showbusiness career to date, Cissy spelled out for Whitney the grim realities of the highly competitive music industry, in which popularity and loyalty were as short-lived as fads in musical styles.

After painstakingly pondering her mother's unvarnished account of the profession, Whitney announced that she still wanted to be a Singer. Finally, the die was cast.

6

The Young Songbird

"[Whitney] didn't date young, I didn't allow it. Period. But she did go through a rebellious teenage phase, mostly small stuff: staying out late, not washing the dishes. She was lazier than hell, stubborn and opinionated. When she was sixteen, I told her she wasn't going to make seventeen because I was gonna kill her."

CISSY HOUSTON, 1987

In the late 1980s, when Whitney Houston was in the first blush of superstardom, she confided to *Ebony* magazine: "My childhood was normal and very simple. I had to be home for dinner at a certain time, and do all the other things that kids have to do—school and homework." This statement was somewhat misleading, for the teenage Whitney already had a complicated, busy existence.

For one thing, she had become deeply immersed in religion and, in her own way, was devout. As she later explained of the spiritual transformation which would be such a key factor in her life, "I was about thirteen or fourteen. I can remember being in church—a church on the corner of Dodd Street, where we lived, that's how much I loved going to church; I would find a church to go to that I loved, that had the same kind of spirit as New Hope [Baptist]. I can remember the Holy Spirit coming into that church and just taking over. I remember just crying and accepting the Savior in my life and in my heart . . . knowing that He was real . . . it wasn't fake."

Given her dedication to the art of singing, it was understandable that one of the facets of her faith most important to Whitney was that emotionally charged, energizing spiritual songs were so much a part of the services. In her own words: "I grew up in the church, and gospel music has always been the center of our lives. . . . At family celebrations, we always end up sitting around the piano and singing. I couldn't get enough of gospel music when I was growing up." Later, as she became an increasingly active and important member of her mother's choir at New Hope Baptist, the thrill of performing gospel songs created a special ecstasy for her that elevated her love of religion: "Nothing is like the sheer joy of singing only for myself and my God."

Yet regular attendance at church services and singing to and for the glory of the Lord did not preclude Whitney from having a "devilish" tomboy side to her personality. While her mother did her best to keep this rebellious streak in check, Whitney was headstrong and pampered, and grew increasingly insistent—whether openly or secretly—on carrying out her rough-and-tumble activities. This rambunctious trait, which cropped up at different points in her childhood (from the Newark projects to the East Orange suburbs), put her in contact with the more streetwise elements of her neighborhood.

In March 1996, the *Globe* tabloid interviewed André Johnson, then a maintenance man, who still resided in the Newark area where he had grown up. He painted an intriguing portrait of the game young girl he knew over the years—a far cry from the picture-perfect, well-behaved beauty that would be established as the 'real' Whitney Houston of the mid-1980s. Johnson recalled, "As a kid, she was a sight. We teased her about her glasses, and her hair looked like she never styled it. You'd never catch her playing jump rope with other girls." Johnson went on to say, "She always wanted to be one of the guys. Whitney wasn't into boys because she was too busy trying to be one herself. . . . I remember one of our guys trying to give her a hug and she had a fit because she didn't want him to touch her. But she'd get right in there and fight with the guys . . . [from the projects]."

According to Johnson, Whitney was usually in the thick of things when it came to playing a pick-up game of football, basketball, or the group's favored activity—jumping rooftops. Johnson described this in detail: "There was a row of garages and she would jump from roof to roof with us. Her skinny little legs carried her like a deer." He also recalled the occasions when Whitney would sing Jackson 5 tunes on the street corner to a crowd of guys and gals. Sometimes, he remembered, Cissy Houston would corral him and the other kids into attending New Hope Baptist Church on a Sunday to hear Whitney sing with the choir.

In the mid-1970s, Whitney passed from being a girl to a fast-maturing teenager. It was during this period that Cissy suddenly felt much closer to her third-born, because now, as one musician to another, they had much more in common. "A lot of typical mother–daughter stuff fell away," Mrs. Houston acknowledged of their growing rapport with each other. "There was an ease with which we related that wasn't there before. . . . I was still Mommy. . . . But there was now an added dimension—we shared a sense of purpose, a call."

For her part, Whitney experienced a special connection with her mother, one that would endure over the coming years—through good times and bad. As the star-to-be explained, "If something is bothering me, she automatically knows it. She doesn't guess, she knows. It's magical and it lets me know how powerful the mother–child link is."

With their new sense of togetherness, Whitney both learned more and enjoyed doing so when she accompanied her mom to recording sessions. These days, Cissy was largely providing background work, since her solo career had failed to take off in any significant way. Meanwhile, to give herself professional exposure in another field, Cissy staged a club act in the New York City area in which she was the featured artist and called on backing singers to provide harmonies for her numbers. On weekends, Whitney frequently attended these cabaret performances at, among other venues, Mikell's jazz club on Manhattan's Upper West Side, Sweetwater's on 68th Street and Amsterdam, and Reno Sweeney's down in Greenwich Village.

Also during this period, thirteen-year-old Whitney began exploring—with Cissy's encouragement—a few showbusiness opportunities of her own. For example, the teenager entered the Garden State Competition and made it as far as one of the five finalists. After further elimination playoffs, it was soon down to Whitney and another contestant. For this key round, she was to sing "Evergreen," Barbra Streisand's song from the movie *A Star Is Born*. Unfortunately, at the crucial moment, Whitney, distracted by the pressures of the event, became nervous about performing in front of the intently watching audience. As a result, her pacing was off. This caused her to exceed the time limit permitted each contestant and she forfeited the singing match. The dejected Whitney certainly had no idea at the time that this defeat would be one of her few showbusiness failures over the exciting years to come. Thankfully, her mother was on hand at the competition to comfort Nippy, and the fledgling performer soon recovered her self-esteem and grew eager for the next career challenge—wherever it might come from.

Under Cissy's continued tutelage, Whitney devoted a lot of her energy and focus to sharpening her vocal skills, learning how to better use her already powerful voice, amazing range, and beautiful tones. Such serious study did not leave her much spare time to enjoy what other teenagers her age would typically be doing—hanging out with friends, playing sports, going to movies, or dating. However, she claims not to have minded such a disciplined way of life at the time. Also, the focused career preparation was a pleasant distraction from the daily grind at Mount Saint Dominic Academy, where, so far, she'd failed to become one of the accepted crowd or really to shine academically.

In fact, most of the time Whitney wished she were anywhere else but in the classroom. She dreamed of becoming a full-time singer, and it couldn't happen fast enough for her. In these formative years, she was lucky to have so many top-flight role models close at hand. Besides having her well-regarded mother to inspire and guide her, there was also her godmother, Aretha Franklin. "Aunt Ree" had already won the Grammy for Best Female Performer in the R&B category eight times between 1967 and 1974. The Queen of Soul continued to record distinctive albums, though she was not achieving the same degree of impact with record buyers as she had in the 1960s. Whitney marveled at Aretha's voice and the impassioned interpretations she brought to her performances.

However, at the time, what really inspired impressionable Whitney to become a professional singer was experiencing first-hand the star treatment that her remarkable cousin Dionne Warwick received on her concert tours. Dionne might not be currently at the top of the charts, but she maintained a loyal, upscale fan base who paid fancy admission prices to attend her concert performances. During a few of her summer breaks from high school, Whitney abandoned East Orange, New Jersey, to be an indulged member of Warwick's entourage as the veteran singer toured the country. In the process, Whitney received a solid education in the art of ordering from room service, traveling on board a private jet plane, and experiencing the special rapport that sophisticated Dionne created on stage with her paying audiences.

Even after Gary Houston went away to college in Illinois, the Houstons seemed—on the surface—to have a fairly tight-knit household. In this family, there had always been a healthy degree of give-and-take between parents and children, and there was an especially strong bond between Nippy and her brother Spikey (Michael). "Whenever we had a disagreement in my family," Whitney recollected, "my mother and father would allow us to call a meeting, and even if we had a problem with them, we could say, 'Hey, Ma. I didn't like the way you did me the other day,' or 'Daddy, can't you talk a little better?' We got a lot of stuff out because we were able to be honest with one another. I would always call the meeting." She went on to say, "It was always my [younger] brother who was picking on me or doing something I didn't like, and my mother would say, 'Michael, why do you do that to your sister?' He'd say, 'Because I love her and I have nothing else to do and she's my younger sister.' From that, I could understand how to deal with him."

Now the Sweet Inspirations has broken away on their own, Cissy was John's only talent-management client. As such, he continued to escort his wife when she had local gigs in the evenings, making sure that everything went as smoothly as possible with the show. However, with her relatively curtailed performance schedule (in order, she insisted, to be at home more with the children), this was not a full-time occupation for Mr. Houston. To keep busy, provide more structure to his day, and pull his own weight financially, he took a position with the City of Newark Planning Board. In holding down a nine-to-five administrative job, plus shepherding Cissy about in the evenings, the fifty-six-year-old—who was already suffering some of the side effects of diabetes—had a more than full schedule. In fact, his schedule was more busy than was physically good for him.

In September 1976, Whitney returned for her second year at Mount Saint Dominic Academy. Now a member of the eighth grade, she settled into her academic routine without enthusiasm. Then, suddenly, later that month, everything changed drastically in the Houston household.

One evening, Cissy was awakened by what she thought was a prank call, and she hung up. The phone rang again, and, this time, Whitney answered. A voice at the other end mumbled something about being a hospital worker and that they had admitted a patient named John Houston who had just suffered a massive heart attack. At first, Nippy thought it was a bad joke. However, on going to her father's bedroom, she discovered he wasn't there. (He had actually awoken, realized how seriously unwell he felt, and, not wanting to disturb or alarm the others, had managed to drive himself to the hospital's emergency room.) Whitney told her mother the bad news and the latter reacted with a brief outburst of hysterics. Then, just as quickly as her panic had erupted, Cissy became calm. In this mode, she organized the family to drive quickly to the hospital. All the way to the medical facility she had visions of arriving only to find that John had died. Fortunately, the reality was not that severe.

Mr. Houston's physical condition remained critical for a few days, but he stabilized and was eventually discharged. Cissy and the others were so thankful to have him back home that it was days before anyone appreciated just how much he had become a changed man. After this traumatic brush with death, his outlook on life had drastically altered. No longer the relaxed and flexible man that he had been, he was now dissatisfied and edgy about nearly everything in his life. This restive state of mind led to accelerating arguments between John and Cissy. It finally came out that after thinking over all that had led to his heart attack, John had elected to believe that his wife was the ultimate cause of his near-death. He decided that he had taken on too many physical and emotional burdens over the years to make life easier for her to follow her dreams in gospel music, the church choir, and the recording industry. There was also an element of guilt that, perhaps, he had somehow failed Cissy in helping her to reach her lofty career goals. His new mindset pushed the couple into a downward spiral. The mounting anxiety and erupting bouts of unpleasantness were bad enough for the parents, but the increased tensions at the Dodd Street home upset the children tremendously.

In the past, Whitney had admired the apparently comfortable dynamics of her parents' give-and-take relationship. "My father showed me how a man treats a lady," Whitney explained. "He demanded respect from my mom but he gave it in return. They were the best of lovers who could fight like cats and dogs but they always went to bed laughing."

Now, there was an undisguised hard edge to the Houstons' quarreling that time did not alleviate. If previously John had seemed comfortable and complacent about living in the shadow of his strong-willed wife so she could operate at the center of her own world, these days he wanted more from life. While this worsening domestic situation was playing itself out, a highly distressed, baffled Cissy distracted herself to a degree by keeping busy with church work, recording sessions with the likes of Bette Midler and the Neville Brothers, and club engagements.

Finally, the couple had to accept that if they hoped to salvage any degree of friendship from their many years together, they would have to physically separate. To bring the situation to a head, John insisted on moving out of the house in late 1977, an action which upset and humiliated his usually stoic spouse.

Whitney, who was very much a daddy's girl, had observed the rapid crumbling of her parents' marriage in puzzlement, but always with the reassuring assumption that somehow her parents would patch things up together. She had never expected that they would really break up. Thus she was shocked when her father actually did leave the family home. What cushioned the blow to a small degree was that John only moved ten minutes away and insisted on remaining part of the family in numerous business and social matters.

Because John chose not to break ties completely at this time and since Cissy hoped that one day they might find a way to be reconciled, the Houstons did not officially divorce in 1977. In fact, they did not even file for a legal separation. Instead, they simply lived in two different locations: Cissy with the children at the Dodd Street home in East Orange, and John in a small apartment in nearby Fort Lee.

Of the two Houston children still at home, Michael had already built up an emotional buffer against this family calamity by becoming enmeshed in a deepening romantic relationship with Donna Jackson, formerly of North Carolina. She had lived in New Jersey for several years and had first met Michael in junior high. Now they were both in high school and were going steady; they would eventually marry.

At the time of this shattering domestic crisis, Nippy had no close friend or boyfriend to be her special confidant. Nor could she turn to brother Michael as much as she would have liked to—he was too preoccupied with Donna.

Whitney's explanation (or rationalization) of why, unlike most girls her age, she didn't already have a boyfriend was that, "The disadvantage of growing up with two boys is that you can't do anything. If they saw me with a boy, it was like . . . 'Who's that?' I was totally like 'Oh, God, please, just go away.' The advantage was that I knew all the raps. I knew all the shit that guys could lay on you from A to Z. I got to hear how guys [really] talk about girls."

Whitney would expound on this theme at greater length in November

1993, when she was interviewed by TV journalist Barbara Walters. She told her: "I learned a lot about men, with my two brothers, my father. They taught me a lot about how men [really] think about women. They didn't say at all: 'Go! You needn't hear this!', it was: 'Come here, I'll tell you about Barbara! Now, Barbara. . . . You know, I had . . . [her] the other day. Gary had her tonight, my friend Joseph is gonna have her tomorrow. Now what kind of girl do you think that is?" And I'd say: 'I don't know, she likes guys!' He said: 'No, she's a whore. That's what she is. And nobody respects her' "

Then, in an almost throwaway climax to this intriguing discussion, Walters and Houston had the following exchange:

BARBARA: Did it change your behavior?
WHITNEY: Yes. It did. I think it made me very cold, in a lot of ways.

As a result of her parents' breakup and her growing sense of abandonment and bewilderment, the already pampered Whitney became even more headstrong, moody, and self-involved. In this accelerated rebellious phase, she wanted to do whatever she pleased whenever she felt like it. She became even more blatantly disinterested in the fair sharing of household chores. At home, she tested her mother's authority in many ways. One day it might be about wearing nylon stockings "like the other girls," with her mother insisting she wasn't old enough to take this step toward adulthood. Sometimes, a frazzled Cissy used sharp words with her recalcitrant teenager when reasonable discussion seemed to make no impact on the girl. Mrs. Houston has alluded to having been pushed to her limits and resorting to other remedies. From the calmness of passing years, she recalled (with a bit of belated humor): "[Nippy's] last spanking came when she was about sixteen. That was the first real spanking she got. A real good one."

Her parents' separation also affected Whitney's attitude and performance at Mount Saint Dominic. Being emotionally wounded, the already shy schoolgirl became even more introverted and distant with her peers at the Academy, where she had always been on the fringe of student activities. She became apathetic in several classes. Her grades slipped badly and she ended up failing four subjects. For the time being, she had lost interest in school almost altogether, a situation which the nuns understood and tried to reverse.

In 1979, when her brother Michael left for college in Kansas, Whitney was left alone in the house with her mother as each dealt in her own individual way with the broken marriage. In reaction to her ongoing unhappiness at the time, Whitney admitted later, "I started hangin' out. In the streets, walkin', hangin', getting' to know another 'family,' I suppose: the world, the music. I was hangin' around a lotta musicians. Singers, background singers, hangin' out in New York. I didn't wanna be at home." Tired of all the arguing she had experienced at the Dodd Street house, she just "wanted peace" from thinking about the troublesome, seemingly insoluble family situation.

Thankfully, at this critical emotional juncture, Whitney's musical career began to blossom.

7

Making First Impressions

"So I got to hear how men really think about women—which left me with not much to be disillusioned about. Guys would walk up to me, and I'd go [folds her arms and frowns]. 'And what do you have to say?' [Laughs] I wasn't goin' for a lot of bullshit. You know, my brother had one girl outside, one upstairs, one in the basement and all three girls would be waiting. Me—'You kept me waiting too long, see ya later.' I knew I was a trip."

WHITNEY HOUSTON, 1993

Through much of the early and mid-1970s, Cissy Houston could not catch a real break in the record industry. "I really don't know what went wrong," she observed once. "I've been in this business a long time, and it discouraged me immensely to see people who seemingly started yesterday ride straight to the top." There were times when the talented but frustrated veteran thought about quitting the business (which she did to a degree when she became more of a homemaker than performer in the early part of the decade), but she said she kept going because "inside I knew I'd be back." Cissy Houston's cycle of bad luck, discouragement and renewed determination about making her true mark in the music business was an ongoing, eye-opening education for Whitney on what might be her own destiny in the industry.

Cissy continued to do background singing on others' albums, sometimes taking a lead vocal on a cut or two of another artist's release (as with niece Dionne Warwick in 1972 and jazz musician Herbie Mann in 1973). While not-so-patiently waiting to be rediscovered by the record industry, she settled for new nightclub engagements in Manhattan.

Before long, Whitney, who initially had been just an onlooker at her mother's cabaret shows, graduated to being one of Cissy's background singers—when the gig did not interfere with her schoolwork. This activity was an outgrowth of her singing occasionally with her mother when the latter was a guest gospel performer at churches in Harlem and elsewhere.

With their overlapping musical styles and similar sound, mother and daughter provided a pleasing, harmonious accompaniment for one another. However, just as had been the case when Whitney joined the choir at New Hope Baptist Church, businesslike Cissy did not show favoritism to her daughter at these club gigs. The teenager had to rehearse as long and hard as the other background singers. In fact, in her mother's demanding eyes, her daughter had to work harder to prove herself worthy of being part of the proceedings. The talented girl met the challenge and made an accomplished addition to Cissy's act. Whitney's initial fears that she was not good enough to take on such club work quickly vanished.

After Whitney became famous in the coming years, club managers and patrons alike enjoyed recounting anecdotes about visiting Mikell's or Sweetwater's in the New York City of the mid-to-late 1970s and witnessing this talented young background singer at Cissy Houston's show. These observers would recall how, on occasion, the shy young lady would timidly step forward to do a solo. Her powerful, wide-ranging voice proved to be of superior quality. Cissy remembers these times well: "I almost had to push her up front. When she did get there, I had to encourage her to make the most of it. 'Show me no mercy.' I'd tell her. 'If it was me out there I wouldn't show any for you.'"

In contrast, there were also instances when Whitney became overwhelmed by a growing sense of her artistic self and her commanding vocal abilities. On these occasions, she could not (or would not) hold herself back from showing off in her solo spot in the self-indulgent manner of a prankish adolescent—and a diva in the making. Such transgressions caused the ever-vigilant Cissy to retaliate with one of her famous super-stern looks, a stare that was powerful enough to make anyone cower back into good behavior. As further punishment, for the next few club performances, Whitney would be relegated to the background group and given *no* solo spots. Such reprimands were effective in reining in the teenager's bouts of unprofessional conduct.

☆

In 1977, the same year that John Houston moved away from the family home and Whitney began her ninth grade at Mount Saint Dominic Academy, Cissy's singing career took a major jump forward. She had begun to include the song "Tomorrow" from the new Broadway musical *Annie* in her club act. She gave the lyrics her special soulful interpretation and it became her signature number as she moved about the Manhattan club circuit, appearing at venues including the Bottom Line and Les Mouches. Also in 1977, she made a new solo album for Private Stock Records entitled *Cissy Houston*. Among the tracks were a memorable version of "Tomorrow" and other standards such as "Make It Easy on Yourself." "Tomorrow" was released as a single, receiving favorable airplay on the radio and becoming popular with record buyers.

The next year, to cash in on the frenetic disco craze, Private Stock issued a new Cissy album (*Think It Over*), on which Whitney participated in the background vocals for nearly every selection. It was great experience for the newcomer to be actually inside the recording studio making "joyful noises" along with her mother. The blazing title song from this upbeat disc became a sizable hit, especially popular in the gay dance clubs. Thus Cissy expanded her fan base, and this lifestyle group became some of her most loyal devotees. Sometimes, gay men would make up almost the entire audience at one of her nightclub appearances, such as at Reno Sweeney's. As Whitney remembered, "My mother used to pack that club out. I mean the queens would be around the corner! Around the corner in a line, waiting to see Miss Cissy." Performing as one of her mother's backup performers, Whitney had her first real experience of mingling with the gay subculture, a group who would support her singing career in years to come.

As a result of Cissy's escalating fame, in 1978 she was asked to headline a concert at Town Hall in New York City. The occasion was to be a benefit fundraiser for the United Negro College Funds. She quickly accepted. With the date set, she decided this might be an excellent showcase for her girl to perform a solo selection. With a mixture of motherly pride and professional concern, she had a serious talk with Whitney about her stepping into the limelight in such a major forum. "Do you believe you can do this?" she asked. Her daughter answered, "Yes, I do." Wanting to be sure they were on the same page, Cissy next asked, "And do you believe in the magic of believing?" Nippy shook her head in the affirmative and said "I do."

Saturday, February 18, 1978 arrived and the audience assembled at

Town Hall on West 43rd Street. Partway through the concert, Cissy informed the audience that her daughter was about to sing a solo number. With the flourish of a proud host, she announced, "Ladies and gentlemen, Miss Whitney Houston." The nervous fourteen-year-old stepped to center stage, accepted the microphone her mother handed to her, and then the musicians began to play the familiar strains of "Tomorrow." After singing the first few stanzas of the song in her powerful voice, Mrs. Houston stepped out of the limelight, and it was time for Whitney to take over.

At first, the novice froze with uncertainty and her stage fright got the better of her. Feeling her mother's ever-vigilant gaze upon her, Whitney regained her composure by closing her eyes, just as she had done before starting that solo at New Hope Baptist Church a few years earlier. Then, risking all, she began to sing: loud, clear, and increasingly confident. By the time she reached that critical part of the number where the singer must perform at full voice, she was in top gear and soared through the difficult section without a problem. The audience, unprepared for this vocal treat, greeted Whitney's rendition with a burst of hearty applause. A beaming Cissy commanded Whitney to do an encore of the splashy part of "Tomorrow." As she finished the song the spectators clapped and cheered and some rose to their feet to give young Whitney her first standing ovation.

The evening was quite a success, but ever-ambitious Cissy made it known to industry friends that she wasn't satisfied yet. She wanted to reach greater heights and did not have forever to wait for what she so rightly deserved. As for Whitney, most reviewers were too preoccupied with raving over Mrs. Houston's performance to make significant mention of her daughter in their write-ups. One reviewer in *Soul* magazine did, but they misspelled her name, referring to her erroneously as "Whiten." Unaware of this unintentional slight, young Whitney was thrilled by the experience and her enthusiastic reception from the audience. "What a night," she enthused. "I found out that there was something inside of me that made me feel incredible when I am singing. It really is like magic." It was just like her mother had said it would be.

By now, Cissy was convinced that the success of her *Think It Over* album would launch her into the big league. But again, luck was against her. Her record label, Private Stock, suddenly went out of business. Mrs. Houston, with husband John helping on the contract negotiations, moved over to

Columbia Records, where she made the album *Warning—Danger* (1979). The disc's title tune and some of the other cuts showcased her strong, gritty song style—with its gospel flavor—applied to the disco format. Yet again, fate intervened. As fast as the disco era had arisen, it just as suddenly came crashing down, and disco songs were now considered passé. Once again, the talented Cissy was at a loose end professionally and was forced to return to club work in the New York City area. Whenever she could, Whitney performed as part of the act. On stage, she was acquiring wonderful experience and gaining the professional poise that would be incredibly useful in the years to come.

While Whitney was experiencing some early success as a showbusiness beginner, other facets of her life were proving troublesome. She was still deeply bothered by her parents' separation and missed having her beloved father at home. Although she saw him frequently, it was not enough for daddy's girl. Meanwhile, at Mount Saint Dominic, she still had not integrated herself into the student body and remained virtually an outsider. At school, she downplayed any mention of her showbusiness ambitions or her performing, not wanting to further alienate her peers, who already thought she was too different from them. To compensate for her shyness, she began displaying occasional outbursts of comic behavior, hoping subconsciously to win her classmates' approval.

An example of this audacious behavior occurred on a school outing. According to Sister Barbara Moore, one of the teaching staff at Mount Saint Dominic Academy during Whitney's tenure there: "One year the class went to Disneyland. There was a circus, one where the children were allowed to get involved. I walked into the arena and there, walking high on the tightrope, was Whitney—and she was waving at me! I knew the career plans her mother had fixed for her and I thought, 'If that child falls and breaks her legs, her mother will break mine.'" The same nun would also note in 1987 that the staff at the Academy were virtually unaware until late in Houston's high-school career that she could sing. Said Sister Barbara, "We just didn't know until there was some event where we heard her. Now it's funny walking into a mall or getting into your car and hearing her voice on the radio. But every time I do, I think, 'Good for you, kiddo.'"

As an antidote to Whitney's distress over her dad's absence from their home life, Cissy Houston suggested that Nippy accept a position as a counselor-in-training at a New Jersey summer camp, a facility which concentrated largely on administering to underprivileged children from the projects. Cissy hoped both the change of scenery and being closely involved with needy youngsters would be good therapy for her unhappy daughter.

Among the staff at the day camp was Robyn Crawford, who at eighteen was two years older than Whitney. Robyn was athletic and quite adept at basketball. In fact, she had plans to attend college on a hoops scholarship once she graduated from high school. Striking in looks, Robyn was slender, with angular features and broad shoulders. She was very driven and well organized, and looking for something special in life that would give her a sense of real purpose. Almost from the first time they met that summer, these two young African-American women became instant comrades.

For Whitney, it was an amazing experience suddenly to have a pal with whom she could share the most sacred confidences, express her ambitions, her concerns, and reveal her confusion and unhappiness over her parents' ongoing separation. Whitney would often describe Robyn as "the sister I never had." Finally, she thought, here was someone she could truly trust with her innermost secrets—someone who would not abandon her as her beloved father essentially had done.

For her part, Robyn found the younger counselor—still not fully past her gawky adolescent stage—refreshing, and her accounts of showbusiness notables such as Cissy Houston, Aretha Franklin, and Dionne Warwick entertaining and exciting. Crawford, unlike others, was amused whenever the now-talkative Whitney would suddenly break into song, but she was careful never to make fun of this habit.

As the bond between the two developed and deepened that summer, Whitney and Robyn became inseparable; one was never seen without the other. To onlookers at the camp, they seemed to be literally joined at the hip. Some more sophisticated observers wondered if there was, perhaps, a sexual relationship going on between them.

When not involved in the charity camp work, Houston and Crawford spent time together in East Orange and thereabouts. Said one bystander about the pair: "They even started to look alike. . . . they would walk arm-in-arm in public. . . . When they were together, they'd act as if no else was even in the room. They had their own world."

The deep friendship caused a lot of talk around East Orange among Whitney's age group. Years later, choosing to laugh about the situation,

Whitney would say, "People used to say we were gay, because when you saw Robyn, you saw me, and when you saw me, you saw Robyn. We were that tight, you know." However, at the time, the situation was not so funny. When anyone called Whitney a dyke to her face, her response was visceral. She shoved the person against a nearby wall and threatened to beat her up if she ever repeated the statement.

The gossip didn't stop, however. Initially, the two targets chose to ignore the volleys of nasty innuendoes and snide remarks. But shrugging off the unpleasant treatment did nothing to resolve matters. The vicious barbs especially began to sting Whitney, who was vulnerable in any case to anything that underlined her status as the outsider she so much hated being. In contrast, Robyn, the older and more emotionally mature of the duo, insisted that it was ridiculous to let the cheap shots of others spoil their growing friendship.

It reached a point where Whitney did not know what to do. As much as she craved and needed the companionship of her new friend, she could not seem to deal with the rumors and remarks circulating about them. The result was a face-off between the two young women. Robyn gave perplexed Whitney an ultimatum: either she had to learn to disregard the slurs of lesbianism, or else they should just go their separate ways.

At first, Whitney took the path of least resistance. She and Robyn stopped spending time together, only barely saying hello when they happened to encounter one another. Neither was happy with this turn of events, but for Whitney, the more emotionally deprived of the two at the time, the rift was heartbreaking. Finally, the two girls met to discuss the situation. In a burst of mutual need, they each agreed that their special friendship should not suffer because of the maliciousness of others. As Whitney would later explain, she told her precious pal, "We're friends. I love you, you love me. Why should we not be friends? Because of what people say and what they think?" She summed up her courageous stance by remarking that "[we] can't let outsiders ruin it [for us]." With this statement—which would become her ruling principle in the years to come with regard to her husband, Bobby Brown—Whitney and Robyn made peace. Their deep friendship, once again, was secure.

Whitney was growing emotionally into a young woman who was beginning to understand herself, her needs, and her goals. She was also growing physically. By 1980, she had shot up to her full height of five feet, eight inches. Looking back at this period, she told *Playboy* magazine's Nelson George in May 1991: "I grew in one year. It was amazing. I'm a little uncomfortable with my body, because I'm usually taller than most of the fellas and it's kind of uncomfortable for them and it's really uncomfortable for me. So now I'm into wearing flats. I've always had long legs. I've been told that's a very sexy thing. I was talking to a friend of mine the other night and he was asking me, 'Whitney, is there anything that you would like to change about yourself?' I said, 'I wish I had short legs.' I didn't mean that I wish I had shorter legs. I love the length of my legs, but it's hard for me to keep weight on rather than take it off. I know if my legs were a bit shorter I could keep that weight on."

Now almost seventeen, Whitney had transformed from a pert, sometimes rambunctious tomboy into a pretty young woman. With her almond-shaped eyes, high cheekbones, and captivating, wide smile (on those occasions when she allowed herself to be joyful about life), she was a radiant figure who required little or no makeup to enhance her beauty. Not unexpectedly for a shy loner, she really had no sense at the time of her physical attractiveness, regardless of what her parents or even her friend Robyn Crawford would tell her. In her mind's eye, she was still the gawky miss who had trouble making friends at school or in the neighborhood and couldn't even keep her father (or brothers, who were away at college) from abandoning her.

What happened next is one of those showbusiness stories that sounds like a press agent's fabrication or a scene from a Hollywood movie. But it truly happened.

One day, Cissy Houston and Nippy were in New York City making their rounds to handle various music-industry matters. As they sauntered along Manhattan's Seventh Avenue, not far from Carnegie Hall on West 57th Street, they stepped into an office building to attend their next meeting. There in the lobby they were spotted by freelance fashion photographer Dean Avedon, who had a knack for discovering fresh talent for the modeling agencies for whom he did assignments. When he saw this young, beautiful, leggy, light-skinned African-American woman walking by, his instincts clicked into gear. He immediately pulled out his business card and handed it to the older of the two, sensing that this woman must be the teenager's mother. He made a quick pitch, urging Mrs. Houston to take her daughter upstairs to the Click modeling agency. He enthused about Whitney's potential, saying he was sure she could become a top model.

As had become her habit, Whitney withdrew into her protective shell in front of this stranger. Having switched into her haughty and cynical mode, she made it clear to Avedon that she knew better than to believe this obvious come-on line. On the other hand, the more seasoned Cissy, never one to let a potential opportunity go untapped, diplomatically smoothed over her daughter's blunt putdown. She suggested to Nippy that they had nothing to lose and it might be fun to see what it was all about.

Cissy's words made sense to her daughter. Her suggestion about a career opportunity was low-key, rather than a command as to what must be done. It was one of the qualities she liked best about her mother. As Whitney phrased it, "My mother didn't force me to be ... anything. She just encouraged me to be what we thought I was good at. If it had been nursing, she would have encouraged me to be a nurse. If it had been sanitation work, she would have said, 'Be the best damn garbage girl in the world.'"

With Dean Avedon leading the way, Mrs. Houston and Whitney got into an elevator and reached the floor where Click Models was based. Avedon quickly swept the two women into the office of Frances Grill, the founder and owner of the firm. The industry veteran took one look at Whitney and agreed with Avedon about Whitney's potential. Recalling that meeting with the Houston women, Grill told Mark Bego, author of *Whitney!* (1986), "she was a very pretty kid, and she had this wonderful mother with her. You can tell very quickly in these kinds of situations; just put them in front of the camera, and something happens. They have a 'language.' The talented ones are really going to do it, and she had that language." Grill elaborated, "She had 'it' somehow all the time. It was quite obvious to everybody who had any contact with her on a professional level."

Since everyone was showing so much enthusiasm about this opportunity, Whitney became much more compliant. John Houston was consulted and he agreed that it certainly couldn't hurt his daughter's chances to gain additional poise, which could only help her as a performer. As Whitney told herself, "Where else could a kid make that kind of money for doing nothing?"

From the start, being a mannequin for pay was nothing more than a job to Whitney. It was a better way than many to earn money to help her mother with running the household and paying for her tuition at Mount Saint Dominic. Besides, it could be the start of a financial cushion for the years ahead as she tried to break into the record industry.

So began Whitney's fashion modeling career. At first, she did a lot of what is known as "editorial" work: pictures used to illustrate feature articles or columns. She did assignments for *Seventeen* and *Mademoiselle* magazines as one of the still relatively few non-Caucasians in the field. Frances Grill remembers, "Everyone adored her. She was 'a very fresh little energy' is all I could call her. And, very 'clean-spirited' is the way I would put it."

As she gained experience and stature in the field, Whitney became the object of interest from bigger modeling agencies intrigued by her haughty look, her ambivalence towards the work, and her seeming indifference to their blandishments. Eventually she left Click Models and began modeling at the gilt-edged Wilhelmina Agency. Evidently holding no grudges against her ex-client, Grill would later say of her shrewd discovery, "What she achieved, I think that it's incredible that she did it so quickly. There was no question that she was going to do it. And she has a quiet determination. She's a very determined young lady."

After a relatively short time, Whitney became a regular on the fashion modeling circuit. She modeled for *Cosmopolitan, Mademoiselle,* and *Young Miss,* and appeared on the covers of publications like *Glamour* and *Seventeen.* In her new line of work, she came to enjoy getting to meet and know her peers such as Phoebe Cates, Brooke Shields, and Tara Fitzpatrick (who made the 1997 documentary *Scratch the Surface,* an insider's look at the modeling industry, in which Whitney was briefly an interviewee). She found the traveling and her growing fees (upwards of $5,000 for two hours' work) appealing, but she disliked the endless primping and prepping: "Too fussy for me. You stand there in front of the camera and just grin."

In the final analysis, what she disliked most about her new craft was having to bury the *real* Whitney beneath the veneer of the pretend, painted image who smiled vacantly at the cameras under the hot lights. All this sudden attention and appreciation of her attractiveness did not make her feel especially beautiful. As she saw it, "Beauty to me is how you feel about yourself."

Added to her growing dislike of the modeling business was the reaction of her classmates back in Caldwell, New Jersey. After she appeared on the cover of *Seventeen,* a few of her peers brought copies of the magazine to school and when Whitney walked into the classroom, they held the publication up in front of their faces and began chanting, "Look at Miss Seventeen. Look at Miss Seventeen." Just then, one of the nuns walked into the room, sized up the situation, and ordered, "Okay, put Miss Seventeen down and let's get to work." Whitney cringed in her seat at this display of pettiness from her schoolmates. Once again, she was being shoved out of the mainstream, out of the "in" crowd, and labeled a pathetic outsider. She might pretend to others that she didn't care, but it was a hurt that never went away. As before, she hid behind a mask of indifference.

One of Whitney's former classmates at Mount Saint Dominic would recall later in life: "She did have this attitude. She wasn't very friendly. She never went out of her way to make any friends, so she didn't have any. Even the boys left her alone. I don't remember her ever going on a date . . . so all us kids just thought she didn't like guys. Besides, she was always hanging out with Robyn Crawford even though Robyn wasn't even in school."

Thus, as she completed her senior year at high school, Whitney was swallowed up by forces that refused to let her true self be recognized and appreciated. She felt no sorrow at leaving the Academy when she graduated in June 1981. While that unsettling experience was finally coming to an end, there was still the bothersome modeling to contend with. At the time, she was in no financial position to quit the business. However, she couldn't wait until that day arrived, because she felt that fashion work was "degrading"—"[it] wasn't a life that I wanted to live."

But on the positive side, the eighteen-year-old had two strong guiding influences: her desire to become a professional singer and her nourishing friendship with Robyn Crawford.

8

Reaching Out for the Big Break

"When I first started out I juiced my mother. I was like 'Ma, Ma, Ma, Ma, Ma, what do I do? What do I say? How do I handle it?' Now I know. You learn, you grow up, and you become your own woman."

WHITNEY HOUSTON, 1993

For reasons best known only to Cissy Houston, in her 1998 memoirs she pointedly makes no reference *whatsoever* to Whitney's good friend and, later, business associate Robyn Crawford. However, back in the early 1980s, Cissy was very much aware of Crawford's influence on Whitney and worried that it was loosening the strong control that the mother had over her youngest child.

Whitney's stabs at independence in personal matters were becoming increasingly frequent, such as the huge amount of time Whitney spent with Robyn. Whenever Cissy walked into the house on Dodd Street, she could almost take bets that Nippy and her friend would be in the midst of a private, deep conversation. On any level, this was irksome to Mrs. Houston. The situation was not helped when Nippy began talking about moving out on her own, now that she had graduated from high school. This led to heated discussions between Cissy and John Houston over how best to handle the delicate and discomforting situation. However, the two had no ready solution to the Whitney–Robyn bond, which continued to generate much speculation in East Orange and wherever else the two inseparable pals went.

On the other hand, Whitney was much more compliant when it came to shaping her vocal career and what the next steps should be. In these matters, she relied heavily on Cissy. Her regard for her mother's abilities in the music field was boundless: "Everything she knows physically and mentally about singing she has passed on to me, and she taught me everything I know about the technology of the recording studio and about the business." When there were contractual matters at hand, Whitney also tapped into her father's expertise.

During this period, Cissy continued to employ Nippy as part of her New York City club act. She had generously decided to give her daughter two solo numbers in each evening's show. By now, it had become commonplace for audiences to rave about the mother–daughter singing team who shared such apparent rapport in front of the spotlight.

At one point, the elder Houston concluded it was high time for her girl to experience headlining a club act herself and get that necessary test under her belt. According to Whitney, they were booked to do a show one evening at Mikell's: "[My mother] called and sounded hoarse and said, 'My voice! I can't sing! You'll have to do it without me.' I said, 'Forget it! I can't do that.' She said, 'Of course you can, you're good.'"

The younger Houston survived the nerve-wracking ordeal; in fact, she acquitted herself well. After the performance, she called her mom to report on the evening. It was then that Whitney discovered the entire thing had been a setup. Cissy admitted, "Well, I was kinda sick, but I really had to show you that you could do this and if that's what you want, you have to go do it."

When Cissy, still much in demand as a top background singer, went into the recording studios, she continued to take Whitney along. Sometimes, the newcomer joined her mother at the microphone, as when Cissy returned to her old stomping ground at Atlantic Records to record two cuts for Chaka Khan's new Warner Bros. album *Naughty* (1980). The Houston women can be heard providing distinctive background harmonies on two tracks: "Our Love's in Danger" and "Clouds." For Whitney, this recording session was extremely exciting and artistically satisfying, as she greatly admired the artist, who was born Yvette Marie Stevens in Great Lakes, Illinois in 1953. In fact, so great was Whitney's esteem for Chaka Khan that, years later, she would record a version of her 1978 hit "I'm Every Woman" and would include her idol in the music video.

Now intent on gaining a toehold in the music industry, Whitney began getting additional recording assignments but still usually in conjunction with Cissy. For instance, the two of them can be heard providing background vocals on the Neville Brothers' *Fiyo on the Bayou*, released in April 1981. Made for the A&M label, the album was an updating of the R&B sound rendered in New Orleans style, boasting a creative mix of reggae, Cajun, and rock to spice up the eight tracks with a contemporary flavor. In addition, the younger Houston was heard on background harmonies for one of Lou Rawls's early-1980s discs.

Over the last few years, as Whitney had become known in tandem with her mother on the club and recording circuit, and had built up her own reputation as a rising model, several producers had offered the young artist a recording contract. Each time, Cissy and John Houston rejected such proposals, insisting that their girl must first graduate high school. Now that she had, and it was clear that her career ambitions and her only average school grades (thanks in part to the distractions of her modeling jobs) precluded going to college, it seemed the right time to put the teenager's career on a more professional footing.

Having failed in his efforts as manager to make Cissy a major name in showbusiness, John Houston wisely did not suggest that he take charge of his talented daughter's future. Instead, he turned to an industry acquaintance, Gene Harvey, who, with his partner Seymour Flics, ran Tara Productions at 230 West 55th Street in Manhattan. Several weeks after her eighteenth birthday in August 1981, Whitney signed a management contract with the small firm.

Under Harvey's guidance, their new client began the grooming process to prepare for her bid at stardom. To gain further visibility, she was advised to continue her modeling chores. But now, in her "spare" time, she took acting and dance classes. She also concentrated her attention on refining her naturally rich singing voice. Meanwhile, Harvey turned down offers from a few major companies to sign up Whitney because "I didn't want her to have to deal with those kinds of pressures at that point."

With her personal manager's sanction, Whitney, as well as Cissy Houston, undertook background vocals on *Experiment in White* (1982), an Atlantic Records offering featuring Janis Siegel, a member of the well-regarded Manhattan Transfer. More exciting for Whitney was a one-shot deal with Elektra Records. They were preparing a new album (*One Down*) by a group known as Material, composed of keyboardist Michael Beinhorn and bassist Bill Laswell. The nine tracks would be a mix of funk and disco and each one would boast a different guest vocalist. Whitney was contracted to sing one of the numbers. On "Memories," with tenor saxophonist Archie Shepp playing a solo, she delivered a smooth vocal performance. The *Village Voice* reviewed the album, paying particular attention to Whitney's contribution. "Guest stars Whitney Houston and Archie Shepp transform 'Memories' into one of the most gorgeous ballads you've heard." It was just the first of the hosannas that were to come Whitney's way.

One can only imagine how conflicted Cissy Houston, who still gained solace from leading the New Hope Baptist Church choirs, must have felt at this juncture. Here was her eighteen-year-old daughter gliding into the music business—albeit with the help of family and friends—while Cissy had struggled for years, and continued to struggle, to gain the recognition she believed was due to her. (The complex relationship between the Houstons was reminiscent of that between Judy Garland and her daughter Liza Minnelli in the 1960s and the 1970s, when the two had seesawed back and forth with their personal agendas, rivalry, and individual successes.)

Kenneth Ammons, who came into Whitney's circle in the early 1990s as the boyfriend of Houston's then publicist, later wrote about his reminiscences of life with the diva in *Good Girl, Bad Girl* (1996). He describes the situation between mother and daughter in the years before he came to know the family personally: "Friends say Cissy was torn between jealousy and pride. Intellectually, Cissy must have known it was time to pass the baton, but she couldn't bear to see her own dream die so her daughter's could live." Ammons also noted that the mother never reined in her daughter professionally. However, she always made sure that Whitney knew "who the real star of the family was."

Now that Whitney's career had focus and guidance, she broke some blood ties by leaving her family's Dodd Street home. She moved into a small, modest apartment in Woodbridge, about twenty-two miles and thirty minutes' drive south of East Orange. But Whitney would not be living alone at the new address. She shared the unpretentious apartment with Robyn Crawford. By then, the latter, who had enrolled at Monmouth University in West Long Branch, New Jersey, on a basketball scholarship, had dropped out of school.

Each of the roommates endured strong reactions from their own families about their new living situation. Said Robyn of the rumors that surrounded the two women's lifestyle together: "I tell my family, 'You can hear anything on the streets, but if you don't hear it from me, it's not true.'" For her part, Whitney insisted: "My mother taught me that when you stand in the truth and someone tells a lie about you, don't fight it. I'm not with any man. I'm not in love. People see Robyn with me and they draw their own conclusions." She insisted vehemently, "Let people talk. It doesn't bother me because I know I'm not gay. I don't care.'"

When not modeling, taking performance classes, or recording songs, Whitney continued to appear in clubs in tandem with Cissy. Increasingly, the daughter was gaining terrific special mentions for her vocal abilities in the reviews of these appearances. *Billboard*, the music industry's trade journal, predicted, "Whitney has the pedigree and the style to be a major vocalist." The *New York Times* was in hearty agreement, deciding the young personality was "a talent with tremendous potential."

As word of mouth about Whitney spread through the music business and among the public, she was signed to perform on the Columbia Records album *Paul Jabara and Friends*. Jabara had written hit songs such as "Last Dance" for Donna Summers, "Enough Is Enough (No More Tears)," a duet for Summers and Barbra Streisand, and "It's Raining Men" for the Weather Girls. Jabara, not a very inspired singer, was now headlining his own album, which would feature him sharing vocals with the Weather Girls, Leata Galloway, and Whitney Houston. Whitney and Jabara teamed up for the ballad "Eternal Love." Released in March 1983, it was a fine, straightforward showcase for Whitney, adding to her standing in the business. (A few years later, when Whitney had gained international prominence, this Jabara album would become something of a collector's item for her fans.)

One of Houston's other professional activities at the time was doing voiceovers for radio and TV commercials, as she had done for the Cosmos campaign with the Average White Band in 1982. The next year, fresh-faced, eager Whitney was one of a small group of singers who also executed a few "dance" movements in a bouncy TV jingle for Canada Dry ginger ale. Later on, when she became more famous, she would do a few commercials for Japan-based corporations.

By now, Gene Harvey was fielding new offers from major record labels eager to sign up Whitney. Elektra and Columbia, which respectively had released *One Down* and *Paul Jabara and Friends*, made overtures towards her. As terms were discussed and Whitney weighed up the various points of Harvey's negotiations, she relied heavily on feedback from her parents. All too aware of the poor label choices that had brought down Cissy's fortunes in the past, Whitney and her family considered the options carefully. Her mother's sage advice was to be sure to pick a company that would steer her responsibly.

When Whitney, in turn, got back to Harvey, she repeated to him her conversations with her parents. She explained later: "I wanted a career that would build over the years, and I didn't want to be just thrown out there to sink or swim. I needed guidance." She added one more requisite for any company intending to become her employer: not only must they respect her as a performer, but they must *also* value her opinions. Voicing what would become her key mantra in years to come, she said, "Nobody makes me do anything I don't want to do."

As time wore on, Columbia dropped out of the bidding and it seemed the nineteen-year-old would soon become part of Elektra's stable. Then, almost by chance, another contender entered the running.

The new player was Arista Records. The successful label was founded in late 1974 by Clive Davis, then and now a kingpin of the music industry. Born in Brooklyn, New York, in 1933, Davis was a devout fan of the Brooklyn Dodgers, a youngster who thrived on playing stickball, and a shrewd scholar; he also discovered he had perfect pitch. After graduating with honors from Erasmus Hall High School, he won a full scholarship to New York University. Both his parents died while he was a college freshman. He graduated from NYU magna cum laude and then moved on to Harvard Law School, again on a full scholarship. He was joined in Cambridge, Massachusetts, by his bride, a social worker. After graduating with honors, he passed the New York bar and then accepted a position with a major Manhattan law practice.

One of the law firm's key clients was the CBS-TV network and its chairman, William S. Paley. After building a strong working relationship with Davis, Paley hired him to come aboard Columbia Records as a corporate attorney in 1960. Six years later, Clive had become the company's general manager and was named its president the next year. By then, he had divorced his first wife and was the single parent of two children. (He would later wed opera singer Janet Adelberg.)

As a record-industry executive, Davis quickly discovered he had a strong knack for finding and signing hot talent. In rapid succession he brought to the label artists such as Janis Joplin and the group Blood, Sweat and Tears, as well as Billy Joel, Aerosmith, and Bruce Springsteen. And under his aegis, the careers of both Bob Dylan and Carlos Santana thrived.

In 1973, Davis suffered a major setback. Columbia Records discharged him, alleging that he was guilty of misusing company funds—to redecorate his Manhattan digs, to rent a Beverly Hills home as a summer retreat, and so forth. As these charges were unfolding, a grand jury in Newark, New Jersey was conducting a major investigation of potential payola and drug usage in the record business. The inquiry involved an associate of Davis as well as a number of other individuals who reputedly had links to the underworld and drug trafficking. The snowballing case led to the conviction of a former talent manager, while Davis was eventually exonerated of any wrongdoing. Both at the time and in his 1974 book, *Clive: Inside the Record Business*, written with James Willwerth, Davis maintained that the taint of suspicion had been cast upon him to make him a scapegoat in the scandal.

In 1974, Davis became a special consultant for Bell Records, a then unprofitable subsidiary of Columbia Pictures International. Within months, Clive had taken over the presidency of the failing label. He renamed it Arista Records and let all its roster go except for Barry Manilow and Melissa Manchester. As before, the astute Davis proved a master at uncovering fresh talent, as well as resurrecting the careers of stars whose popularity had waned. In the latter category was Dionne Warwick, who came to Arista in 1979. Her first LP for Arista, *Dionne*, which Clive had Barry Manilow produce, proved to be a big winner. It was the best-selling disc of her career to date. By the next year, Aretha Franklin had left Atlantic Records to join Arista, after being wooed by Davis and having been impressed by his success with Warwick. She soon made a dramatic comeback under the Arista banner. Also in 1980, Arista was acquired by BMG, which was in turn owned by the German conglomerate Bertelsmann AG.

Davis, who could be imperious and self-aggrandizing, developed such a successful track record in the notoriously precarious music business that he was esteemed as one of its prime movers and shakers. Never shy about tooting his own horn, the 'workaholic,' always impeccably dressed Davis frequently took the opportunity to explain his philosophy for success in the business: "You gotta find artists who are unique, you gotta find material that could become standards."

On another occasion, the starmaker further enunciated his thinking on that most pivotal of all abilities—picking winning talent: "If it's someone who can write . . . they have to . . . say something that's special." On the other hand, he insisted, if the artist does not write, "they have to bring songs to life in a manner never thought of." According to Davis, when all was said and done: "Ultimately, it's no fun to be in this business if you don't have hits."

This was the industry giant who was about to cross professional paths with Whitney Houston.

9

Finding a Mentor

"I come from a long line of singing perfectionists, and I'm just the same way."

WHITNEY HOUSTON, 1985

Back in June 1980, Gerry Griffith, the young A&R director at Arista Records, had caught Cissy Houston's cabaret act at the Bottom Line club in Greenwich Village. At the time, both her son Gary (then wavering between playing professional basketball and trying to break into showbusiness himself) and Whitney were part of the lineup, along with the evening's headliner, flautist Dave Valentin. For whatever reason, Nippy was having an off night. On such occasions, she would go into robotic mode, unwilling—or unable—to put much soul or energy into her singing. Griffith was not impressed by her rather perfunctory performance of "Home," and he dismissed her as a possible new member of the Arista stable.

Two years passed. In 1982, Griffith, always keeping attuned to the goings-on within the music industry, learned that Elektra Records was rumored to be on the verge of signing Whitney. Suddenly, the artist represented a new commercial appeal for Gerry. Maybe, he told himself, he should revisit her potential. Fortuitously, he noted that Cissy, along with Gary and Whitney, was scheduled to perform at Seventh Avenue South. He attended their show at the Greenwich Village club, where Whitney gave an impassioned rendition of her two standby numbers: "Tomorrow" and "Home." When she finished her selections, Griffith had to admit to himself that there had been a tremendous overall improvement in her presentation since he'd last seen her perform in front of an audience back in mid-1980. "She wiped me out," is how he described his enthusiastic reaction to the new and improved Whitney Houston.

Griffith immediately contacted Whitney's manager and mentioned that Arista might now be in the market to sign her up. This prompted Gene Harvey to repeat what Griffith already knew: that Elektra was about to cement a deal with the exciting young vocalist, but nothing was finalized yet. The following day, Griffith met with the artist and was struck by her "cool confidence." Unlike other aspiring artists, who would likely have been bowled over with excitement at being the object of a bidding war, Whitney maintained an intriguing air of cool indifference. This display of emotional control made Griffith try all the harder to woo her into the Arista camp. Obviously, he thought, she was even more of a pro than he had anticipated. He made a mental note never again to underestimate her.

What happened next is open to interpretation. Griffith maintains that when he met with his boss to rave about Whitney Houston being a hot contender to join the Arista lineup, Clive Davis greeted his sales pitch with a significant lack of interest. According to Griffith, his superior "didn't exactly jump out of his seat." In fact, he was "a bit nonchalant about it."

It is understandable that the busy head of Arista might be wary of subordinates extravagantly praising new talent they have just "found." However, it also seems likely that somehow, over recent years, Davis would have heard about the impressive talents of Whitney from two people who knew him very well—Arista artists Dionne Warwick and Aretha Franklin. It is unlikely that one or the other would not have already extolled Whitney's virtues to their mentor, the man who had resuscitated their careers. Since one of these celebrated performers was Whitney's cousin and the other was her godmother, one would have thought they must have already made a case for Davis taking notice of her—unless some subconscious sense of pending rivalry from this newcomer had muted such possible recommendations.

On the other hand, perhaps Aretha and Dionne *had* discussed Whitney's abilities with Davis. However, he might have been skeptical about their enthusiastic endorsements, coming as they did from less than impartial sources. Yet another possibility was that Davis, ever the calculating executive, wanted to be really sold on a new talent before giving the green light. As such, perhaps, he might have played devil's advocate by refusing to make it easy for anyone who couldn't give him a convincing argument for gambling on Whitney. In any event, at the end of their conference,

Davis yielded to Griffith's blandishments to the extent that he agreed to attend a special showcase of Whitney's singing.

Anxious to make the occasion an unqualified success, Griffith worked directly with Whitney and her mother to select an appropriate gown for her to wear and the right songs for her to sing (it was agreed that "Home" and "Tomorrow" were perfect), and consulted with his "discovery" and others to create dance movements and bridging stage patter to give the presentation a polished flow.

The venue was to be Manhattan's Top Hat Rehearsal Hall. At the last minute, the always-busy Davis almost backed out of attending the showcase set up expressly for him. Griffith refused to give in to this latest obstacle. He used all his ingenuity to get his distracted boss to keep his promise to see Whitney perform. At the appointed hour, the seemingly cool and collected Whitney began going through her paces—with the recently added showbusiness embellishments—in first-rate style.

Griffith was convinced that Arista's top executive would now have to agree that he had been right about Whitney. However, when the subordinate dared to surreptitiously look over in Davis's direction, the latter had a bored—even blank—expression on his face. A crestfallen Griffith glanced back again to be sure that the overworked Davis wasn't perhaps taking a catnap. Leaning back in his chair, he seemed, at the very least, lost in deep thought. When the short show ended, Davis arose, chatted briefly and politely with Whitney and Griffith, and then vanished into the night as his limousine whisked him to his next appointment.

The following morning, an apprehensive Griffith met with his employer. While allowing that Whitney was "good," Davis declared himself unconvinced that she was, indeed, "special." After further discussion, with Griffith recounting all of Whitney's finest selling points, Davis said that his best offer would be a one-shot recording deal for two sides of a single. This was the type of low-risk arrangement record companies typically offered to marginal talent; the financial and time risks to the label were relatively minimal. Griffith immediately protested that Whitney had far too much industry savvy to accept such an insulting offer, pointing out that there was already a better offer from Elektra on the table.

When Davis remained fixed in his decision, Griffith put forth what he considered his trump card. He informed his boss that just recently, CBS Records (who had unceremoniously dumped Davis years ago) had entered the running to bring Whitney into their fold. Wouldn't it be great, he insinuated, to beat his former company to the punch? Still refusing to budge, Davis insisted a "single deal" was the best he could offer. Whitney would have to take it or leave it. With that, he sent a crestfallen Griffith out of the executive suite. (Interestingly, later on, Davis would state that, from the start, he'd been "stunned by [Whitney's] talent" and that he "wanted to sign her immediately.")

As a dedicated A&R man, Griffith was determined not to abandon an artist he believed in so strongly. Thus, several days thereafter, he attended Whitney's appearance at Sweetwater's. He visited the singer backstage before her performance, where he found her already talking with the head of Elektra Records. During the show, Whitney acknowledged to the crowd the presence of the Elektra executive in the audience, but made no mention of Griffith or Arista. It was her way of letting everyone in earshot know that Elektra was the main player in the competition to claim her. It was a bitter moment for Griffith.

In the coming weeks, there was a fortuitous turn of events. For one thing, Davis began reconsidering his past ambivalence towards Whitney and tapped into his industry contacts to find out what others thought of her. When he received highly favorable feedback about the artist, he had second thoughts about his past—perhaps too hasty—judgment. The ace star-picker then came up with an alternative plan that made financial sense to him.

As he would explain later to Griffith, Arista was now prepared to offer Whitney a one-album contract. The gimmick of this particular deal was that he would pick four top record producers and make each one of them responsible for supervising three tracks on the debut disc. This way, he would ensure that Arista got a flock of hit singles out of the album. That, in his estimation, would cover the substantial investment in producing Whitney's debut and marketing her to the world.

At this juncture, another interesting factor came to light. Paul Marshall, the seasoned industry lawyer whom the Houstons had hired to negotiate the finer points of the contract with Elektra, learned that Bruce Lundvall, then the head of Elektra, was embroiled in a struggle for control with the company's chairman. The uncertainty as to Lundvall's future with the label caused the attorney great concern. If Lundvall should leave Elektra, where would that leave Whitney?

On the other hand, as Marshall was quick to point out to the three Houstons (Cissy, John and Whitney), Arista had now made a proposition that made sense. Their proposal outlined a definite plan of attack to be followed by Davis in order to launch Whitney's recording career. The

Houstons were certainly well aware of what Clive had accomplished for Dionne Warwick and Aretha Franklin in recent years; they agreed that he'd done exceptionally well by both performers with his smart, hands-on approach, and, hopefully, he could and would do the same for Whitney.

When Marshall finished reviewing the two record companies' offers, the senior Houstons voted in favor of Arista. However, the parents agreed, the final choice must be Whitney's. In making this pivotal decision, Cissy cautioned her daughter not to pick the company that gave her the most freedom, but, instead, choose the one that would use its expertise to guide her in the right direction to success. Obviously, Mrs. Houston had profited from her past errors of judgment. The nineteen-year-old heeded her mother's guidance and soon concluded that Arista was indeed the place for her to call home.

As negotiations continued, another term was added to the agreement between Whitney and Arista. It was called in the industry a "key man" clause, which meant, in essence, that if Davis should leave Arista, Whitney could leave the label with him. This made practical sense to both Whitney and Davis, although Arista's parent company was understandably displeased, fearing that if Davis ever dissolved his working relationship with the label—or vice versa—the heavy investment in Whitney would vanish with him.

By April 1983, the contract was a done deal and was duly announced in industry journals with all appropriate fanfare. Flattering articles detailed how Clive Davis had done it yet again by finding another unknown quantity whom he would bless with his magic touch and savvy and turn into a recording superstar. Pictures of Davis and Whitney illustrated such write-ups, with squint-eyed Clive affecting his shrewd but avuncular grin. In contrast, Whitney, with her short, curly hairdo and lack of makeup, sported a blasé, "big deal" look. In retrospect, studying the body language of the two figures at this key moment, one could sense that this pair, each of whom possessed a sizable ego, were already squaring off in a contest of wills as to who would call the shots in the singer's rise up the ladder of success.

In signing Whitney, Davis had not anticipated that he would have to deal not only one-on-one with the strong-minded young girl, but also with her mother, an old hand in showbusiness. By now, Mrs. Houston was full of elation over her daughter's success. In fact, for the veteran gospel performer, this remarkable achievement went beyond motherly pride. As she confided to others, "My daughter's success at signing with Arista was my success. My heart was filled with gratitude to God for guiding us to this point." In meetings with Davis, Cissy unhesitatingly let the executive know the types of songs she would permit her daughter to sing and the types of numbers that she considered vulgar and in bad taste. As she repeatedly reminded Clive: 'She's a church girl at heart.'"

The sophisticated music mogul admitted he had no problem with that reasoning. Then, assertive Cissy, who was so enjoying living vicariously through her baby, launched into another topic of concern: the matter of wardrobe. She described how, when Nippy had signed with Tara, Gene Harvey and Seymour Flics had mapped out a strategy in which Whitney would be required to wear revealing outfits for her club appearances. When Cissy had seen the sexy wardrobe they had commissioned, she had flown into a rage, informing the managers, "You can put all that crap right back. I don't know who you got that for, but Whitney's not wearing any of that. She is not shakin' no butt, showin' no skin, nothing like that." The fuming woman reminded the others that her daughter was a singer and did *not* need to rely on lewd gimmicks. At the end of the discussion, Mrs. Houston issued an order: "I'll take care of the clothes; you manage." The mighty Davis acceded to Cissy's dictates—largely because they were in line with his plans for promoting his new singer to the public in a tasteful manner.

Clive had already formulated a list of ingredients that would be key to making Whitney Houston a saleable property: she was young, eye-catching (and a former model to boot), had stage presence, came from a church background, and boasted a pedigree which included Cissy Houston for a mother, Dionne Warwick for a cousin, and Aretha Franklin for a godmother. At this point, the executive was still not all that wowed by her voice, but he told himself and his staff that with all these marketable ingredients there was no reason in the world why they couldn't turn Houston into a household name. The more he talked about the challenge, the more he became convinced that he had a winner in the making.

Davis directed the Arista team to approach record producers about working on tracks with Whitney, while other staff members were delegated to search out potentially best-selling songs. Meanwhile, an opportunity too good to pass up fell into his lap. It would give the public a special preview of his recent find and cost Arista virtually nothing. Veteran TV talk-show host and former big-band singer Merv Griffin, a longtime friend of Davis, had just arranged to devote one whole episode of his syndicated show to saluting the record-industry big shot. Davis decided this would be an excellent opportunity to introduce Whitney to the viewing public. What made his decision so remarkable was that, at that moment, he really had no idea when her debut album—as yet not even started—would be ready for release. It was an unorthodox tactic, but Davis was now set on launching his find in a big way.

Merv Griffin broadcast his popular variety program from his own theater on Vine Street in Hollywood, not far from Hollywood Boulevard. Late in April 1983, Davis flew out to the West Coast with Cissy and Nippy. Mrs. Houston was bursting with pride for her daughter and full of excitement for herself: she and her girl would sing a duet on the program, thus giving Cissy her own excellent exposure.

In contrast to her jubilant mother, Whitney was a bundle of exploding emotions. Suddenly realizing how important this showcase was to her future, her nerves were getting the better of her. In fact, while rehearsing her numbers back in New Jersey, she had one day broken down in tears. Cissy had made light of this, not wanting to add to the mounting pressure on Whitney as she prepared to make her debut on national TV. Now, as they flew to Los Angeles, Whitney seemed more in control of herself—at least on the surface. Already she had assumed the haughty demeanor she had come to rely on in order to mask her inner turmoil. Her attitude now appeared to onlookers to suggest, "Okay, I'm here, but, folks, I'm doing you a big favor." This attitude would become increasingly familiar to Whitney's staff, coworkers, and audiences in the years to come.

Once settled in L.A., Cissy and Whitney were collected by limousine and driven to the Merv Griffin Theater. After being introduced to the host, there were brief rehearsals with the house band, a session in makeup, and the usual light conversation in the green room while waiting to go on air. After Merv's opening song, the convivial host brought Clive Davis on stage and the two friends engaged in amiable banter about the executive's incredibly successful career in the record industry. Then it was time for Clive to introduce his latest protégée. The Arista chief pulled out all the stops. In his trademark manner of talking with the utmost conviction that he spoke the truth, Davis leaned over the desk to inform Merv: "There was Lena Horne. There's Dionne Warwick. But if the mantle is to pass to someone who is nineteen, who is elegant, who is sensuous, who is innocent, who's got an incredible range of talent, but got soul at the same time, it will be Whitney Houston in my opinion." He went on to add, "She's a beautiful girl and her poise doesn't hurt." After emphasizing his discovery's "natural charm," Clive concluded, "You either got it or you don't. She's got it."

With that, a smiling Merv Griffin announced Whitney Houston, and she came forth from behind the stage curtain. She was wearing a striped lavender (her favorite color) blouse and dark slacks, a gold neck chain and earring, and a ring on her left hand. Her hair was still in the short, curly style that gave her a Michael Jackson look. Smiling rather nervously, Whitney launched into "Home." As she sang the number, she brought a full range of emotions to the lyrics, with hand gestures that seemingly pulled energy into her lithe body.

What the audience probably did not observe at the time was the unusual presence, standing behind the stage curtain, of Cissy herself, leading the show's musicians! Determined that nothing should go amiss with this crucial performance, she had been unhappy with the way the house conductor had been directing the tempo of "Home." So Cissy insisted on taking over as conductor. With baton in hand, she stood behind the blue spangled curtain guiding the band through their proper paces as her daughter pulled out all the stops in her rendition of the song. At the end of the number, both Griffin and a beaming Davis congratulated the young songbird as the appreciative studio audience applauded loud and long. Later in the same program, Cissy, wearing a gold lamé gown with all the trappings befitting an established star, did an unvarnished duet of "Ain't No Way" with Whitney. It was the same song that Cissy had performed with Aretha Franklin at Philharmonic Hall in New York several years earlier.

When the show came to a close, Clive Davis felt well pleased with this special launch of Whitney's recording career. But his jubilation proved to be short-lived. Backstage, he, along with Gerry Griffith, who had come along on the trip, held an impromptu meeting with Ray Parker Jr. The latter, a guitarist, songwriter, vocalist, and producer, was under contract to Arista and had a close personal relationship with Davis. The label's chief had especially requested that Parker attend the taping, as he wanted him to watch Whitney in action. Davis hoped that Parker, one of the hottest producers around, would take charge of some of the songs on Whitney's debut album.

In plain language, Parker told the music entrepreneur that he was not overly impressed by Whitney Houston. In his estimation, the singer was not yet seasoned enough to embark on a professional recording career, and she played with the notes in her songs too much in a show-off manner. In short, Parker felt she was not ready for the big league and he did not want to waste his time producing her work.

Momentarily crestfallen, Davis returned to New York. He scouted around other key producers to come on board. To his growing dismay, several others felt the same as Ray Parker Jr. The consensus was that while there was no doubt Whitney could sing, that by itself wasn't enough. They failed to spot anything sufficiently unique about the performer to warrant gambling their time, energy, and reputations on her. This onslaught of unexpected negative feedback stunned the Arista boss and left Gerry Griffith astonished.

Davis was in a quandary. Who could he turn to in order to salvage Whitney's already-aborting career?

10

Cementing an Image

"Everybody wants to be loved, everyone wants to feel love, so that's what I try to sing about."

WHITNEY HOUSTON, 1989

As Clive Davis and his Arista staff struggled to line up appropriate producers and songs for Whitney Houston's debut album, the artist was experiencing changes in her private life.

For one thing, Nippy became an aunt when Donna Houston, brother Michael's wife, gave birth in 1983 to a baby boy, whom they named Gary, after the Houstons' older son. Since Whitney continued to live in her own apartment in Woodbridge, New Jersey, with Robyn Crawford, Cissy was now alone in the East Orange house, except when her mother-in-law stayed with her. Spreading his own wings, John Houston, still not yet divorced from Cissy, not only had his Fort Lee apartment, but also a modest getaway place out of state. Meanwhile, Cissy kept busy with her church choir work, background singing assignments, and club engagements, which often featured Whitney and Gary. By now, Michael was also thinking of entering the music business and was trying his hand at writing songs.

As for her social life, Whitney has said of this period in the early 1980s that she became a regular at popular nightclubs in New Jersey and in Manhattan. As she phrased it, "When I was sixteen, seventeen, eighteen, nineteen, I partied my brains out. I was a partying monkey."

But now, as an Arista Records contractee, she was no longer a relatively anonymous person when she went out in search of fun and relaxation. She had to be more conscious of where she was seen in public and, once there, how she conducted herself. At this juncture, as Arista worked in overdrive to mold and promote their new artist, any wrong step on her part could cause the marketing campaign to implode and spoil her relationship with the record label. There must certainly have been heart-to-heart talks between Davis (and other senior Arista executives) and Whitney (and most likely Cissy). At such meetings, it would have been discussed how best to present the artist to her future record-buying public. As part of this presentation, it was deemed essential that their new vocalist maintain—at least in public—a fairly wholesome image, that of a refined, church-going young lady with a lot of talent and energy who was eager to entertain the public with her God-given gifts.

There was, of course, the matter of Whitney being black. In bygone years, when racial discrimination was still virulent and overt, the likes of Lena Horne, Dorothy Dandridge, and Diahann Carroll had to fight long and hard to break into the mainstream. Their least action in public was subject to tremendous scrutiny, especially by those forces looking to discredit them. However, by the mid-1980s, rock, disco, and R&B had changed the musical climate, and with so many of the leading artists in these genres being black, it was no long the obstacle to success it had been in prior decades. It also helped that the 1960s civil rights legislation and demonstrations had altered, to a degree, the general public's attitude towards integration in the U.S. It was now an era in which unique African-American singers such as Michael Jackson, Tina Turner, Prince, and Donna Summer could achieve major success in the U.S. with urban black audiences *and* Middle America. The key to achieving this was to acknowledge the subject's racial roots, but then to downplay any strong ethnic aspects—diction, wardrobe, and the like—that might seem too alien to the white majority.

With her light skin, pleasing facial features, and sleek body, combined with the poise gained through modeling, Whitney could easily be promoted as a refined, blossoming young American. Then, too, there was her background as a church-going young lady who had attended a private high school. The only potential glitch was that Whitney did not always feel in tune with this carefully constructed image. Sometimes, she gave in to her urge to be more urban and streetwise than church-pew-refined.

To accentuate Whitney's image of respectability and credibility to both the music industry and the public, hardly an Arista press release failed to mention her ties to Cissy Houston, Dionne Warwick, and Aretha Franklin.

In her early years with the company, this litany of the artist's pedigree would be recited endlessly.

Whitney had already given early indications to her new employers that she was an individual who sometimes marched to her own tune, especially in her private life. There must therefore have been a delicate process of give-and-take in planning councils at Arista on how best to corral the artist's wilder partying instincts, what spin to put on her close friendship with Robyn Crawford, and how to treat her lack of any visible boyfriend.

Singer Barry Manilow once quipped about his Arista boss Clive Davis: "He has the mind of a banker and the ears of a teenager." Indeed, Davis had his finger on the pulse of what young record-buyers—the most important sector of the market—wanted in the way of music. He showed this knack again when assembling the elements for Whitney's debut album. After Ray Parker Jr. and several other producers rejected invitations to work on the disc, Davis continued to bring other candidates to hear her sing at Sweetwater's and other New York clubs and to give out tapes of her demo sessions.

Then, Davis had the brainwave of matching her with Jermaine Jackson. The latter had recently moved over to Arista from Motown in the capacity of singer, producer, and arranger. Jackson agreed to work with Whitney. Now that one of Michael Jackson's older brothers was part of the project, Davis began negotiations with veteran singer Teddy Pendergrass. A car accident in 1982 had left Pendergrass paralyzed from the waist down, but he was making a comeback at Elektra/Asylum. Teddy agreed to record a duet with Whitney on the West Coast for his upcoming album. Arista negotiated with his label so that the joint number could also be included on Whitney's record. Slowly, through such maneuvering, the elements for Whitney's much-trumpeted, but so far hardly begun, debut were finally coming together.

While Davis was involved in the painstaking process of shaping Whitney's first full-blown recording, her managers explored other options. By now, except for publicity in connection with her recording career, Whitney had abandoned modeling. Despite the financial benefits and other perks it had brought her, she was glad to be out of that field. On the other hand, she was not totally opposed to trying her hand at acting, as had, for example, Janet Jackson.

To start with, getting a part on a TV sitcom would be good experience for Whitney. It would enhance her recognition with the public and provide a basis for deciding if she had a future in this sector of the entertainment business. Twenty-year-old Whitney was therefore touted to casting agents. Before long, she was hired for a one-shot TV assignment. She made a guest appearance on *Gimme a Break* (1981–1987), the comedic vehicle starring Nell Carter, a talented, short, and rotund African American. In an episode of this NBC-TV network comedy series broadcast on March 15, 1984, entitled "Katie's College," Whitney played a friend of Kari Michaelson's character who convinces her Caucasian pal to open a boutique. In her relatively brief scenes, she looked fresh and wholesome but seemed, understandably, a bit uneasy in front of the cameras.

Whitney having survived this induction, her managers sought more such work. One potential project was a new NBC-TV sitcom starring Bill Cosby. It was to be recorded in New York City and was due to premiere in fall 1984. Established comedian and raconteur Cosby was set to play an obstetrician whose upscale household included a wife (Phylicia Rashad) and five children. Whitney was put forward for the role of Sondra, the twenty-year-old daughter. After the usual auditions and discussion of how she would blend in with the others already chosen to play family members, she remained in the running to be a series regular. As time went on, however, it became clear to Whitney how much time the recording would take up and that it might detract from her focus on her singing career. She also had concerns about her ability to carry off such a central role. Although no contract had yet been offered, she decided to withdraw. Later, when asked if Whitney had indeed been seriously considered for the role, which eventually went to Sabrina La Beauf, Jay Sandrich, who directed *The Cosby Show* (1984–1992), said diplomatically—and enigmatically, "She knew she was a good enough singer that she was gonna do very well without being on *The Cosby Show*."

During this formative period, Houston would make one additional foray into TV sitcom. On NBC-TV's *Silver Spoons* (1982–1986), starring teenager Ricky Schroder, she turned up on the September 15, 1985 installment ("Head Over Heels"). She was cast as the sudden object of affection of Franklyn Seales's character, the fussy business manager to Schroder's colead, Joel Higgins. Whitney appeared as a pert young singer who raises Seales's body temperature, but politely advises him that her career is more important at this juncture. Before the end of the episode, her character has disappeared from the story line. The script allowed for

Houston to sing briefly in a club sequence in which she is seen rehearsing a forthcoming music video. As before, she did not bring much energy or conviction to her paper-thin role.

Returning to the arena where she was far more comfortable, Whitney flew to Los Angeles to record her duet ("Hold Me") with Teddy Pendergrass. Producer and songwriter Michael Masser, who worked on this number, would recall the Whitney of this period thus: "She was a young kid who was eighteen years old with everything in front of her." Released on the Pendergrass album *Love Language* (1984), as a single it only reached number forty-six on the U.S. charts, peaking at number fifty in Great Britain. Clive Davis was, of course, disappointed with this result, but the song served its purpose of helping to create an identity for Whitney by matching her with established soul crooners.

There was greater rapport when Whitney and Jermaine Jackson worked together on the track "Take Good Care of My Heart." They displayed a solid chemistry that came across well when the single received radio airplay. It also helped to build sales when it appeared on Jackson's self-titled Arista album in 1984. That and a second number ("Nobody Loves Me Like You Do") that the two recorded together would be used for Whitney's future album.

Meanwhile, the team of Houston and Jackson made a guest appearance in 1984 on the popular daytime television soap opera *As the World Turns*, lip synching to "Nobody Loves Me Like You Do" in a segment involving a benefit performance for the homeless. Still later, Houston would duet with Jackson on the song "Shock Me," included on the soundtrack of the John Travolta–Jamie Lee Curtis movie *Perfect* (1985). Next, she did a duet ("If You Say My Eyes Are Beautiful") which appeared on Jermaine's 1986 album, *Precious Moments*. During this time, there were rumors of a romance between Whitney and Jackson, who was then married to the daughter of Berry Gordy, the founder of Motown Records and once the mentor to Jermaine and the other Jacksons. Both singers repeatedly denied any such romantic entanglement, although for Whitney, such gossip created intriguing new facets—albeit fanciful ones—to her personal life.

In the fall of 1984, Arista stepped up their elaborate promotion of Whitney. She had already performed at an Arista-hosted event for Jermaine Jackson at a downtown Manhattan disco and had also made an appearance at a fundraiser for the Dance Theater of Harlem. Now, the record company included her as a key part of the lineup for their tenth anniversary celebration in November, held in Manhattan at the Museum of the City of New York. At this black-tie affair, where other artists such as Dionne Warwick, Patti Smith, and Alan Parson were in attendance, Houston performed "I Am Changing" (from *Dreamgirls*) and her tried-and-true number "Home." Among the guests at the bash was entertainment journalist Mark Bego, who later wrote *Whitney!* (1986). His recollection of this memorable night was that "[Whitney's] emotional interpretation of those two songs held the entire crowd transfixed in a mesmerized trance."

Later that same month, the Arista celebration was restaged for the West Coast media. Journalists were invited to the company's Los Angeles headquarters to meet, among others, the much-touted Whitney Houston. Among those in attendance was music reporter J. Randy Taraborrelli. Years later, he would recollect, "Physically, Whitney Houston was average and not as glamorous as many other female recording stars I'd interviewed. Clive Davis claimed she'd been a model, but I recall thinking that she certainly didn't seem the type. Her hair was short and curly; she wore just a little makeup. She was reed-thin. Carrying an air of cool amiability, she had a winning smile but didn't seem very approachable. In other words, Whitney Houston clearly didn't possess any special qualities that suggested superstardom was in her future. She wasn't even exactly enthusiastic." When Taraborrelli and the songstress did chat briefly one-on-one, she referred frequently to "my Lord and Savior." Before the news people left, Clive Davis handed out cassettes of songs that Houston had recorded. He told the guests, "When you hear this tape, you'll know why I am so enthusiastic."

As the album launch date of February 1985 grew nearer, Arista staff members did their best to generate positive press attention for Whitney. In publicity photo shoots or carefully staged interviews, she came across in a manner agreeable to building her image. However, in person at media gatherings, she was not always such a useful asset. While she could make a strong impact when singing, she was not at her best when she was required to mingle with the guests and hype herself and her forthcoming album. In fact, she had a knack of fading into the wallpaper at such functions. A former Arista employee would remember, "We used to joke that you could invite Whitney to a party, put her in the room, and there she'd stay for the rest of the evening. She'd be like a piece of wood."

Therefore, whenever possible, the Arista force arranged for industry folk and the press to experience Whitney when she was singing and not force her to engage in face-to-face conversation. In front of a microphone playing to a club crowd, she displayed an increasingly appealing persona. For example, after witnessing a nightclub performance she gave in February 1985, the *New York Post*'s critic enthused, "What is happiest to those who have watched her grow is that she's not just a voice; with gestures and with poise, she takes command of her stage and her moment, and thus her time is limitless. When at the end of a song she opens her arms, roses cannot fill them—the universe rushes in to embrace her."

Ever the perfectionist, Clive Davis continued to tinker with the strategy of his ongoing promotional campaign to launch Whitney. At the same time, he was cajoling and maneuvering producers to work with his unknown protégée, moving on from initial refusals to other likely candidates. That the overall process took so long was partially due to Davis's instinct that every element of this album must be just right if it, and Whitney, were to make a major impact on the charts. As such, the cost of the project, originally budgeted at under $200,000 (already a hefty sum in those days, especially for a neophyte), reportedly soared close to $400,000. Such a sizable investment was both a tremendous vote of confidence on Arista's part and a huge gamble for Whitney's mentor, Davis.

One of the solo numbers recorded for the album—now entitled *Whitney Houston*—was "Saving All My Love for You," written by Michael Masser and Gerry Goffin. The song had appeared first on a Marilyn McCoo and Billy Davis Jr. album in the late 1970s. Even as revamped for the mid-1980s, Davis was not happy when he heard the first takes. As Kenneth Reynolds, then marketing director at the label, explained, "Clive had a formula already. Whitney was just a talent to mold. She had to lose the gospel roots. The early version of 'Saving All My Love' sounded like the new Aretha Franklin. But Clive didn't like it—'No, it's too black.'"

In short, the Arista honcho wanted it both ways: for Houston to keep some of her urban, black roots in order to reach that lucrative marketplace, but not enough to scare away the white majority audience. It was a tough tightrope to walk. No matter how diplomatically the situation was presented to the singer, it could never be disguised enough to avoid the implicit message: "You've got to be less black."

There was another problem with "Saving All My Love for You." Cissy Houston didn't at all like the scenario described in the lyrics, which told the story of a woman pining with love for a married man. Mrs. Houston thought the song's message would reflect badly on her daughter. Whitney herself had more urgent reasons for resisting the recording of this number—it hit far too close to home. As she herself has confessed, "I was going through a terrible love affair. He was married, and that will never work out for anybody. Never, no way. Forget about it." Nevertheless, for the sake of her art and the album's wellbeing she was eventually persuaded to do the song.

Another of the disc's selections, "How Will I Know" by George Merrill and Shannon Rubicam, had originally been intended for Janet Jackson, but Jackson had vetoed it. Later, when Arista's Gerry Griffith heard it, he was convinced that this was "absolutely perfect" as a "pop crossover song" for Whitney. Davis, in turn, was very excited by the tune and together they contacted producer Narada Michael Walden, who they believed could make it a smashing showcase for Whitney. Ironically, at the time, the latter was working with Houston's godmother, Aretha Franklin, on her new album and initially said he was too busy to produce "How Will I Know." He told Davis, "I don't know who Whitney Houston is. I don't have time to mess with her."

The ever-persuasive Davis convinced Walden to reconsider, and the veteran producer came on board once he had gained permission from cowriters Merrill and Rubicam to revamp part of the song. With the adjustments made, Narada came to New York, where Whitney did her vocals in one day-long session. The following day, the producer persuaded Whitney to join with her mother Cissy on the background harmonies. Said Walden of Whitney: "She was reluctant because she wanted to enjoy hearing her mother sing. I said, 'No, get out there and sing,' so she did." According to Narada, when Davis listened to the results, he "immediately proclaimed it a 10, which is outrageous for him, because he doesn't like anything."

"Greatest Love of All" had initially been written by Michael Masser and Linda Creed (the same team that penned "Hold Me") for the 1977 film *The Greatest*, the Muhammad Ali biopic. George Benson had recorded the number for that movie's soundtrack, and the single, released by Arista, had risen to number twenty-four in the charts. In recent years, Whitney had been including the song in her club appearances. In fact, she had wanted to include it in her special audition showcase for Clive Davis back in 1983, but it had been dropped because of time constraints. By now, Whitney and Masser had become friendly and agreed that the track should be part of her new album. Masser then informed Davis, who was not keen on the song because of its past unremarkable track record, that either the number went on the album or he would quit working on the project. Thus, it went in. But even then, there was great debate as to which of the several takes recorded should be chosen.

Also included on the album were two entries produced by Kashif (born Michael Jones in Brooklyn, New York), a singer-songwriter who had joined the Arista stable in 1983. He wrote "Thinking about You" with LaLa, while the latter was responsible for creating "You Give Good Love." With the Michael Masser–Jeffrey Osborne collaboration "All at Once," "Someone for Me" by Raymond Jones and Freddie Washington, plus the aforementioned two duets with Jermaine Jackson and the one with Teddy Pendergrass, the album of ten tracks was finally finished.

But not quite. Having gone the distance, Clive Davis was still not yet satisfied with the photos suggested for the album cover. Before long, Whitney had endured a total of ten photo shoots to capture the "real" her. Such lavishness regarding cover artwork was almost unprecedented in the business at that time. The front cover of the album shows Whitney in a Giovanne De Maura-designed off-white, African-style sari, sporting long earrings and a strand of beads around her neck. Together with her close-cropped hairdo, Davis believed the album cover made her look much "too ethnic." He kept telling staff members that he "wanted her to look more like everyone else." To appease him, on the back cover was a strikingly dramatic shot of Whitney in a tight white one-piece bathing suit, standing with legs astride by the ocean shore.

With time running out before the album's much ballyhooed release date, Clive Davis finally approved the album packaging. Thus *Whitney Houston* officially debuted on February 14, 1985. It was quite a Valentine for the world.

11

Riding High

"The songs that I sing don't fit into any category, so I don't think about it at all. But I believe that music does influence people. It's a universal thing. Everybody listens to music and knows about it. I think that the lyrics can have a lot to do with influencing whoever you're singing to."

WHITNEY HOUSTON, 1988

Every industry has its rules. In the music business it was a given that an album would use only one producer so that the disc would reflect a consistent theme and flavor. *Whitney Houston* had four producers. Another key principle was that a singer's debut should *not* contain duets because they would distract the listener from getting acquainted with the new vocalist's style. *Whitney Houston* contained three duets. Yet another established trade guideline was that an album should kick off with an upbeat number, one that would really grab the listener. *Whitney Houston* opened with two ballads. Once again, industry shaker Clive Davis had broken with tradition. But he had his reasons. As he explained, "We wanted to establish her in the black marketplace first, otherwise you can fall between [the] cracks, where Top 40 radio won't play you and R&B radio won't consider you their own. We felt that 'You Give Good Love' would be, at the very least, a major black hit, though we didn't think it would cross over the way it did." He elaborated further, "We wanted 'You Give Good Love' to solidify the black base. To our surprise, it went to number 1 on the R&B charts and number 3 pop. Then 'Saving All My Love for You' hit number 1 R&B and number 1 pop. It's ironic, but Top 40 stations give more exposure to ballads by certain black artists than to those by most whites. Whitney is helping to maintain the ballad tradition."

While Arista was deliberately ignoring several established marketing principles with Whitney's debut album, they were careful to take advantage of an increasingly popular sales tool—the music video. The MTV cable network had been launched in 1980 and quickly made its reputation by showcasing musical talent in flashy video shorts geared to promote singles from an artist's latest album. In the early 1980s, savvy operator Madonna had merchandized her distinctive image and sound so effectively in this format that it quickly propelled her into the realm of superstardom.

In its first years, MTV had focused largely on Caucasian artists. Then, as the 1980s progressed, Michael Jackson, Tina Turner, Prince, and other ethnic-minority talents had broken through the racial barrier with effective, cutting-edge videos that found a ready viewing audience. By 1985, when Whitney Houston's recording career began to take off, it was already feasible for an African-American performer to follow the music-video route and be assured of airtime on MTV.

Whitney had already proven in her modeling years that she was extremely photogenic. That she was not an experienced actress, nor indeed an accomplished dancer, did not matter in this form, where lighting, mood, sound, style, and special effects were the key ingredients. Because a slick music video typically intercuts shots in rapid succession to create a cumulative effect, a novice thespian and untrained dancer like Whitney could still make a powerful impact.

During the second half of 1985 and into 1986, Whitney made four music videos in support of singles from her debut album. The first, "You Give Good Love," was directed by Michael Lindsay-Hogg and was shot at a Greenwich Village restaurant. It opens with a video cameraman setting up his camcorder and suddenly being drawn to another room of the club by the voice of a songstress. He follows the beautiful sounds and soon he and his camera are flirting with the vocalist (Whitney). She is dressed in a clinging light-colored pantsuit and a black leather jacket. Through the perspective of the cameraman's lens, the viewer is treated to a multitude of close-up shots of Whitney, some so magnified that one can even spot a few acne blemishes beneath her makeup. For those in the know, the video includes shots of important people in Whitney's life at the time. In the midst of the extras playing restaurant workers and so forth was Arista executive Kenneth Reynolds as a cook. In one segment of "You Give Good Love," two young black females are seen standing in the background, grooving to Houston's singing. The woman on the right is Whitney's good friend Robyn Crawford, making her performing debut.

The second video, "Saving All My Love for You," was shot by cutting-edge music-video director Stuart Orme in London, where Whitney was on a promotional tour. The narrative for this slickly executed short follows the song's theme: Whitney's character is a recording artist who is emotionally involved with her married producer. By the finale, he has returned to his wife and family, leaving the heroine—the rejected "other woman"—romantically out in the cold.

At the time of release, the adultery theme of "Saving All My Love for You" generated much media controversy. It led Whitney to insist, "I could never see myself in that position. I wouldn't just take whatever someone wants to give to me, especially if I am giving a lot to him but not getting that much back. I could never find myself in that situation, but someone else might. The video tells a story but it's by no means my story." Some commentators wondered if Houston wasn't protesting too much on this issue.

The next video, "How Will I Know," helmed by Brian Grant, was the entry that gave Whitney tremendous presence on MTV. The film is supercharged with high energy and presents the young artist at her most visually fetching and sexually appealing. In this outing, she sports a curly blond wig (which one reviewer likened to her "wearing a basket of dyed poodles on her head") and her makeup is designed to make her already-light black skin seem even lighter. The camera tracks her running helter-skelter through a maze of corridors as a troupe of dancers intersect and bypass her. Wearing a form-fitting, revealing metallic dress, Whitney stops to open various doors, hoping that behind one of them she will find the answer to the lyrical question, "How will I know if I'm in love?" During her frantic search, there is even some brief footage of Whitney's godmother, Aretha Franklin, in a clip from the latter's video for "Freeway of Love."

The fourth and most personal of the videos from Whitney's debut album is the one that accompanied "Greatest Love of All." It was shot at Harlem's Apollo Theater and its story line features Whitney as a little girl (played by Keara Janine Hailey) about to perform in a children's amateur talent contest. Standing next to her is her mother (played by Cissy Houston), who is encouraging her child to take the plunge and do her best. The story flashes forward to the present as the adult Whitney wanders about the same theater, then applies her makeup for the coming performance. Next, both the child and adult Whitney meet center stage. Then, as the youngster disappears, the grownup Whitney completes "Greatest Love of All," and then rushes into the wings, where she and her mother embrace. Full of pleasing nostalgia, this loosely autobiographical piece is one of the most inspired videos that the artist has made to date.

☆

To Clive Davis's great satisfaction and to the surprise of many in the music business, the slow-starting *Whitney Houston* album, as well as its single releases, built steadily on the industry charts. By May 17, 1986, "Greatest Love of All" had climbed to number one on the *Billboard* charts in the U.S., rising to number eight in the U.K. It was a milestone for Whitney in the industry, for, following "Saving All My Love for You" (also her first number-one hit in the U.K.) and "How Will I Know," it was her third number-one success from the same album. It was the first time a female artist had achieved this distinction in the U.S. marketplace. Capping her triumph, *Whitney Houston* reached the top of the album charts on March 8, 1986, remaining in that lofty position for fourteen nonconsecutive weeks.

While the record-buying public and music-video-watching TV viewers fully endorsed the Whitney Houston explosion, reviewers were more qualified in their praise. *Rolling Stone* magazine reported, "Blessed with the most exciting new voice in years, Whitney Houston sings the hell out of the pleasant but undistinguished pop-soul tunes on her album . . . many of the songs here are so featureless they could be sung by anyone. They make what could have been a stunning debut merely promising."

The *New York Times* concluded, "Artistically, her debut album is a personal triumph over material that, generally speaking, hews to conservative pop formulas." *Newsweek* observed, "Houston does bring a charming combination of innocence and seductiveness to the glitzily produced arrangements. But her style and clear voice is more akin to Diana Ross's than to the rich rolling sound of her soul idol, Aretha Franklin."

The consensus among the critics was that this newcomer possessed a remarkable voice and had the useful ability to change like a chameleon from one style and tempo to another—*but* her material was so one-dimensional that it emphasized the general lack of conviction the artist was bringing to the lyrics. Nevertheless, most record-buyers paid little heed to this critical carping. Over time, *Whitney Houston*, which was a best-selling album for forty-six weeks, would eventually sell over 13 million copies in

America, with several million more sold overseas. At the time, it was the biggest-selling debut album by a solo artist. Literally in a matter of months, Cissy Houston's girl had gone from background singer to solo superstar.

Whitney's phenomenal success led *People* magazine to predict: "It will take an act of congress to keep this woman from becoming a megastar."

The enormous success of Whitney's debut album caught everyone off guard, including the singer herself. Over the years, she had witnessed how Cissy's showbusiness expectations had been built way up by a pending gig or album, only to be deflated by a quirk of fate. It had taught Whitney to maintain a measured emotional investment in what could be, to avoid the disappointment of anticipating what might not happen. Such an approach made her seem to many others to be blasé about her sudden burst of popularity.

Even after her initially slow-selling album begin its meteoric rise up the charts, Whitney was still cautious about expressing excitement over her good fortune. She explained, "You know, it gets to a point where the first couple of million you go, 'Oh, thank you, Jesus!' [Laughs] I mean let's face it, you make a record, you want people to buy your record—period. Anybody who tells you 'I'm makin' a record 'cause I want to be creative' is a fucking liar. They want to sell records. As it went on—and it went on—I took a very humble attitude. . . . My mother always told me, 'Before the fall goeth pride.'"

As Whitney's celebrity status mounted, the media plied her for reactions to her escalating fame. They wanted to know how she felt about being transformed into both a role model (especially for young African-American girls) and a sex symbol. She told *Us* magazine, "People ask me if [my success] is fair. There's nothing unfair about working hard and getting what you want. . . . I [have] worked hard and I'm very serious about what I do." She confessed to another media outlet (*Toronto Sun*), "It's . . . embarrassing to be famous. . . . People tell me, 'You've started something. People are trying to look like you.' I can't imagine anyone wanting to look like me."

To the *Detroit Free Press* she commented, "I think that image is created on something that is not there. Being . . . a sex symbol, to me, is something that is made up. Being a sexy person doesn't come from wearing sexy dresses. It's more of an inner thing. . . . So I didn't need an image. My image was already there—whatever I am is what I am." She also began discovering, "I can't go anywhere. Everybody recognizes me. But . . . personally, I'm the same. Sometimes I want to be alone—like when I'm out having dinner. . . . [But it's hard] to make people understand that you're hungry and you [just] want to eat dinner."

Meanwhile, Whitney's family had varying reactions to her sudden burst into the public eye. When John Houston was questioned about the mantle of superstardom settling on his daughter, he responded, "It seemed to come so much out of the blue. I know if I asked her about it, she would say, 'Daddy, I have no feeling for it at all.'"

As for Cissy Houston, she presented the public image of the beaming mother whose girl had done her proud. There was also a sense of joy at finding herself at last in the spotlight, thanks to her increasingly famous last-born child. Said one neighbor of Mrs. Houston, "Cissy basked in Whitney's limelight like a big cat stretching in the sun. The way she went on and on about record sales and concert dates and all that money, it was like it was happening to her. She'd praise the Lord and say things like, 'It's finally happening after all these years.' Well, she wasn't talking about Whitney because it didn't take Whitney 'all those years' to make it."

For Whitney's parents and brothers, as well as loyal friend Robyn Crawford, all of whom would soon come to work for the artist in one capacity or another, it certainly must have taken a good deal of clear-thinking not to let Nippy's budding success distort their own self-worth or their ambitions and needs.

As Whitney's fame continued to mount, her income abruptly accelerated far beyond her expectations. Soon, the now-wealthy twenty-two-year-old began indulging herself and her loved ones with material acquisitions. However, not everyone out there was thrilled with her success. Whitney recalls, "I drove a Mercedes back home to see my mother when she still lived in East Orange, New Jersey. I parked my car in the driveway and when I came back, mayonnaise and mustard and all kinds of shit had been smeared on my car. That's how things had changed. Because I had achieved, some people didn't like it." It taught her that "You never go back home."

For Whitney Houston, as with any fast-rising recording artist, "just" making the album and accompanying music videos was not all that was required of her professionally. Part of Arista's program to maximize her sales potential and build for her future was to gain her exposure on national TV and on tour so she could meet and expand her fan base.

One of her first small-screen showcases as a new singing star was a prestigious event. She was booked on *The Tonight Show Starring Johnny Carson*. On her first visit to the famed late-night TV talkfest, she shared airtime with Joan Collins and got to sing "You Give Good Love." Houston would return to the program on December 4, 1985, when Joan Rivers was sitting in for Johnny Carson, and again on December 4, 1990 when Jay Leno was the substitute host.

A less formal television outing for Whitney was the syndicated *Mike Douglas Show*, which was taped in Philadelphia. As the TV program got underway that particular day, Whitney stepped front and center to sing "How Will I Know." During her rendition, she suddenly noticed that the men in the front rows of the audience were leaning forward with bug-eyed looks on their faces. She was puzzled, but nevertheless continued singing. Then she spotted a woman out front who kept pointing a finger in a jabbing motion at Whitney. This prompted the artist to glance down and she realized that the shoulder strap of her dress was coming down, putting her in quite a revealing position. Without losing a beat and still singing away, she turned around, fixed the unruly strap, and swiveled back to face the audience so the show could go on.

To create media buzz in Europe for their new artist, Arista flew Whitney to England and the Continent in the spring of 1985. Essentially it was the first time that Whitney had been away from home. She became homesick. As she related to *Ebony* magazine, "I cried every day. You've got to remember that I'm still young. I'm still a baby in a lot of [ways]."

Occasionally, something happened on the trip to distract the American singer from her lonesomeness. For example, she was in Paris and booked to appear on a popular French TV talk show. Besides the host, there was another guest, a *bon vivant* whose behavior quickly revealed that he had already had more than a few hard drinks before the program began. As the show proceeded, Whitney sat on stage smiling politely at the host and the camera and occasionally glancing at the tipsy Frenchman, who was chattering with the emcee in their native language. Suddenly, this middle-aged male looked lasciviously at Whitney and blurted out in heavily accented English, "I want to fuck you." At first, Whitney couldn't believe what he had just said on air. Then she smiled politely, but looked perplexed at what to do next. The look of bemused surprise on her face was priceless, even more so than when the host prompts the inebriated guest to apologize.

Back in the United States, Whitney embarked on a short concert tour to small venues. It was an opportunity for her to gain much-needed experience in this challenging medium. Towards the end of May 1985, she played The Roxy (Los Angeles), Judge's Chambers (Dallas, Texas), Park West (Chicago), and Moonshadow (Atlanta, Georgia).

Next, Arista and her personal management team arranged for Whitney to tour as the opening act for the A&M label artist Jeffrey Osborne (who had cowritten "All at Once" with Michael Masser for her album). As Whitney and headliner Osborne crisscrossed the country to appear at bigger sites than she had ever played before, it was she who received the best reviews. The industry journal *Cashbox* reported, "Her poise and confidence on stage are readily apparent." When she and Osborne were at the Holiday Star Theater in Merrillville, Indiana, the *Chicago Tribune*'s Steve Dale observed that Whitney "has a voice more reminiscent of a young Lena Horne than of her pop contemporaries. And she certainly looks and dresses differently. For one thing, when she models she does so with her clothes on, and for publications such as *Glamour* or *Cosmopolitan*."

The end of August 1985 found the Osborne–Houston team singing at the open-air Greek Theater in Los Angeles. Paul Grein (*Los Angeles Times*) enthused, "Whitney Houston isn't your run-of-the-mill opening act: She's the hottest newcomer of the year and a promising addition to the lineage of top-flight, mass-appeal singers. ... Houston combines [Dionne] Warwick's classy demeanor and cool attitude with a vocal style that ranges from the volcanic power of Chaka Khan to the angelic sweetness of the late Minnie Riperton. Just 22, Houston seems by turns little girl, classy lady and red-hot mama."

As that tour wound down, Whitney realized just how exhausted she was from the grind. She told one reporter, "Sometimes I feel like I'm really 42. I guess that's because I started so young." The singer had also begun experiencing a problem that plagues many vocalists—losing her voice. Occasionally, there would be days when she would wake up and could hardly utter a sound. Panicked by each sudden loss of voice, she soon discovered that lots of tea with honey was an excellent remedy and that her priceless gift of singing was not always under her control. In subsequent years, this onslaught of hoarseness or an inability to sing at full voice would become an increasing problem—or, sometimes, merely an excuse when the other stresses intervened.

☆

In the fall of 1985, with Whitney's album selling so well, there was no difficulty in booking her as the headline attraction on a road tour. Said the artist of her elevated status: "I always enjoy performing, so it doesn't matter to me whether I'm the opening act or the headliner. But it will be fun to get to do a whole sixty-minute show."

In early October, Whitney was due to appear in concert in Chicago, and later that month, on the twenty-eighth, she was to be the featured artist at Carnegie Hall. Among the celebrity crowd in attendance that night were the performing and songwriting husband-and-wife team of Valerie Simpson and Nickolas Ashford, and movie star Eddie Murphy, as well as Whitney's doting parents. During the concert, Whitney learned that Ed Koch, New York City's controversial mayor, was in the audience. She asked him to join her on stage, only to be greeted with booing from various quarters of the theater. Embarrassed for Koch and unmindful of her own discomfort, she nevertheless insisted that the official come up on stage. It was an early example of Whitney the individualist, refusing to be cowed by others' opinions.

At the end of November that year, Whitney was performing in Southern California. Robert Hilburn (*Los Angeles Times*) caught her performance at Golden Hall in San Diego and enthused, "Whitney Houston has three things that money can't buy a performer: a sensational voice, captivating poise and uncommonly good looks." He continued, "The show lasted about 75 minutes, but Houston used her voice so dramatically—moving in quick spurts from one intensity level to another—that it sometimes was breathtaking. . . . She didn't even need time to warm up. On the opening number . . . [she] stretched the word 'children' into all sorts of tuneful shapes. . . . Part of the impact is the suddenness of these vocal moves. Houston will start a line routinely . . . then [break away] . . . increasing the volume threefold and holding a syllable for several seconds. . . . It's called control, and Houston . . . has so much of it she can give you chills."

But the *Times* reviewer—if not the audience, who afforded her a standing ovation—had reservations about her choice of material and her degree of commitment to the lyrics she sang. "Once you got past the dazzle of her vocal ability, you realized there was a gap. You didn't feel at the end of the evening that you're learning anything about her or yourself."

By year's end, Whitney was back on the East Coast. At Christmastime, she and her mother cohosted a holiday program on MTV's new sister station, VH1. The pair introduced music videos and provided amiable chitchat in between. It proved to be a delightful outing as they talked extemporaneously about their family life, their careers, and other matters. In one interval, the duo sang a cappella "You and Me Against the World." Later, the pair engaged in a family-tree discussion which showed that, although Whitney might be a rising megastar, her mother intended to top her daughter in this particular conversation. Cissy explained to home viewers that contrary to what the media was stating, Dionne Warwick was in actuality her niece and Whitney's cousin. When the younger Houston chirped up that Dionne's mother and Cissy were sisters, the elder Houston gave her daughter a sharp look, gripped her microphone a bit tighter, and added, "She is my much *older* sister, of course."

12

Leader of the Pack

"Everything I have done has worked. I didn't plan to sell this many copies of my record the first time. Arista and I obviously did the right things, and if that's success—and if it is orchestrated—then I want to orchestrate it for the rest of my life."

WHITNEY HOUSTON, 1986

By the end of 1985, much of America and the world were ecstatic worshippers of Whitney Houston. Her face appeared on the covers of countless magazines around the globe and interviews with the skyrocketing star were being circulated in a wide assortment of publications. Some naysayers predicted that such overexposure would surely result in a backlash from the press and/or the public, but, at the time, it seemed that nothing could halt the Whitney Houston frenzy. Certainly her mentor (some labeled him the singer's puppetmaster) Clive Davis was not about to cut back on the massive publicity campaign that Arista had constructed for Whitney. His company was enjoying large profits from *Whitney Houston* and Davis was savoring each aspect of this well-crafted success. He proclaimed proudly to the press, "To carefully nurture a young artist for two years and then have your dreams come true is like a storybook tale."

Whitney's Cinderella-like story continued as the music industry's annual handing-out of awards got underway. In *Billboard* magazine's year-end roundup of the best performers in various categories, she was cited in sixteen fields and came out on top in two: New Pop Artist and New Black Artist. In January 1986, at the 13th Annual American Music Awards televised from Los Angeles, Whitney was nominated in six categories and scored a victory in two: Best R&B Single ("You Give Good Love") and Best R&B Video ("Saving All My Love for You").

The young and beautiful singer was the perfect poster child for the AMA ceremony. Accompanied by her parents (who, although separated, put on a public show of togetherness), Whitney's beauty, enthusiasm, and freshness made her a very winning presence at the star-studded occasion. The audience responded well when she displayed humility and religious piety by thanking Almighty God for all her recent blessings. After the gala, the Houstons made an appearance at Clive Davis's bash and then adjourned to the Beverly Hills home of Dionne Warwick, where they held a family celebration.

Wanting the best (that is, the most) for both Whitney and Arista, Clive Davis took great offense when the nominations for the prestigious Grammy Awards were announced in mid-January 1986. Although Whitney was nominated in several categories, she had been omitted from the Best New Artist Category, where the nominees included a-ha, Freddie Jackson, Katrina and the Waves, Julian Lennon, and Sade. The infuriated Arista chief wrote a highly controversial article published in the January 18, 1986 issue of *Billboard* magazine, asking, "What Does 'New Artist' Really Mean?" He inquired angrily, "How is it that a recording artist can be voted 'Favorite New Female Artist' by the readers of *Rolling Stone*, named 'Newcomer of the Year' in music by *Entertainment Tonight* [TV show], 'Top New Artist' [in two categories] by *Billboard*, sell nearly four million copies worldwide of her very first album, and not be considered a candidate for 'Best New Artist' by the National Academy of Recording Arts and Sciences?" The Academy's answer was that "The rule that disqualifies Whitney is perfectly clear. . . . an artist is not eligible if . . . [he or she had a previous] label credit or album credit."

Davis upbraided the Grammys for the unfairness of their ruling as applied to Whitney. (He had a point, since previous Best New Artist Grammy winners such as Carly Simon and Cyndi Lauper had similarly performed on others' albums before their official "debuts.") Meanwhile, Whitney remained calm in public about the situation, reasoning, "These things happen," though others claimed that on the night of the awards she was steaming with rage about being omitted as Best New Artist. She said of her nominations in general: "If I win, I win. It's an honor, of course, but I feel the same as I did before."

For the Grammys, held at the Shrine Auditorium in Los Angeles on

February 25, 1986, Whitney wore a red taffeta dress. It was an outfit Cissy had picked out and insisted her daughter should wear, although Whitney was against it. During the evening, it was Dionne Warwick who presented the award for Best Pop Vocal Performance—Female. After reading the list of nominees (which included Whitney, Pat Benatar, Madonna, Linda Ronstadt, and Tina Turner), Dionne opened the envelope. A huge grin spread across her face as she announced her cousin to be the winner for her rendition of "Saving All My Love for You." Whitney raced to the stage and the two hugged in a long victory clinch. A genuinely touched Whitney blurted out to the audience, "Oh, my goodness. I must thank God, who makes it all possible for me!" She continued, "To my mommy and daddy, the two most important people in the world to me. To Clive [Davis]. You are the best." She also found occasion on air that evening to thank Robyn Crawford for her support. During the gala show, Whitney sang "Saving All My Love for You," which would later earn her an Emmy Award in the category of Outstanding Performance in a Variety or Music Program.

One part of the merriment that Whitney had hoped to avoid was attending Clive Davis's annual Arista bash in honor of the Grammys. This year it was being held at the swanky Beverly Hills Hilton Hotel. Whitney had had enough of being treated like a queen. She explained, "It was this whole 'princess of the industry' kind of thing and I was feelin' kind of weird about all this admiration. I guess it was also this transformation you go through from being totally unknown to being really [well] known. And all these accolades, all these new people admiring you, calling your name, and you don't even know 'em. It was just a little much for me."

However, the ever-vigilant Cissy insisted that Nippy at least make an appearance at the event. She told her reluctant daughter: "They don't know you're scared. If you don't go, they'll take it for something else." Whitney surrendered once again to her mother's authority, but she recalls, "I got to the party and I started hyperventilating. I went to the bathroom and my mother went with me. And I couldn't believe she was so calm. I couldn't breathe."

Adding to her recent run of accolades, in April 1986, the mayor of Newark, New Jersey presented Whitney with the Key to the City. It was a testimonial that was especially meaningful to her parents, who had grown up in Newark, and in particular for John Houston, who still was employed by the city and had a close working relationship with the mayor, Kenneth Gibson. Solidifying the singer's impressive showbusiness status, the readers of *People* magazine voted her the Top New Star in May 1986. The next month, Arista announced that *Whitney Houston* had already sold over 6 million copies in the domestic marketplace.

☆

With her megasuccess, Whitney had not only become a celebrity—she had also become a corporation: Nippy, Inc. Her father asked that he be allowed to comanage his daughter with Gene Harvey and Seymour Flics, and thus it was arranged. By now, Gary Houston was singing background vocals and occasional solos in Whitney's concert program, and younger brother Michael was hired as assistant road manager for her tours. As for Robyn Crawford, she was officially deemed the star's personal assistant and unofficially remained her chief confidante. Cissy was always on hand, volunteering industry tips to her daughter, as well as offering career guidance and general feedback—whether requested or not. It was too ingrained in the mother and choirmaster not to be always the teacher, one who demands and expects perfection from her prize pupil.

Occasionally, Whitney stole away from the limelight for a vacation—her favorite new spot was a secluded destination in the Caribbean—and she claimed she was learning to relax by "starting to get into writing music" (an occupation which has yet to really get off the ground for her). Mostly, she existed in career overdrive. She was featured in a major TV ad campaign for Diet Coke, which strikingly showcased her pep and beauty, leading a columnist from the *New York Daily News* to ask, "How could I watch Whitney Houston sing her heart out for Diet Coke and then consider drinking something else?" Her "Greatest Love of All" video and single were still getting tremendous airplay. On July 4, 1986, as part of the centennial celebration for the Statue of Liberty, she was part of a nationally televised salute (originating from Jersey City, New Jersey), singing "Greatest Love of All," which had become her personal anthem. By now, the video compilation *Whitney Houston: The #1 Video Hits* was on release and was quickly rising to the top of *Cash Box* magazine's music-video chart.

As the national and international media explored, exploited, and questioned the swelling Whitney Houston mystique, journalists increasingly asked about her personal life. In particular, they wanted to know if there was any boyfriend on the scene. Already some journalists were including in their coverage of Whitney veiled references and inferences about her close ties to Robyn Crawford. For public consumption, Houston quipped that Miste (one of her two Angora cats; the other was Marilyn) was "the only man in my life at the moment."

Reporters also wondered aloud how Whitney had maintained such a squeaky-clean image (at least to the general public) in such a permissive era as the 1980s. Her response was: "I believe in God the Almighty. My parents raised me in such a way that I don't have to do all those things that others are doing around me. If you just anchor yourself with God, you can resist a lot of temptations. Prayer helps a lot."

Because of the remarkable selling and staying power of the *Whitney Houston* album, Arista was not in a great rush to push a follow-up disc into record stores. Instead, Whitney chose to put together her first world tour. As she explained—and would repeat at the start of each of her shows, "This tour is your tour. This show is your show." Now a headliner able to pack huge forums and to persuade fans to pay an average ticket price of $16 to $20, it was necessary to expand the format of her program. "The show has to be a lot bigger," she explained. "It's kind of like a production thing now." As a consequence, she hired a choreographer and a lighting designer, as well as frequently consulting with Cissy Houston on song selections. To open her show, she signed a young New Jersey comedian, Sylvia Treymore, whose specialty was doing impersonations of Dionne Warwick, Tina Turner, Cher, and others. Backed by a nine-piece band, Whitney also employed four background vocalists (including brother Gary), as well as a stage crew.

The tour began in late summer 1986 on Long Island, New York, where the *Newsday* reviewer described Whitney's presentation as "silky-smooth and slinky fast . . . her body a graceful, spikey motion machine." As her opening number, she offered her rendition of Michael Jackson's "Wanna Be Startin' Somethin'" (which, under bizarre circumstances, Whitney would perform in 2001 at Jackson's thirtieth anniversary salute at New York City's Madison Square Garden).

Besides singing the hit tunes from her first album and a few tracks—including "I Wanna Dance with Somebody (Who Loves Me)" and "Didn't We Almost Have It All"—being considered for her next one, Houston included a gospel song, "I Believe." Whitney reasoned, "I don't think I could do a show without . . . [gospel] being a part of it. It's a part of me. It's part of my voice and part of my life. Someday I would like to do a gospel album and record with my mother and Dionne [Warwick]." Expanding further on her desire to show her respect for the Lord, she said, "I'm just so grateful and I'm so thankful to Him for what He's given me. So many things can happen to one who is successful, so that you can just get taken away. But the Father has kept me level. I know I can't get any bigger than Him."

The end of August saw her performing at the Poplar Creek Theater in Illinois. Daniel Brogan of the *Chicago Tribune* was on hand to report on the sold-out concert, in which she stopped her band during the first number to tell the crowd: "Clap if you want to. Sing along if you want to." Brogan was much more impressed with the luminary in person than he had been with her debut album and enthusiastically detailed the evening's entertainment. "She let the crowd know they were in for a few surprises almost from the moment Saturday's show began. From behind a partition she teasingly sang a few lines from her most recent no. 1 hit, 'Greatest Love of All' before bursting into the spotlight for a funky rendition of Michael Jackson's 'Wanna Be Startin' Somethin'. . . . Then as if to insist that she isn't entirely an overnight sensation, she sang 'Eternal Love,' which she recorded several years ago on a compilation album."

The Chicago critic was particularly impressed with the vivid interpretations Houston gave to her repertoire of songs: "To each she added dimensions far beyond their vinyl counterparts. . . . 'How Will I Know' was transformed from a schoolgirl's timid daydream into something bordering on a bold come-on. 'You Give Good Love' took on a bluesy growl, and 'Saving All My Love for You'—performed on a stage bathed in red—exuded an earthy ache that carried easily up Poplar's big hill. Strutting across the elaborately lit and designed stage during 'Someone For Me' she looked like a sort of uptown Tina Turner in her tight, glittery miniskirt and high heels."

Forgiving the star for indulgently showing off her vocal range by drawing out some of the lyrics in overly extended notes, he praised her ardent rendition of Jennifer Holliday's "I Am Changing" (from the Broadway musical *Dreamgirls*). Said Brogan of Whitney's powerhouse interpretation, "You couldn't help wondering if she was issuing a challenge for her audience to follow her in the new directions she is beginning to take."

By January 1987, Whitney was back on the East Coast, appearing at the Grand Ballroom in Baltimore, Maryland. Special added attractions on the bill that evening were Tina Turner and Ben E. King. The latter had been the headliner back in May 1968, when the Sweet Inspirations had appeared at Atlantic Records' annual revue at the Apollo Theater in Harlem. A very young Whitney had been standing in the wings that night watching her mother and the others perform; now, she was the star attraction and King was a featured guest.

Later that month, Houston returned to Los Angeles for the annual American Music Awards. The City of Angels was not one of her favorite spots, even though she was already in discussions with film studios about making her big-screen debut. As she had pronounced a few months earlier, "I'm not into L.A. at all. I'm your basic East Coast person. I'm a New Jersey girl. I'm very secure here, so I don't want to go anywhere else."

At the AMA festivities held at the Shrine Auditorium, superstar Janet Jackson had the largest number of nominations—nine in total, while Houston had seven. However, Whitney was the much bigger winner of the evening, claiming five trophies against Janet's two. As had become customary with Whitney, her award acceptance speeches would not be complete without a religious reference. When she received her prize in the Favorite Video Single—Soul and R&B category for "Greatest Love of All," the evening's biggest winner, she said, "I want to give thanks to Almighty God for love and strength." Also among the winners that evening, in the Soul/R&B Favorite Band, Duo or Group category, were New Edition, the funky group featuring fast-rising talent Bobby Brown.

Weeks later, on February 24, 1987, also at the Shrine Auditorium in Los Angeles, the 29th annual Grammy Awards were held. Whitney, with a few of the later singles from her two-year-old first album released in the time span covered by that year's Grammys, was nominated in one category: Record of the Year ("Greatest Love of All"). However, she lost to Steve Winwood, for "Higher Love." It must have been some consolation that Madonna, one of Whitney's least favorite peers, lost out that evening in the Best Pop Vocal Performance, Female category to Barbra Streisand.

For some months already, the media had been pitting Madonna and Whitney, two of the public's current favorite popular-music artists, against one another. The Material Girl was not fond of the seemingly overly pious Whitney, whose wholesome image had, for the time being, superseded her racy persona in popularity. She had let her displeasure be known in a number of veiled statements. In contrast, Whitney was more direct in her criticism, chastising the earthy singer who was responsible for such controversial numbers as "Like a Virgin" and "Papa Don't Preach."

Speaking frankly, Houston told one reporter, "I find Madonna particularly revolting. . . . Madonna says horrible, nasty things like, 'Go to bed with anyone you want.' She's not really lady-like, is she? I don't know what she has—but I don't like it. In the long term, I'm sure she will just be forgotten."

Another diva with whom Whitney would have an even more contentious skirmish was Diana Ross. The latter was nineteen years older than Whitney and her career (both as a solo recording artist and in films) seemed past its peak. Reviewers were labeling Houston the "new" Ross, and that had an understandably negative effect on the older star. In addition, gossip columnists kept insisting that Whitney was considering starring in the screen version of the musical *Dreamgirls*, a thinly veiled account of Diana Ross and the Supremes. Ross took offense at this, remarking, "Fat chance!" She insisted that if anyone was going to play the lead role in *Dreamgirls* on screen, it would be herself. Whitney reportedly countered to friends that if Diana were to star in the film, it would have to be called *Dream-Grannies*. Nor was Whitney shy about dissecting her rival in print. For one publication, she obligingly analyzed the reason for Ross's drop in popularity: "Diana got boring. *Lady Sings the Blues* [1972] was amazing. And then *Mahogany* [1975] and *The Wiz* [1978]. She got boring. I don't know what happened."

For months, there had been speculation about when Houston would actually begin work on her second album. Sporadically throughout 1986 she went into the studios to record potential numbers for the album, telling journalists, "I'll give it everything I have. If you can't do your best, why even bother?"

But even when a song was deemed of the proper caliber to be considered for the new release, Clive Davis was still reluctant to divert potential sales from Whitney's debut platter to her new offering. Because Davis's decision was the final word at Arista, Whitney had to abide by his dictates on the scheduling of her second album. However, this didn't mean that the increasingly independent-minded star, now a multi-millionaire, didn't bridle at the public perception that she was solely the creation of her all-knowing mentor.

Several years thereafter, in June 1993, Whitney would express her thoughts on this sensitive subject to *Rolling Stone*'s Anthony DeCurtis. As had become her stock-in-trade, she spelled out her opinions in an unvarnished manner: "I don't like it when they see me as this little person who doesn't know what to do with herself—like I have no idea what I want, like I'm just a puppet and Clive's got the strings. That's bullshit. That's demeaning to me, because that ain't how it is, and it never was. And never will be." Furthermore, she added, "I wouldn't be with anybody who didn't respect my opinions. Nobody makes me do anything I don't want to do. You can't make me sing something I don't want to sing." But the singer's complex feelings about her guru also embraced praise: "Clive and I work well together. We basically like the same things, which, thank God, allowed us to get along all these years. We get on each other's nerves sometimes, but we've been together ten years now. Anybody can get on anybody's nerves over that long a period."

The young Whitney Houston.

Whitney's parents, Cissy and John Houston, in the mid-1980s.

Cissy, John, and Whitney Houston at their East Orange, New Jersey home in 1987.

The Sweet Inspirations singing group in London, December 1968. *Left to right:* Cissy Houston, Myrna Smith, Sylvia Shemwell, and Estelle Brown.

Whitney's cousin Dionne Warwick, the legendary singing star.

Whitney's "Aunt Ree": Aretha Franklin, the Queen of Soul, with Arista Records chieftain Clive Davis in 1981.

The young Whitney harmonizing on stage with her mother.

A radiant Whitney Houston during a December 1983 fashion shoot for *Mademoiselle* magazine.

Top: Whitney Houston performing in concert with her brother Gary, *c.*1985.

Above: Siblings Michael and Whitney Houston.

Above left: With mentor Clive Davis, head of Arista Records, in the mid-1980s.

Above right: Accepting her first Grammy Award in February 1986.

Left: Cissy and Whitney Houston performing at the seventieth-birthday tribute to South Africa's Nelson Mandela in London, November 6, 1988.

Jermaine Jackson and Whitney Houston rehearse their 1984 guest appearance on the TV soap *As the World Turns.*

Multi-talented musician and producer Kenneth "Babyface" Edmonds with his frequent collaborator, Whitney Houston.

Above: Robyn Crawford, longtime friend and business associate of Whitney Houston.

Right: Performing "The Star Spangled Banner" at Super Bowl XXV, January 27, 1991.

Visiting the U.S.S. *Saratoga* for the cable TV special *Welcome Home Heroes from the Gulf War*, March 31, 1991.

Comedian and movie star Eddie Murphy, whom Whitney Houston dated in the late 1980s.

Singer Bobby Brown – Whitney Houston's future husband – captured in one of his famous stage moves.

A young Bobby Brown (second from left) with his original band, New Edition, in 1983.

Top: Bobby Brown and Whitney Houston on their wedding day: July 18, 1992.

Above: (left) An aerial view of Whitney Houston's Mendham Township, New Jersey estate; (right) the monogrammed swimming pool.

Whitney Houston embraces President Nelson Mandela during her November 1994 concert tour of South Africa.

Attending the annual Whitney Houston Foundation Christmas Party in 1992.

Greeting a guest at her Christmas get-together for homeless children at Newark Symphony Hall, December 17, 1995.

13

How Will I Know

"When I finished that first album, I felt successful. I made some great songs, and people liked it. But with the second album coming, you know what people said to me? 'Whitney, this is the most important album you will ever do.' And I was like 'Huh?' I just sold 13–14 million albums, and now you tell me I have to work at success. [I decided] not to get into that thing where you have to try and beat yourself. That's gone, that's done."

WHITNEY HOUSTON, 1992

Having hit on such a successful formula for Whitney Houston's debut album, Arista was not about to mess with the recipe for the follow-up, *Whitney* (1987). Again, there were four producers in charge of the various tracks. Three—Narada Michael Walden, Michael Masser, and Kashif—were holdovers from the first album; the new member of the quartet was Jellybean Benitez.

The opening number was the high-energy "I Wanna Dance with Somebody (Who Loves Me)," written by George Merrill and Shannon Rubicam, the composers of Whitney's highly successful "How Will I Know." Merrill and Rubicam had attended a Houston concert at the Greek Theater in Los Angeles. Impressed by the audience's response to her singing "How Will I Know" and, at the same time, observing a falling star in the sky, they were inspired to write "Waiting for a Star to Fall." When that song failed to please Clive Davis and his staff, the duo created a replacement song, "I Wanna Dance with Somebody (Who Loves Me)," which Davis liked a good deal.

The head of Arista contracted Narada Michael Walden to produce "I Wanna Dance with Somebody" and several other tracks on the *Whitney* album. For Walden, the offer created a potentially delicate situation. After working with Houston on "How Will I Know" many months earlier, Walden had suggested they be friends. He asked her if "we could exchange phone numbers, but she said no. She didn't want to give me her phone number. . . . I took it in [my] stride. She was a top model who had guys hit on her all the time, so she didn't want to give out her phone number."

Despite the awkward state of affairs, Narada agreed to listen to the demo of "I Wanna Dance with Somebody (Who Loves Me)." Initially, he did not share Davis's positive response to the track, feeling "it was too country and western. It reminded me of a rodeo song with Olivia Newton-John." Nevertheless, he told himself: "[there has] gotta be some way I can make it . . . funkier." His challenge was "to figure out how to make it black and more R&B, because I wanted her to keep her fans at black radio." After much deliberation, Walden, Houston, and the crew went into the recording studio. "Whitney just knocked it out and then I knew we had a good record."

The catchy, uptempo single debuted on U.S. radio at the end of April 1987 and, by the week of June 27, 1987, "I Wanna Dance with Somebody (Who Loves Me)" had risen to the top of the charts. It provided Whitney with her fourth number-one single in the U.S. (and her second in the U.K.). Walden's other offerings on the album included two further number-one hits: "So Emotional" and "Where Do Broken Hearts Go." The star's vocals for these tracks were recorded relatively quickly. As the producer recalled, "Sometimes she didn't know the songs, so it may have taken her a day to sing it through a bunch of times to learn it, but then on the next day, she would knock things out in one or two takes."

The melodramatic "Didn't We Almost Have It All" was produced by Michael Masser from a song he composed with Will Jennings. It rose to the top of the U.S. music charts in late September 1987 (although on the British charts it only reached number fourteen). When "Where Do Broken Hearts Go" reached the top spot in late April 1988, it marked Whitney Houston's seventh consecutive number-one hit and in doing so broke an industry record, surpassing past achievements by the Beatles and the Bee Gees. Already by this time the *Whitney* album had achieved a special distinction of its own: it was the first by a female artist to enter the charts at number one. These victories provided Arista's marketing arm with plenty of promotional ammunition.

Not to be overlooked on the *Whitney* album is the eleventh track, "I Know Him So Well" by Tim Rice, Benny Andersson, and Björn Ulvaeus, a number written for the British stage musical *Chess*. This cut gave Whitney and Cissy Houston the opportunity to record a duet.

As Arista wanted to give the album's packaging a chic look, distinguished fashion photographer Richard Avedon was hired to capture Whitney's likeness—wearing a man's white T-shirt and jeans—for the cover photo. The inner sleeve boasted a high-fashion Avedon shot of a sleek Houston posing in a stylish black gown, while a snapshot of baby Nippy graced the album's reverse side.

Having waited so long for a new Whitney Houston disc to analyze, music reviewers were quick to jump into the fray with their assessments. *Newsweek*'s Richard Corliss wrote, "The new album showcases a Whitney Houston who sings bolder, blacker, badder." He concluded, "*Whitney* marks graduation day for the prom queen of soul."

Vince Aletti of *Rolling Stone* judged, "On one hearing, it's easy to dismiss Whitney Houston's new album as overcalculated, hollowed-out pop product, so suffocated by professionalism that only the faintest pulse of soul remains. But after several listens, it's nearly impossible to dislodge *Whitney* from your brain. Like Houston's debut, this is a mess of an album that succeeds in spite of itself." He dissected further, "There are plenty of young singers out there with more passion, guts, subtlety, street smarts and sass . . . but Whitney is like the pop pros of an earlier generation. Her work is cool, authoritative, no-nonsense and delivered with a facility that is almost off-putting. If it's sometimes hard to locate an emotional heart in Houston's songs, the sheer talent is obvious. Still, the narrow channel through which this talent has been directed is frustrating."

Meanwhile, *Rolling Stone* used the release of *Whitney* as an opportunity to label her a "crossover queen" and a "yuppie icon." It was precisely these two elements in the Whitney Houston story that were now arousing the open ire of the black press, who felt Whitney was ignoring her black roots to cater to the white establishment—which was to some degree true. The ethnic media complained that Houston was directing her efforts towards mainstream radio and to providing a series of safe, derivative hits suitable for the largely Caucasian audiences who could afford the steep ticket prices at her concerts. Upset by her supposed defection to the Man, the black press took to referring to the singer as "Whitey" Houston or "Whiteney" Houston.

Increasingly angered by such allegations, Whitney would later remark to *Essence* magazine: "What is 'Black'? I don't know how to sing 'Black,' and I don't know how to sing 'White,' either. I know how to sing. Music is not a color to me. It's an art." On another occasion, she asserted, "There's no way I would attempt to make myself less black, whatever that entails, to be more commercial. I'm comfortable with myself and I don't want to change anything. I stay close to my roots. I don't pretend to be anything other than what I am—nor do I want to be. But for so long we've been tortured with this image problem—it used to be that if you wanted to sell records as a black artist, you didn't put your face on the sleeve. I'm not saying there's anything wrong with anyone who chooses to change their look for those reasons . . . but I don't want to sell out and I don't have the need to."

Cissy Houston couldn't resist entering the fray and used a *Los Angeles Times* interview as her public forum: "What is the problem with crossover anyway? It's the only way you can reach your public. And if her voice is not as hoarse as what one normally thinks of for a black artist, that's not Whitney's fault."

The controversial race issue refused to fade away, but for the time being Clive Davis and Arista ignored the matter—at least in public. After all, they could tell themselves, her second album had sold enormously well and had done very nicely in the annual record-industry awards marathon. Among her victories, Whitney earned two American Music Awards in the Pop/Rock categories of Favorite Female Artist and Favorite Single for "I Wanna Dance with Somebody (Who Loves Me)," as well as a Grammy for Best Pop Vocal Performance, Female for the same track.

Alternately overwhelmed, embarrassed, excited, and worn down by her dazzling professional success, Whitney chose not to rock the successful luxury ship on which she was cruising. As she confided, "I told my people to give me a plan and I'd follow it. And it worked. I traveled and smiled, and it worked."

Once again back in front of the cameras, making music videos in support of singles from her second album, a cigarette-smoking Whitney confirmed that she had been offered the lead in the screen version of *Dreamgirls*. However, she pointed out, "Whether I do it depends on how good the script is and what it says. If you're offering someone a specific part, I think the person who plays it should have some input." There was also talk of Whitney starring in the movie adaptation of Toni Morrison's *Tar Baby*, a project that did not come to be.

Putting aside thoughts of (and serious fears about) conquering Hollywood, Houston agreed to tour to enhance sales of *Whitney*. On what was called the *Moment of Truth* tour, she headlined multiple shows in twenty-five North American cities, opening in Tampa, Florida on July 4, 1987 and winding up in Montreal, Canada on August 28. The show was again staged in the round, and she now had two full albums of hits from which to draw.

On September 8, Houston was at New York City's Madison Square Garden for the first of two sold-out performances at which the top admission price was a then-hefty $25 a seat. In reviewing the event for the *New York Times*, Jon Pareles remarked that the star "often lets her voice get buried in busy, frantic stage versions of her hits" and that "too much of the concert distracted from her singing, as if she were insecure about her considerable talents."

Pareles acknowledged that the headliner can "deliver a gospel rasp, a velvety coo, a floating soprano and a cheerleader's whoop." However, he pointed out, "Ms. Houston treats songs the way many video directors treat narratives: as a series of quick cuts, each just seconds long. In concert, the approach makes an impressive display of improvisation, but it atomizes the songs."

The *Times* reviewer had particular reservations about the relatively stark set-up of the concert, in which Whitney stood atop a circular platform with the band literally at her feet. As he observed, "Ms. Houston, on a stationary stage, shifted her angle almost continually in an effort to face everyone. As a result, she'd start a phrase and turn her back before it was over." He added, "In most selections, she had to battle band and backup singers to be heard; the arrangements sounded like they were intended to cover up mediocre vocals." He was much more impressed with her renditions of "Greatest Love of All," "Didn't We Almost Have It All," and the gospel number "I Believe" (for which Cissy joined the background singers).

Despite the shortcomings of the staging and the imbalance of sound between the star and her band and background singers, the national tour was a major commercial success.

Thanks to her album sales, concerts, and so forth, twenty-three-year-old Whitney Houston was already worth $44 million by 1987. According to a *New York Times* estimate, she was only topped by Madonna and Steven Spielberg as the highest-earning Americans in the entertainment business. With her affluent status, Whitney's image altered from that of a humble gospel singer whose relatives included mother Cissy Houston and cousin Dionne Warwick to a superstar who stood entirely on her own terms.

As befitted a major diva of her stature and wealth, in late July 1987, Houston purchased a 5.1-acre spread in upscale Mendham Township, New Jersey (about thirty miles and nearly an hour's drive to the west of East Orange). There, over the next few years, she would have a modern, circular home constructed. Because Whitney was often on the road during this period, she would have her architects, builders, and interior designers fly to meet her at a tour destination to discuss the progress of the construction and show her their latest floor plans and samples of materials. With another portion of her enormous earnings, Houston also purchased a luxury condo apartment on the twenty-sixth floor of a high-rise on Island Boulevard, on pricey Williams Island in North Miami Beach, Florida. From the balcony of her expensively decorated digs, she had a gorgeous view of the Atlantic Ocean.

Also in 1987, Cissy Houston finally sold the family's East Orange home and purchased a compact, sunny condo in Verona, New Jersey, about five miles northwest of the Dodd Street family home. John Houston continued to maintain his place in Fort Lee, New Jersey. By now, Whitney's older brother, Gary, had wed, and his firstborn, daughter Aja, arrived in 1987. Two years later, he and his wife had a son, Jonathan.

Despite career successes and material rewards, Houston expressed surprise—almost concern—that the world at large no longer regarded her as the wholesome young church-going soul of before. She insisted to *Us* magazine, "I really do very ordinary things with my life. I eat, sleep, sing, play tennis, play with my cats. Being alone is very important to me, but when I'm with friends I laugh, joke, fool around. Act normal."

Referring to the ongoing speculation about her private life, especially which—if any—men were in her life and what role Robyn Crawford was playing in her personal sphere, Whitney complained to *Us*, "Why should people know everything? There have to be surprises." By way of illustration, she said, "One of the best things about my act is that I come out like this frail thing with these skinny little legs, and then people hear this great big voice and say, 'How did that come out of this little thing?'"

But no matter how hard Houston tried to diffuse the issue, the apparent lack of romance in her otherwise successful life preoccupied the media. Fielding the question once again, she admitted to a TV reporter that year: "I have felt the feeling of being in love but I've also turned away from it. 'Cause I've known people who have been in love and how they react, and I just ain't got there yet."

While Whitney steadfastly refused to provide the media, and especially the tabloids, with fodder about her private life, the supermarket papers invented their own stories. They insisted she was "seeing" assorted celebrities, ranging from the diminutive musician Prince, to baseball player Darryl Strawberry, to Manhattan restaurant entrepreneur Brad Johnson. Occasionally, and very rarely at that, the press reported that Houston was being seen in the company of hard-living, edgy movie star Eddie Murphy, who was two years the singer's senior.

Murphy had first met Whitney when he attended her Carnegie Hall concert in October 1985. After the show, he went backstage to introduce himself. Periodically, over the next few years, their relationship developed beyond casual acquaintance into a sporadic romance. It was not exactly a connection favored by the gods. At that time, Murphy lived mostly on the West Coast, making pictures and hanging out with his posse of friends, staff, and hangers-on. By this period he had passed the first blush of fame he acquired in TV (*Saturday Night Live*) and in the movies (*48 Hrs, Trading Places, Beverly Hills Cop*). Now, in the late 1980s, he was earning over $35 million a year, but he had gained a reputation as a loose cannon on his recent tours, such as *Eddie Murphy Raw*. These days, Eddie was distracted from filmmaking by his obsession with expanding his recording career as a vocalist beyond his one successful R&B album, released in 1985.

If Whitney was discreet about her romantic life in the mid-to-late 1980s, Murphy was building up quite a public track record. For example, in September 1988, he became engaged to Musanna Overra, an eighteen-year-old Howard University student. But that union, set to take place in December, never occurred. Nor did a short-lived romance later that year with British singer Lorraine Pearson, a member of the pop group Five Star, lead to a walk down the wedding aisle.

When Murphy and Houston were not having occasional quiet get-togethers, he was seen about town with TV actress Jasmine Guy. A year later, in November 1989, the comedian became a father for the first time when girlfriend Nicole Mitchell, a model, gave birth to their daughter, Bria. Also in 1989, Murphy parented a son, Eddie Jr., with a young former flight attendant, Paulette McNelly. These days, when not on a Hollywood set, Murphy was ensconced in his colonial-style brick mansion, Bubble Hill, in Englewood Cliffs, New Jersey, while Nicole and their child lived mostly in Sacramento, California.

Perhaps in reaction to the increasing number of media stories focusing on her special rapport with Robyn Crawford, Whitney would occasionally suggest publicly that she and Murphy—whom she referred to as Edward—were more than "just friends." Another time, and in a different mood, she might refer to Murphy fleetingly, saying, "Like with any man, he can get on your nerves." But mostly she made ambiguous statements about her supposed suitor, saying such things as, "Yeah, we're friends. Just two very friendly people, the kind of friends that don't really have a got-to-see-you, got-to-have-you kind of relationship. Because of my career and his career—I'm here and he's there, I'm there and he's here—it's hard to establish a relationship. Even when you have two people who have the money, the fame and the same kind of status, it's the time factor—having the time to establish a relationship and to try to keep it."

At other points during the late 1980s, Whitney was more often seen publicly in the company of Murphy's good pal, comedian and actor Arsenio Hall, than with Murphy himself. When bachelor Hall began his late-night TV talk show in 1989, he would sometimes mention Whitney on air, inferring that he and she were actually dating. But, insisted Whitney, "Arsenio is my buddy. We have a different kind of closeness than Eddie and I." Still later, Whitney would appear on Arsenio's TV show on several occasions. On one such outing, she playfully teased the host into admitting to the audience that there was nothing of an amorous nature going on between the two of them.

Sometime in the late 1980s, Murphy, who handed out more gems than a jewelry shop, gave Houston a five-karat diamond ring. It was allegedly intended to cement their growing closeness as a couple, despite his other current female distractions. However, a major turning point in their on-again, off-again rapport occurred one evening when she invited him to her Mendham Township home. She had her staff prepare dinner for two, but according to her, he never showed up, nor did he ever apologize. If Murphy's extremely busy dating schedule and his fathering two children had not taught her anything about the man she was seeing, this broken dinner engagement gave her pause to consider his role in her future. However, none of these revelations prevented Whitney from periodically hooking up with Murphy throughout the late 1980s and very early 1990s. It seemed that once she had a yen for a relationship, no one or nothing could make her leave it alone until it finally suited her needs to do so.

Murphy wasn't the only movie star to be drawn to Whitney. Another who was smitten was actor Robert De Niro, who had already won two Academy Awards for his lead roles in *The Godfather Part II* (1974) and *Raging Bull* (1980). Born in 1941, De Niro was more than twice Whitney's age. He also had a complicated personal life. In 1976, he had married black actress Diahnne Abbott, by whom he had a son. By the late 1970s, the marriage was essentially over. Then, in 1982, De Niro had fathered a baby girl with singer-songwriter Helena Springs.

Given De Niro's penchant for African-American women, it was predictable that he would eventually set his sights on fine-looking Whitney Houston. As she would later tease in a TV interview with Byron Allen, "Yeah, he was sweatin' me." Reportedly, the Oscar-winning actor was so intent on getting to know Houston that he began a campaign of sending her a massive number of bouquets, making sure that his home phone number accompanied each one.

When the elusive Whitney did not respond to these blandishments, De Niro raised the stakes by sending her an assortment of pricey trinkets, including diamond earrings attached to a cute teddy bear. Whitney may not have been aware that he was at this time dating black model Doris "Toukie" Smith, who would later have a brief bit part in Whitney's 1996 feature *The Preacher's Wife*. Either way, she was sufficiently intrigued to call and thank the actor for his tokens of esteem. They chatted pleasantly and he mentioned the notion of them working together in a film. She made polite noises about the suggestion. However, when she eventually saw the script, which dealt with unsavory filmmakers and their mistresses, she lost interest in the idea.

As De Niro's game of conquest continued, rumors of his pursuit came to the attention of Arista executives, who politely but firmly told Whitney that to embark on a mixed-race relationship would be disastrous for her career (and their coffers). Cissy and John Houston seconded this opinion, and informed their offspring in no uncertain terms of their strong feelings on the matter. By now, even Whitney had tired somewhat of De Niro's perseverance. Apparently, however, her indifference to his charms only whetted the actor's appetite even more. He appeared to be ready to wait out her reluctance and in the meantime continue dallying elsewhere.

It seems that Mrs. Houston finally decided to put an end to the potentially inflammable situation, which her ambivalent daughter had allowed to drag on for far too long. One day while visiting Whitney, Cissy got into an argument with her daughter on the subject of De Niro. When Whitney walked out with Robyn Crawford in tow, the still-angry Mrs. Houston rushed around the building gathering up the assorted expensive tokens that the actor had sent over recent weeks. She supposedly packed them up in a box and returned them with a brief note saying: "Thanks, but no thanks."

That feat accomplished, Mrs. Houston returned to giving reporters her usual statement about her still-single daughter: "What Whitney really wants is to get married. It's a matter of finding the right person and the time. She's a loving girl, and wants to be certain. She's going to make a great mother."

14

The Changing Wind

"The press won't let me be a regular person. It used to hurt me really badly. Because I'm a true-to-myself person. I was raised that way. I don't live lies. It was hard to accept, because you go out in public and people watch what you do. Now I know it's a commodity, a business for them. . . . To me, our society is very weird about what they get off on."

WHITNEY HOUSTON, 1995

Over the years, Whitney Houston had observed her mother coping with the unpredictable ups and downs of her own showbusiness career. Having experienced such life lessons vicariously, Whitney thought she was prepared for dealing with twists of fate in her own professional life. However, what she never counted on was the powerful effect the media could have on the public's perception of the "real" Whitney. In a 1993 interview with *Rolling Stone*, she professed herself amazed to find that the press "always distorts shit. It's never, never what I said; it's never how I said it; it's never how I thought that person perceived it. It's always some other crazy shit—which is why I don't like doing interviews. Because they lie. They just outright lie." In dealing with the media, Houston proved to be somewhat naïve, frequently stubborn, and often self-defeating.

To start with, Arista Records had used the power of the press to promote Whitney as a definable image to the public, even before her debut album had been released. It should therefore have been clear to Whitney that if the media could be employed to help make her a household name, they could just as easily break her. But she neither acknowledged nor accepted this fact.

In her obstinacy, Whitney was either vastly overestimating her charismatic power over her fan base or underestimating the influence of journalists in presenting her "true" persona to the world. In not understanding that the press must, in the long run, be indulged, or else its members would one day seek their revenge, she was undermining the health of her career. Meanwhile, as time went on, she increasingly resented the media for their intrusions on her privacy, ignoring the fact that this public attention was the price of being a celebrated popular artist.

Adding to Whitney's escalating public relations quagmire was the fact that she frequently inflamed reporters by hitting back—in her increasingly colorful street language—rather than ignoring them when they baited her with leading questions. The press soon came to realize that certain sensitive subjects (her emotional closeness to Robyn Crawford; her "selling out" to the world of white pop) would push her emotional buttons. The hoped-for public explosions provided sensational quotes, such as: "No, I am not a lesbo. Guys that say that about me are the same ones who want to jump into my pants!" This bait-and-print practice was nothing new in the media business, but Whitney refused to understand how effectively she was being played by reporters. Had she merely bitten her tongue or offered a bland "no comment," she frequently could have saved herself much grief.

It also didn't help matters that Whitney increasingly exhibited an at best neutral and sometimes overtly hostile attitude to the media at press conferences, leading them to view her increasingly as an "enemy" and thus undeserving of sympathetic coverage. If only she had learned to "act" offstage and present a seemingly friendly image to the press, pretending that the ritual of answering their volley of questions was not such a bore and such a waste of her precious time, she could have sidestepped a good deal of media backlash.

Another showbusiness truism also seemed to elude Whitney. If the fickle public can make someone a star, it can similarly knock that person down at whim. Her phenomenal success in the mid-1980s had placed her on a high pedestal where she became a ready target for hard-to-please critics and envious onlookers. Rather than dodge such bullets gracefully, she flung back salvos of her own, increasingly going off the deep end in emotional responses to leading questions about Robyn Crawford, Eddie Murphy, her loyalty to the black community, her artistic growth, and so forth.

Furthermore, Houston seemed not to fathom that when some reviewers sniped about her lack of artistic growth, her refusal (or inability) to write her own songs as many other leading artists did, or her shortcomings as a dancer in her live shows, they might, perhaps, have been giving her backhanded compliments. In essence, many of these critics were subtly suggesting that since she had already exhibited such incredible artistic ability, expanding her creative range was well within her grasp—if only she cared enough to try.

The 1980s wore on, and the Whitney–Arista team followed an "if it ain't broke, don't fix it" policy with a conventional, commercially safe second album. It prompted some sources to be less polite in their criticism of the already-frozen Whitney Houston format and style. For example, in October 1987, the American Comedy Network, which syndicated programming to 215 radio stations in North America, took a potshot at Whitney. On one of its morning shows, hosted by Mark Wallengren and Kim Arnidon, the network presented a parody of Whitney's "Didn't We Almost Have It All," entitled "Don't My Songs All Sound the Same." The spoof song referred to the artist "taking no chances" in sticking to her assembly-line method of making hit tunes, and ended with a pledge to "keep on yelling" in the recording studios. Bertilla Baker provided the Houston-esque vocals for the skit.

Later, in the early 1990s, Fox-TV's satirical comedy series *In Living Color* would present a biting parody of the artist entitled "Whitney's Rhythmless Nation." Using Janet Jackson's 1989 song "Rhythm Nation" as its basis, the spoof poked fun at Whitney's music videos and concerts, in which her dancers did all the splashy choreography while she typically engaged in only the most simple steps. Worse was to come when the Fox Network's *Mad TV* (in the mid-1990s) and Black Entertainment Television's ComicView (in 2001) savagely parodied Whitney with references to her diva-like behavior, reputed drug usage, and the many shenanigans and peccadilloes of her bad-boy husband, Bobby Brown.

Further fuelling the deterioration of her once-wholesome, girlish, gospel-loving image was Whitney's prima donna-style behavior in public appearances, especially on the concert trail. When she initiated her road tours in 1985, there was an ingratiating exuberance about her as a performer and it seemed obvious to audiences that she was anxious to please and eager to learn more about presenting herself to best effect. At that time, concertgoers, new to seeing the artist live on stage, were forgiving about the definite undertone of artificiality and mechanical slickness to her live act.

As the grind, monotony, and pressure of later tours took their toll on the now-established star, she chose to further bury her emotions when in front of the spotlight. Especially now that her onstage performances were no longer a novelty, her presentation at such outings was now being likened to that of a well-conceived, windup doll. Matters were not helped as news leaked out in these years that Whitney was increasingly behaving like a diva at concert venues, issuing a long list of excessive demands to be met at each site in order to pacify her royal highness. Her requirements included sufficient backstage accommodations and a detailed list of amenities for her imposing entourage of support performers, technicians, and bodyguards, among others. Then there was her insistence that the air conditioning in such facilities must be kept to a minimum—or turned off—even in very hot weather, due to her susceptibility to colds, which always went right to her throat. Thus it was bandied about that the star was unconcerned that ticketholders, having paid substantial sums for the privilege of seeing her sing, might have to sweat through a long, sweltering evening with no respite.

On stage, Whitney liked to be in total control, which minimized the chance of the audience witnessing any refreshing acts of spontaneity. Her attitude became increasingly indifferent to her fans: she would do her concert her way, and if the audience was not sufficiently thrilled by the privilege of seeing her perform, that was their problem and not hers.

This icy, regal attitude first came to the fore when Houston was headlining at London's Wembley Stadium in 1988. The star seemed resistant to performing on this particular occasion. For whatever reason, she wasn't in the mood to exert herself—despite her high fee. Apparently, it did not faze her that thousands of paying fans were seated in the arena waiting for her to start singing. Finally willing herself to walk on stage, she was greeted enthusiastically. Next, she waved to the audience and shouted out, "Hello, London!" This was followed by a boastful, "I've had seven consecutive number-one singles!" Then she capped that remark with, "I am bigger than the Beatles!" To make such a statement in the quartet's homeland showed bad judgment. However, this was not the end of it. When portions of the audience took offense at this apparent Beatles-bashing, they began booing. Houston's reaction was not, "Oops, I made a mistake," but rather, "Why are they responding that way to *me*?" Her ire now aroused, she gave what some spectators labeled a perfunctory performance, listlessly going through her paces. The frostiness that existed between Whitney and her audience was palpable.

Whitney's troubled love–hate relationship with the British public soon had another occasion to manifest itself. She was among the celebrities set to perform in London at a tribute concert in honor of the seventieth birthday of South African anti-apartheid activist Nelson Mandela, then still a political prisoner in his homeland, on November 6, 1988. At this eleven-hour gig, aired live on TV by the BBC, there were rumors that Whitney was being difficult. Reputedly, she was upset when the program lineup didn't include a spot for her mother, Cissy. In addition, the autocratic artist supposedly resisted relinquishing part of her allotted forty-five minutes of stage time to Stevie Wonder. Then there was an encounter with comedian and actress Whoopi Goldberg, who was also performing at the fundraiser. Backstage, as Whitney prepared to make her entrance, her phalanx of bodyguards purportedly shoved Whoopi aside to clear the path for the singer. Such treatment prompted Goldberg to retort, "I'm black, too!"

This, then, was the emerging diva who demanded complete obeisance from her audiences and fellow artists—even when she was guilty of gaffs.

During Whitney's British concert tour in mid-1988, she recorded a new single entitled "One Moment in Time." The song had been written in honor of the 1988 Olympic Games, to be held in Seoul, South Korea, that fall, and was to be included on a special Olympics album from Arista. That September, "One Moment in Time" became Whitney's third British number one; it peaked at number five in the U.S. For this song, Houston was nominated for a Grammy in the Best Pop Vocal Performance—Female category, but at the February 1989 awards ceremony she lost to Tracy Chapman for "Fast Car."

In the fall of 1988, Whitney could also be heard on the Capitol album *Heaven*, which featured BeBe and CeCe Winans, a highly regarded duo who specialized in soulful black gospel music. The siblings were part of a musical dynasty rooted in Detroit's Mount Zion Church of God in Christ, which had been founded by their great-great-grandfather and was now presided over by their preacher father. Whitney had first encountered the Winans at an industry awards ceremony in Los Angeles in 1987, when she told them, "I listen to your tape every morning. It really inspires me." CeCe acknowledged that the first time she had heard Whitney sing had been on a radio jingle, and she was unaware who the vocalist was. Winans recalled, "She's a gospel singer. She was singing a commercial for Steak & Ale like she'd been saved!"

Later at the function, Whitney joined BeBe and CeCe on stage. Even with no rehearsal, the trio harmonized perfectly on their rendition of her favorite Winans song, "Love Said Not So." Thereafter, Whitney often surprised the Winans duo on stage with a special guest appearance whenever they all simultaneously happened to be in the same city.

As the 1980s drew to a close, Whitney began to count more and more on her mother to mediate for her with the press, to be her special representative at award ceremonies she could not (or could not be bothered to) attend, and to be her official spokesperson on various matters. Cissy seemed both willing to accept the demanding task and adept at it; after all, it did keep her in the spotlight.

Cissy Houston felt well qualified to be her daughter's ambassador at large because, as she reasoned, family are "the only people you can always count on." When it came to responding to media enquiries about such controversial matters as Whitney's links to Robyn Crawford, or her diva-like behavior on concert tours, Cissy either neatly sidestepped the issue at hand, or tossed out one of her home-spun retorts for consumption. For example, at one such question-and-answer session with the ever-curious press, she noted of her celebrity daughter: "I tell her, 'If you're on a firm foundation, no one can destroy you, whatever they say.' She knows that, and I think she's learning that you cannot even give credence to those things that are not true by talking about them." Never at a loss for words on any topic, Cissy even had thoughts about her girl's much-touted offers to try her hand at moviemaking. Regarding Tinseltown and its supposedly racy lifestyle, Cissy raised her eyes heavenward and said, "Hollywood, I don't know. All I can do is talk to her and pray a lot."

These media opportunities sometimes allowed Mrs. Houston to touch on how Whitney's fame reflected on her. "I don't feel regretful about anything in my career. I am happy with my status. But sure, I hear some of my style in Whitney, more so as she gets older. A lot of people have tried to take my style over the years—so who better to do it than my own daughter? Maybe God meant for me to see this through her."

Occasionally, Cissy came out with remarks that really made one ponder the possible subtext. For instance, she informed a news outlet of her famous offspring: "The thing is I really like her now. You don't always like your kids, you know? Sometimes when I hear her sing, I get chills. She's got such a gift. When I think about people who want to say things that tear her down—well, I don't even like to think about it. Gets me so crazy." Usually, though, Mrs. Houston returned to the established concept of her superstar daughter still being humble and family-oriented. Cissy insisted, "She's not a star when she comes home to the family. She's just Nippy. But she's a gutsy little broad. That's how I raised her. There are so many ways we're proud of her, so many."

Left unaired in public were the apparently increasingly frequent arguments between mother and daughter, as Whitney, now the top act of the family, exerted her independence and allowed career pressures to color her fast-shifting frame of mind. One of those who experienced the many mood shifts of the star was veteran Aretha Franklin. Since both artists were under contract to the same label, Arista thought it would be a good marketing gimmick for Whitney and her Aunt Ree to record a song together for the latter's new album, *Through the Storm* (1989). The much-hyped joint number, entitled "It Isn't, It Wasn't, It Ain't Never Gonna Be," misfired, and both parties wished it had indeed never come to be.

In her autobiography, *Aretha: From These Roots* (1999), the Queen of Soul makes some intriguing observations about recording this duet: "As it went down, some things were misunderstood and we miscommunicated; we were very badly mismatched in terms of maturity and experience and sensitivity. It was something that never should have happened. I think Nippy felt unappreciated, and nothing could have been further from the truth." The finished track did not make the top twenty on the U.S. charts (but did reach number twenty-nine in the U.K.). In contrast, another duet—the title song, performed with Elton John—from the same album reached number sixteen in the U.S.

Having performed so steadily over recent years, in 1989 Whitney chose to cut back her professional schedule a great deal. At certain times, career ambitions seemed to be a very low priority for the artist. The way she phrased it, the time off would allow her and her public to have a break from each other. With more free time on her hands that year, she founded the Whitney Houston Foundation for Children, Inc. The charitable institution especially focused its activities on children suffering from AIDS, as well as illiteracy among the young. Genuinely concerned about the welfare of disadvantaged kids—especially from the black ghettos—the celebrity devoted a great deal of personal energy over the years to the organization, which was based in Newark, New Jersey. She often worked behind the scenes promoting its cause, not wishing her efforts to be viewed as bids for publicity. Before long, Nippy would appoint Cissy Houston as chief executive officer of the Foundation, and her sister-in-law, Donna Houston, was to become very active in its operation.

Whitney also supported other charities, including St. Jude's Children's Hospital, the Children's Diabetes Fund, and several AIDS-related organizations. As time went on, Houston received recognition of her humanitarian work: she was awarded such accolades as the Fredrick D. Patterson Award from the United Negro College Fund, and both the Brass Ring Award and the High Hopes Award from the Children's Diabetes Foundation.

In the spring of 1989, at nearly twenty-six years old, Whitney was still a single woman. However, there had been changes in her domestic life. Years in the building, her elaborate compound in Mendham Township, New Jersey was now nearing completion. She would soon move into her spacious new quarters, with swimming pool, tennis courts, recording studio, and the main house with its modern, circular design. Besides Robyn Crawford and a growing staff of helpers, bodyguards, and domestics—including her mother's longtime friend Aunt Bae—Whitney made further additions to her household. She purchased two Akitas (a Japanese breed of large, muscular dog), whom she named Lucy and Ethel in honor of the classic TV series *I Love Lucy*. They joined her menagerie, which already included her two cats, Miste and Marilyn.

During this time of revitalization, Whitney was in no great rush to put together a third album for Arista. She felt no particular creative need to do so, and there was certainly no pressing financial incentive—she was already quite wealthy. On the other hand, she realized the importance of maintaining a public presence. This was accomplished with a high-caliber, high-earning national TV commercial for AT&T, who wanted to promote the clarity of sound reproduction on its phone lines. The hip small-screen advert presented Whitney at her high-fashion, well-coiffured (in wigs) best.

Similarly, Whitney, her managers (with decisions now funneled through Nippy, Inc., of which her father, John, was in charge), and Arista all appreciated the value of her attending key music-industry functions. She therefore agreed to perform at the 3rd Annual Soul Train Music Awards in mid-April 1989. When she accepted the invitation to this Los Angeles-based fête, she had no idea that the decision would alter her entire life.

15

That Guy from Roxbury, Massachusetts

"When you love, you love. I mean, do you stop loving somebody because you have different images?"

WHITNEY HOUSTON, 1993

The 3rd Annual Soul Train Music Awards were held on Wednesday, April 12, 1989 at the Shrine Auditorium. Singers Dionne Warwick and Patti LaBelle were among the evening's cohosts. Because Elizabeth Taylor's good friend Michael Jackson was receiving the Entertainer of the Year and the Heritage Award (for outstanding achievement in the field of entertainment), she also agreed to be a presenter at the gala. Other celebrity prizegivers that night included Anita Baker, LL Cool J, Heather Locklear, Stephanie Mills, Pebbles, Public Enemy, Sinbad, Billy Dee Williams, and Eddie Murphy, Whitney's sometime suitor.

The previous year, Houston had won the Soul Train Music Award for Best Album of the Year—Female for *Whitney*. The choice had not pleased some members of the audience, who thought the album ignored the artist's black roots—they felt Whitney was an "Oreo," who, like the famous cookie, was chocolate on the outside and white on the inside—and they had booed her when she accepted her trophy. At the time, a surprised and upset Whitney had tried not to let the hissing and catcalls bother her, but the negative response from her own community had deeply affected her.

She would later try to dismiss the disturbing incident, rationalizing that some people in the audience "had just gotten sick of me and just didn't want me to win another award."

Tonight, Houston was toughing it out, returning to the scene of her past embarrassment. Robyn Crawford was part of her entourage as moral support. During the ceremony, there were performances from entertainers including Ashford & Simpson, Sheena Easton, Patti LaBelle, Dionne Warwick, Rob Base, the Clark Sisters, Thelma Houston, and BeBe & CeCe Winans. Whitney was particularly impressed with R&B hotshot Bobby Brown, whose album *Don't Be Cruel* had risen to the top of the music charts in late January 1989; it would remain at number one for six non-consecutive weeks. Bobby performed an energetic rendition of the title track that night. Said Whitney of Bobby: "He was kicking 'Don't Be Cruel'—he was hot, he was on fire." She was very taken with this sexy young man who definitely knew all the right slick moves on stage.

During the event, Whitney had a much more personal and up-close encounter with the rakish Bobby. According to Houston: "I and some friends [Bebe and CeCe Winans] of mine were sitting behind him. I was hugging them, we were laughing, and I kept hitting Bobby in the back of the head. Robyn [Crawford] said, 'Whitney, you keep hittin' Bobby, he's goin' to be mad at you.' I leaned over and said, 'Bobby I'm so sorry.' And he turned around and looked at me like 'Yeah, well just don't let it happen again.' And I was like 'Oooooh, this guy doesn't like me.'"

Intrigued by this successful artist who seemed to be unimpressed by her ("I always get curious when somebody doesn't like me. I want to know why"), Whitney was determined not to let their meeting be a one-off. She decided to pursue him. Waiting for a few weeks, so it would not seem as though she was chasing him, she invited Brown to her twenty-sixth birthday party that August. To her surprise and pleasure, he called back and said, "I'd love to come." When he arrived at the festivities, held at her impressive New Jersey estate, he was careful to maintain an air of casual respect. He kept to himself how physically attracted he was to his hostess, and, on his most polite behavior, chatted intermittently with her throughout the party. Later, a deeply impressed Whitney would say, "He was the first male I met in the business that I could talk to and be real with. He was so down and so cool. I was like 'I like him.'"

Thereafter, because each was busy with his or her own professional and personal activities, it was another four months before the two encountered one another again. The occasion was a BeBe and CeCe Winans concert.

After the show, CeCe hosted a party, inviting a group of friends and notables to share dinner. At the end of the meal, Bobby Brown walked over to Whitney and said, "If I asked you to go out with me, would you?" Houston recollects, "At the time I was dating someone, but it was kind of ehhhh. So I said, 'Yeah, I would.' And he said, 'You really would?'—he's so cool—'I'll pick you up tomorrow at eight.' And we've been friends ever since. See, our whole relationship started out as friends. We'd have dinner, laugh, talk and go home. It wasn't intimate. And then it kind of dawned on us, 'What's going on here?'"

Soon, much of America and the world would be asking that same tantalizing question over and over again.

Robert Baresford Brown was born on February 5, 1969 in Boston, Massachusetts. The fifth of eight children of a construction-worker father and a junior-high-school-teacher mother, he grew up in the inner-city Orchard Parks projects, part of Roxbury's rough black ghetto. There was a great deal of racist feeling in the city at the time, which made being poor and black even more difficult. Brown has recalled, "We had our hard times. You live to get past them. But it was rough growing up in the streets and having to fight someone for the stupidest reasons." As he elaborated further to *Rolling Stone* magazine in 1989, "I grew up with the frame of mind that I wanted expensive things. I always wanted the $100 sneakers. I always wanted the better things in life. If I seen anything, a sweat suit I wanted in the store, I'd have to get some money to get that suit. I had to get mine the way I knew how to get it—stealing and whatever I had to do. A lot of my friends either they're passed away, in jail, or on drugs."

Bobby first developed a taste for the spotlight when, at the age of three, his mother lifted him onto the stage at a James Brown show and the child began to strut around to the music. Tommy Brown, his brother and manager, remembers, "He was never shy. Not Bobby." Before long, the musically inclined youngster began winning talent shows—when he wasn't acting on his impulse of becoming a juvenile delinquent. Considering his shaky formative years, Brown said once, "I don't think I ever felt like a kid. I always hung around older guys, doing the older things. . . . You knew they were going to get money. And if they got money, you got money. Mo' money, mo' money, mo' money is better. That's why I still have boyish ways about myself."

Brown was only eleven when he underwent a shattering experience. His boyhood friend James "Jimbo" Flint was stabbed to death in a stupid fight, dying as a griefstricken Bobby looked on. Recalling the traumatic incident, the star said, "That was the turning point in my life. That's when I realized that running the streets can't last forever. You don't always have good luck. Right after that, we got New Edition started."

In short order, this bubble-gum music group, patterned after the old Jackson 5, were placed second in a major Boston talent show. Local talent agent and record producer Maurice Starr quickly signed up the group. The boys dropped out of junior high school to go on tour. Brown had already achieved his initial goal of getting out of the projects. In 1983, their first song, "Candy Girl," was a hit, and New Edition, whose members' average age was fourteen, became an instant success. But there were rumors that the group's raucous offstage behavior was perhaps fueled by substance abuse. Brown would always deny this, insisting, "We were a bunch of brats, but we wasn't into drugs, we wasn't into liquor. We was into girls." As he explained, "There were little girls chasing around us. Little panties onstage. Some of the girls were [sexually] fast and it broke a lot of us down."

Despite the enormous success of New Edition, the ambitious Brown constantly felt frustrated. At the time, the teenager believed that Starr was being unfair in his financial dealings with the band. Even more importantly, he was irritated because he wasn't being allowed to sing lead vocals or given more of a say in the group's artistic direction. Brown's unhappiness led to a great deal of tension between him and the others. He recalls: "I was sad. Very sad. I got real sick, but I kept performing, and it just got worse and worse. It all came down on me. I was feeling alone, not knowing if tomorrow was promised to me."

In 1986, Bobby Brown went solo. Almost immediately, there was industry buzz that the artist was an out-and-out drug addict (and, later, that he had actually died). A few years after the fact, Brown would give his version of these career-damaging rumors: "[Some of the business people] we had and I were fighting all the time, and in order to try and blacklist my name, that's what they did. But I've never used drugs and never been on drugs. My only drug is, I think, alcohol. I drink beer a lot. That's my best drug."

By the age of seventeen, Bobby Brown had a solo recording contract with the giant MCA label. He had also become a dad: "It was one of those nights. It was my birthday and the guys had given me a party at the hotel. I was drunk and one thing led to another, and another thing led to that thing, and I forgot the bag and POW! My little boy [Landon] came."

His first solo album, *King of Stage* (1987), contained the hit R&B ballad "Girlfriend," but otherwise was creatively and commercially undistinguished. In contrast, the 1988 follow-up *Don't Be Cruel* was a notable success. It spawned four consecutive hit songs, including the title tune, for which producer Teddy Riley combined the musical genres of hip-hop, pop, and funk to make the first real "New Jack Swing" record. The album's most popular track, the sassy, driving "My Prerogative," went to number one on the charts in mid-November 1988. The *Don't Be Cruel* album would eventually sell a massive 8 million copies, and one of its cuts, "Every Little Step," would earn Brown a Grammy in the Best Rhythm & Blues Vocal Performance—Male category.

A good deal of Brown's continuing success was attributed to his live shows, part of an exhausting tour schedule designed to take full advantage of his white-hot popularity. What made his live performances so exciting to women in the audience was his athletic dancing style, which combined grinding pelvis thrusts with nimble long sliding steps. Alternately mixing slick and smooth steps with hard pounding actions, the act was further enhanced by the star's heavy-duty bad-boy image, the result of speculation about his raw private life. This led John Leland of *Newsday* to judge, "Bobby Brown is the most electrifying performer of his day."

By 1989, when not on tour, Brown was living in a new home he had purchased for his parents in Los Angeles' San Fernando Valley. He had recently purchased a Mercedes coupé, and a favorite pastime of his was to cruise the mountains east of LA in his brand-new jeep. At the time, the playboy claimed to have no steady girlfriend: "only friends, and I won't say who." In fact, that fall he became a father for the second time when Kim Ward, from his old neighborhood and his first love, gave birth to their daughter, LaPrincia.

As to his financial future, the wealthy twenty-year-old boasted, "I'm investing. I wanna know what I've got down to the penny. Then I wanna build things. And help the poor. So many people like [real-estate entrepreneur] Donald Trump have all that money and don't know what to do with it. I want to be like a Trump. Only a kinder Trump."

Early in 1989, Brown had his first major brush with the law as an adult. On tour in Columbus, Georgia, he was arrested by a local police officer for having violated the city's legislation prohibiting performers from "simulating sexual intercourse" in public. The arresting officer claimed Brown was "hunching" an eighteen-year-old fan on stage, while the singer insisted he was dancing several feet away from the girl—"I didn't even touch her." After being taken off to police headquarters, the entertainer was released on bail of $652 and was free to resume his concert an hour later. Back in action, Brown was angry about "the Lust Bust" (as the press termed it). He reasoned, "I invite a fan onstage at all my shows. I just did a couple of pumps with my hips. There's nothing wrong or nasty about it. It's just a dance." A few months later, again in the South, he was arrested for a similar offense. Once again, he paid his fine and then went about his business.

Although Brown made his film debut in 1989 (in a small role in the hugely successful *Ghostbusters*; his soundtrack song "On Our Own" rose to number two on the charts), he decided that neither Los Angeles nor the East Coast was for him. Instead, he was in the process of moving to Atlanta, Georgia, where he had purchased a $2.2 million estate (with a 14,000-square-foot home) at a bargain rate. There he lived with his first-born child, as well as his father (recently separated from Mrs. Brown), and began recording in his own home studio, a facility he named Bosstown. Brown's relocation put him in close proximity to his collaborators Antonio L. A. Reid and Kenneth "Babyface" Edmonds, the in-vogue musician-producer team who had earlier moved their business to Atlanta.

During this period, Brown, who had endured past disputes and ongoing lawsuits with previous representatives, was being managed by his brother and himself. The artist cancelled twenty concerts of his summer 1989 tour. Engulfed in courtroom actions and amid rumors that he was a major substance abuser, he countered: "I see what drugs can do to a person, so why would I be into 'em? Having the top male slot now, drugs would just bring me down, and down is not a place I want to go."

His public remarks in this period reflect just how much this young man, with seemingly everything to look forward to, was going through an emotionally testing time. "No matter what happens in life, you gotta deal with the problems. I was always taught this by my mom and dad. No matter what, you can't let them break you down. Once they see that you're broke down and you can't take it no more, boom, right over the edge you go. That's when you lose it all." He also declared, "A million dollars ain't nothin' now. Once you get that million, you want more millions. Some of the happiest people are poor people. I been there. I love money but I'm not happy right now. I can be happy, at times. I'm happy onstage. That's the only place I'm happy. I'm not happy unless I'm onstage." As to the potential of pursuing an acting career, the singer commented wryly, "One day maybe they'll give me a chance to play the boy next door. Yeah, *right*—the guy everybody says is on drugs."

But, on some occasions, Brown claimed he was content to put his often-troubled past behind him, confiding, "I'm just happy God showed me the way. God showed me the light." At other times, Brown's bragging, arrogant side would kick in and, in typically hyperbolic fashion, he'd insist to the world: "I'll be the biggest thing since Michael Jackson, since Elvis. I want to be that large."

This, then, was the complicated, talented man who had so captured Whitney's attention.

As Whitney moved into the new decade, her professional activities accelerated. For example, she was in Japan on January 8, 1990 to perform in concert at Yokohama Arena. A month later, Houston was among the stars who appeared on the ABC-TV special *Sammy Davis Jr. 60th Anniversary Celebration.* In April that year, she took part in *That's What Friends Are For,* a two-hour CBS-TV celebration (and AIDS fundraiser) marking the fifteenth anniversary of Arista Records. The celebrity hosts included Lauren Bacall, Chevy Chase, and Whoopi Goldberg, and the diverse lineup featured—besides Whitney—the likes of Air Supply, Burt Bacharach, the Four Tops, Alan Jackson, Kenny G, Melissa Manchester, Barry Manilow, Carly Simon, Patti Smith, and Dionne Warwick.

Despite all the rumors and false starts to date, Whitney had yet to star in a feature film. However, in May 1990, it was announced that she had signed a multi-picture development deal with Twentieth Century-Fox for screen projects in which she would star as well as produce (through her own company, Nippy Productions). Commenting in the trade press on the deal, Joe Roth, chairman and chief executive officer of Fox, proclaimed Houston to be "a star of the first magnitude in the world of music, and it will be exciting for us to work with her."

During this increasingly hectic professional period, Whitney continued occasionally to see Eddie Murphy and, more quietly, to become better acquainted with Bobby Brown. She was also getting settled into her lavish new digs in New Jersey, a home constructed largely of glass, with few solid traditional walls. The house boasted a cinema and a huge imported Italian bath, said to be big enough to hold six. The structure's entrance hall had an impressive waterfall decorated with artistically arranged vines and flowers. The immense living room was dominated by a massive circular couch and an ornate purple-glass coffee table. The numerous rooms contained remote-control units to operate everything from the lights to the curtains. There was even a specially constructed conveyer belt linking the kitchen to the dining room.

While Whitney was mistress of her lavish domain, there was much about her home that Houston delegated to the supervision of others. For example, except for visits to the refrigerator or a closet food shelf, she was a virtual stranger to her own kitchen. When pal Arsenio Hall conducted a satellite interview with Houston in 1990 for his TV talk show, he had his staff tour on camera a few rooms of her impressive new abode. In the process, he teased the bespectacled Houston for pretending that she actually knew where everything was in each room. To prove his point, he asked her to open one of the kitchen drawers in front of her. When she did, she was surprised to find that they contained pots and pans and laughingly conceded that his hunch about her culinary ignorance was correct.

It was three years since Whitney had recorded her last album. In the meantime, the success of her first two offerings had spawned several new big-voiced talents with multi-octave ranges, two of whom—Mariah Carey and Toni Braxton—were now on the verge of great breakthroughs. Other black female vocalists with whom Houston was competing for listeners' favor included Janet Jackson, Anita Baker, Sade, and Vanessa Williams, as well as seasoned veterans Aretha Franklin and Tina Turner, both of whom had recently rekindled their popularity.

These days, just as Houston's remarkable sound was no longer considered unique, the standby musical genres that had made numbers such as "Saving All My Love for You" and "I Wanna Dance with Somebody (Who Loves Me)" so popular were now regarded as passé. The ever-changing recording industry was going through new developments, increasingly moving away from pop music to the more gritty styles of hip-hop and urban R&B.

Assessing the new times and the roster of fresh favorites, Clive Davis agreed that it was now time for Whitney to head in different musical directions. He wanted her to gravitate back to her African-American roots and to recapture that core audience which had turned away from her mainstream ballads and uptempo pop numbers.

Ever mindful of her nightmare experience at the 1988 Soul Train Music Awards and the increasing harsh criticism from the black community, Houston was in full agreement with Davis's career plan. However, as she explained to *USA Today*'s Tom Green, "I would rather say to people that this new album is not different. It's just an extension of what Whitney has in store for them." (Like many divas, Houston sometimes fell into the habit of referring to herself in the third person.) She was a bit upset to think that people were buying into the allegation that black audiences were not among her most faithful fans. She scoffed, "I get my flak like everybody else . . . but I'm just doing what I do best." Then, going on the offensive, she added, "I would think black people would be proud. . . . I don't sing music thinking this is black, or this is white . . . I sing songs that everybody's going to like."

With his finger on the pulse of who was hip in the contemporary music field, Clive decreed that his prized singer should work with, among others, L. A. Reid and Babyface (Kenneth Edmonds). That youngish team, whose company was known as LaFace, had done a terrific job for artists such as Bobby Brown, Pebbles, and Karyn White. According to Reid, "We wanted to come up with something that was different than anything Whitney had sung, so we approached it from that angle. We wanted to give her a new direction, and pick up where we felt she was lacking. We felt she needed more of a black base."

L.A. and Babyface went to work on songs for Whitney's upcoming album. When they had completed several possibilities, they invited the singer to Atlanta, Georgia so they could finally meet face to face and get her first-hand reaction to their work so far. The collaborators had dinner with the artist and afterwards played her their composition "I'm Your Baby Tonight." Said Reid: "She was very happy." Within a few weeks, Houston was ready to step into the studios to record the number.

At the time, it must have seemed to Whitney that fate had brought her together with the LaFace pair. She certainly respected their strong reputation and must have had confirmation from her new boyfriend, Bobby Brown, of how inspired they had been in preparing numbers for him. Furthermore, visiting the Peachtree area to work with L.A. and Babyface gave Houston a good excuse to spend time with her main man, Bobby.

The *I'm Your Baby Tonight* album was released in November 1990. A quick study of its cover artwork is sufficient to indicate that this disc intended to showcase a "new" Whitney Houston. The black-and-white front-cover photo by André Blanch shows the star casually dressed in a gray, long-sleeved sweater, white slacks, and white sneakers, seated sideways on a Harley Davidson motorcycle (whose license plate reads "NIPPY"). In the choice of makeup and lighting, there is no attempt to lighten her skin shade; in fact, in the color inner-sleeve photos by Blanch and Timothy White, spunky Whitney strives for a strongly ethnic look with her copper-toned wigs and informal wardrobe. In one shot she wears weathered jeans torn at the knee; in another she has moved from leopard-skin boots to being barefooted. An unpublicized aspect of the photo shoot for this album was that Houston reportedly kept the crew waiting for over twelve hours before she deigned to make her first appearance in front of the cameras. When she finally did so, she offered no apology or explanation; in fact, to those there that arduous day, she didn't indicate the slightest embarrassment about her self-indulgent behavior.

To create the whole album package required a total of eight producers, thirty-four recording engineers, sixteen songwriters, six makeup people, plus Whitney's assorted auxiliary contributions as vocal arranger and background singer. The LaFace pair produced four tracks: the title cut, "My Name Is Not Susan," "Anymore," and "Miracle." It was their "I'm Your Baby Tonight," released in October 1990, that became the album's first number-one hit in the U.S. (although in England it only reached number five). The hip-hop-tinged "My Name Is Not Susan" peaked at number twenty in America, while "Miracle" (written by Eric Foster White) topped out at the number-nine spot in domestic release. (Later, when there was some controversy suggesting that the lyrics to "Miracle" contained either an anti-abortion or pro-life message, Whitney would put an end to the discussion by saying, "It wasn't geared toward any of that mess. . . . Birth and life are miracles. When I sang the song, I just went into my spirit and I said, 'Father, give me the right spirit to sing this song.' I try to stay as neutral as I can, because I don't want to be seen to be on this side or on that side.")

Luther Vandross cowrote and produced "Who Do You Love," which provided an opportunity for his good friend Cissy Houston to contribute background vocals to her daughter's new release. "We Didn't Know," added at the last minute, was written and produced by Stevie Wonder as a duet for himself and Whitney.

As a throwback to her prior successful albums, and to hedge his bets, Clive rematched Whitney with two of her past producers. Narada Michael Walden supervised "All the Man That I Need" (the album's second number-one hit in the U.S.; in England it stalled at number thirteen), "Lover for Life," and "I Belong to You." Michael Masser produced (and wrote with Gerry Goffin) "After We Make Love," which failed to recreate the magic of the team's earlier "Saving All My Love for You." The final track was "I'm Knockin'," a collaboration between Rhett Lawrence, Benjamin [BeBe] Winans, and Rickey Minor (Whitney's musical director for her concerts).

In reviewing Houston's third album, David Browne of *Entertainment Weekly* rated it only a D+. He poked fun at Whitney's "blank-slate quality" and her diction, which allowed "everything" to come out as "everythang." Building up steam, he panned the release because "*Baby* adheres doggedly to one agenda: to prove Houston is a get-down, funky human being who can party with the best of them. ... The album is relentlessly superficial—and proud of it." In contrast, *Rolling Stone* was far more favorable, ranking it worthy of three out of four stars. The reviewer noted that the disc "amounts to a case study in how much she can get out of her luscious and straightforward vocal gifts within a dance-pop framework" and that here Houston "refines two of her signature styles: state-of-the-art dance pop and baroque ballads."

Time magazine judged that Whitney "comes within striking distance of classic saloon soul here and proves she's stepping up to fast company." An approving *Q* magazine commented, "At the age of 27, Whitney Houston has the world at her feet and a string of supremely impressive statistics to her name." The publication concluded, "Her seemingly effortless range and phrasing turn an up-beat blubber of a tune into instantly seductive high class pop soul of the first order . . . there is no doubting that this album confirms her right to sit atop her own particular pile."

If the powers involved in creating *I'm Your Baby Tonight* hoped its new direction would enlarge Whitney's record-buying base, they were sorely disappointed. At the time, the disc sold "only" 3 million copies, eventually clocking up sales of over 6 million worldwide. It was also a relatively low-achiever when it came to chalking up prizes, winning two from the American Music Awards and three from the Billboard Music Awards. Although Houston was nominated for a Grammy in the Best Pop Vocal Performance—Female for "All the Man That I Need," she lost to Bonnie Raitt for "Something to Talk About".

Disappointed by record-buyers' response to *I'm Your Baby Tonight*, Whitney would also nurse other grudges about this critical release. She found it ironic that Clive Davis had received the lion's share of credit for the high-flying success of her first two albums, whereas when it came to the new disc, which did not fare as well commercially, she got most of the blame. Still smarting about the situation two years later, Houston voiced her thoughts to a national magazine: "What disappointed me was that my record company did not do what they should have done to make *Baby Tonight* more of a success. They bungled." But then, taking another tack, she reasoned, "Three million people buying records? That doesn't sound like a bad number to me." To prove her point and to banish the issue from further discussion, she added, "I know a lot of folks who would like to sell that many."

16

The Super Bowl and Beyond

"You're supposed to be partying in your twenties. I was on tour and making records. I sacrificed those years. When Bobby came along, I started having a ball. He taught me how to have fun."

WHITNEY HOUSTON, 1996

When interviewed on cable TV's *BET Video Soul* in 1991, Whitney Houston revealed that she would like to work with Michael Jackson: "I think he and I probably would create a lot of magic . . . Incredible!" She mentioned that two or three years earlier they had talked about it, but it didn't happen. "He hasn't called me," she smiled, "but I can wait." She also confided, "Now you know that's another person I'd love to do something with. Bobby [Brown] and I would be explosive. As a matter of fact I wanted to do a duet with Bobby for the album *I'm Your Baby Tonight*, but that didn't work out either."

Viewers of the program must have been surprised that there was actually something that the Prom Queen of Soul—now transforming herself into a hipper urban diva for the 1990s—could not have accomplished on her behalf. After all, here she was, six years into her star tenure in the notoriously fickle recording industry and still a major player. In fact, so pervasive was Whitney Houston's impact on popular culture that writer Bret Easton Ellis, in the midst of his dark novel *American Psycho* (1991), includes a chapter recounting her professional achievements.

Besides a shift in musical genre, there were other noticeable differences about the new Whitney. For example, in this last decade of the millennium she began to adopt a more outrageous sartorial look, appearing in a glittery body suit by Gianni Versace and bold creations by Azzedine Alaia and Jean Paul Gaultier.

By now, Whitney and Eddie Murphy were no longer an item. Romantically, he had been unwilling to focus on just one woman. On the other hand, he was upset to discover that the rumors about his on-off girlfriend dating Bobby Brown were true. Some onlookers said that he grew incensed when gossip columns linked Whitney to Philadelphia Eagles quarterback Randall Cunningham, although the singer insisted, "We're only friends." When the tenuous relationship between Murphy and Whitney came to an end, he reputedly asked her to return the diamond "engagement" ring he'd once given her. The two celebrities eventually re-established a rapport, and when Murphy married Nicole Mitchell in an extravagant wedding at New York City's Plaza Hotel in March 1993, Whitney and Bobby Brown would be among the guests.

Back in early 1990, Clive Davis had approved Whitney's acceptance of an invitation to sing "The Star Spangled Banner" at the upcoming Super Bowl XXV football game in January 1991. It proved to be a savvy decision indeed. By then, Whitney's recording career seemed to be stalling—that is, in relation to her enormous past album sales—following the release of *I'm Your Baby Tonight*. Disgruntled members of the black community were still dogging her for selling out to the white establishment. Other segments of the public were puzzled that she was in her late twenties and still single. Still others were discomforted by the recurrent tabloid rumors about the artist and her longtime pal Robyn Crawford. Yet another contingent were disappointed or upset by the seemingly wholesome Whitney Houston becoming so close to out-and-out bad boy Bobby Brown.

As the January 27, 1991 gridiron play date between the New York Giants and the Buffalo Bills approached, the United States officially embarked on the Gulf War. With American troops fighting overseas as part of the coalition to drive Saddam Hussein out of Kuwait, there was much debate over whether the playoff should go ahead as planned. It was decided that the game would be good for morale, distracting the public from their mounting concerns about Operation Desert Storm. Thus, in mid-January, Whitney went into a Los Angeles studio to record "The Star Spangled Banner." Soon afterwards, in Tampa, the Florida Orchestra recorded the music track.

On the last Sunday of January 1991, 73,813 fans packed the security-controlled Tampa Stadium, while a TV audience of 115 million watched at home. A few weeks earlier, when appearing as a guest on Arsenio Hall's TV show, Whitney had been given solid advice about proper decorum on her forthcoming appearance. The words of wisdom came from comedian Roseanne, another guest on Hall's program that evening. Roseanne told a bemused Houston to remember two things on that momentous occasion: do not spit on the ground and do not scratch your crotch. The comedian knew what she was talking about, having caused a national controversy when she had sung "The Star Spangled Banner" at a televised baseball event in Southern California and punctuated her screeching rendition by an impromptu send-up of the macho behavior of major-league ball players.

Forewarned, Whitney made no such gaffes at the Super Bowl. Instead, she was at her most appealing. Wearing a sweat suit and headband, she looked completely like a wholesome teenager as she jubilantly took her position in front of the microphone. She would recall of this pivotal moment, "I think it was a time when Americans needed to believe in our country. I remember standing there and looking at all those people, and it was like I could see in their faces the hopes and prayers and fears of the entire country." She launched into an impassioned, flamboyant rendition of the song, her voice soaring majestically through the well-known lyrics. As she explained later, "I didn't want [my rendition] to be the traditional 'Star Spangled Banner.' I wanted an arrangement everyone could sing along with. It's a pretty tough song to sing. It goes from very low to very high, and it's very delicate." Her fervent interpretation mesmerized the audience, who were inevitably reflecting on the men and women serving in the Gulf War, now ten days old. When the song came to an end, the stadium crowd clapped and cheered unrestrainedly. The pleased star smiled widely and waved at the adoring masses.

Thereafter, the attention of the stadium and home audiences turned to the playing field as the two opposing football squads prepared for the kick-off. As for Whitney, she adjourned to a stadium sky booth to watch the proceedings, joined by Robyn Crawford and singer MC Hammer, as well as a contingent of friends and bodyguards. According to onlookers, partway through the game, a three-way argument developed between Whitney, Crawford, and Hammer, with the latter two vying as to who would be favored with the lion's share of Whitney's attention. Some insist the shouting match went on for several minutes before everyone calmed down.

Later, Whitney would recall, "It wasn't until a day or two later that I realized the whole country was in an uproar." She was referring to the fact that thousands of Americans, currently in a hugely patriotic mood, were clamoring to buy a recording of Whitney singing "The Star Spangled Banner." It just so happened that prescient Clive Davis had anticipated the public's wish, and in short order, Arista arranged for singles of "The Star Spangled Banner," with Whitney's interpretation of "America the Beautiful" thrown in for good measure, to be distributed to stores nationwide. There was even a video of Houston's rousing performance of the anthem on sale. The single proved enormously popular, rising to the top twenty of the *Billboard* music charts, where it remained for fourteen weeks.

Meanwhile, as would increasingly prove the case with anything that Whitney Houston did, a controversy burst forth. Suddenly, the press was claiming that her rendition of "The Star Spangled Banner" had *not* been a live performance, but was in fact pre-recorded. Buried in this superficially shocking news story was the fact that this was conventional practice at such major sporting events to avert the danger of anything going amiss. Instead, journalists focused on Houston's canned vocals (even though she had sung live along with the pre-recording at the Super Bowl). Some reporters also editorialized about her diction and how the musical arrangement had been shaped in order to give the offering a more ethnic sound, so that finally there was a black voice of America. As the hullabaloo escalated, the press threw mud at Arista Records for capitalizing on a time of international tension by pandering to Americans' patriotism.

To distill this "wrong" impression of "The Star Spangled Banner," the record label announced that a large percentage of all sales would be donated to charity. It was duly reported that over $500,000 of the $1 million earned by the single went to the American Red Cross Gulf Crisis Fund. (Still later, and on a much smaller scale, there was a further backlash when the Florida Orchestra claimed it had not received its proper portion of royalties from the popular recording. This led to a legal dispute that was eventually settled between the parties.)

Originally, in the spring of 1991, Whitney was contracted to undertake a concert tour of Europe, with eighteen dates set in the United Kingdom during March and April. However, because of the Gulf War, the tour was pushed back to late summer. But by March, Operation Desert Storm had ended and the troops were returning home. To take advantage of Houston's new burst of popularity, Arista, her management team, and the HBO cable channel arranged with the U.S. military for Whitney to give a free live concert in honor of the returning combat forces. This was an outgrowth of the original plan for Whitney to sing for the troops stationed near the front lines of Operation Desert Storm, which was not finalized by the time the Gulf War ended. To avoid any possible new taint of "war profiteering," the proceeds from this cable TV special were earmarked for established charities.

Welcome Home Heroes from the Gulf War aired as a special on Easter Sunday, March 31, 1991. The ninety-minute offering began with footage showing Houston being flown by helicopter to the U.S.S. *Saratoga*, anchored off the Virginia coast. Once on board, she met and ate with the servicepeople who were soon to disembark and be reunited with their families. The scene then shifted to a jammed makeshift auditorium in Norfolk, Virginia, where Houston performed in front of combat veterans and their families.

For this more informal event, the star ran through her repertoire of hits and made a concerted effort to interact with the attendees, especially the young children. The program was a huge success, proving to be the third-highest-rated music event in the cable network's history, and it would be nominated for two Emmy Awards.

While Whitney was receiving kudos for this successful outing, there was much publicity devoted to her loving family, in particular her parents. However, behind the scenes, the seemingly always smiling and good-humored John and Cissy Houston were at loggerheads. By now, John's deepening relationship with Whitney's maid, Barbara "Peggy" Griffith, had come to light, and Cissy was furious that her husband (they still had not yet divorced after all these years of separation) was dating this much younger woman from Trinidad. Cissy felt humiliated in front of her friends and the congregation at New Hope Baptist Church and wondered if this would damage her working relationship with the pastor there. The domestic situation so upset Cissy that she developed a severe case of bleeding ulcers. Furthermore, John, now reaching an age where he should be thinking of retirement, was frustrated that his dreams of becoming a self-made record-industry entrepreneur, on the same level as Motown's Berry Gordy, seemed unlikely ever to be realized. He had to content himself with the annual salary of approximately $125,000 he earned working for Whitney.

In spring 1991, Bobby Brown professed to his pals that he was deeply in love with Whitney Houston. But at that time, Whitney was still ambivalent about the depth of her feelings for this high-spirited, moody man and how she truly felt about giving up her freedom in exchange for marriage. Thus, she recalls, "The first time he asked me to marry him, I said 'Forget about it, no way. It's just not in my plans.'"

Complicating Whitney's situation, of course, was her ongoing association with Robyn Crawford, who was an integral part of her life. But, behind the scenes, the threads of their friendship had been frayed severely by the unending rumors that the two close pals must be lesbians. In a relatively rare moment of public frankness (these moments almost always occurred when she was speaking to the black press), Whitney told Joy Duckett of *Essence* magazine: "It got to be a pain in the ass. No matter how much you try not to let them bother you, [rumors] do bother you. So we just said, 'Hey, if this is what's gonna happen, then let's not be friends anymore.' But that wasn't the answer, either. After a while you start thinking, We're friends. I love you, you love me. Why should we do this because of what people say and what they think? She was here before and I know she'd be here if my career ended tomorrow."

What became clearer to onlookers as time went on was that the two women had decided—or at least Whitney had—to focus their friendship more on their joint career activities, and to downplay leisure time spent together. Thus, while Whitney would still describe Crawford as "my best friend, who knows me better than any woman has known me," she would reveal, "Robyn and I had had enough time together, and our relationship changed from friendship to more of an employer–employee arrangement."

Just as Whitney was orienting all her thoughts toward having a close personal relationship with Bobby Brown, it became known that Kim Ward was again pregnant by Brown. While Brown claimed that he would do right by his future child, he insisted that this situation had nothing to do with his strong feelings for Whitney. He reasoned that Kim had become pregnant during a period when he and Whitney were not seeing much of one another. However Whitney really felt about the latest development, publicly she seemed unfazed by a circumstance that would have embarrassed and angered most other women. Instead of rebuffing his further romantic overtures, she and Brown became even closer.

In late April 1991, Whitney captured the headlines again after an incident that occurred in Lexington, Kentucky, where she had a concert engagement. She and her large entourage (including, among others, her brother Michael, Robyn Crawford, and British bodyguard David Jones) had checked into that city's Radisson Plaza Hotel. After a relaxing evening at the Red Mile Harness racetrack, the group returned to the hotel, where they decided to watch a sports match on the big-screen TV in the lounge. In now-standard fashion, Whitney's protectors kept fans away from her, insisting she was unavailable to sign autographs or speak with them. According to some accounts, a group of men in the lounge began conversing loudly, hoping to gain the singer's attention. When this did not work, they allegedly began throwing out lewd remarks and racial slurs, but Whitney and her party ignored them. Soon afterwards, Whitney, Robyn, and Michael took the elevator up to their rooms on the seventeenth floor.

According to Whitney's account, her party found three of the rude men from downstairs up in the hospitality area of the seventeenth floor. The three strangers, apparently drunk, continued their verbal abuse, and then one of them attacked Michael. Before long, an incensed Whitney had literally jumped into the fray to protect her sibling. The trio of men had a different account of what transpired before police arrived on the scene. They claimed that when Whitney and her set disembarked on the seventeenth floor, one of them requested an autograph and was rebuffed by an openly antagonistic Whitney. In their version, Michael then attacked one of their number, with the singer quickly entering into the fracas. The men also alleged that the enraged star even tossed out a death threat at them.

During the coming week, the three men (one of whom had required hospital treatment for a bad cut over one eye) filed a lawsuit against the Houston siblings, charging them with fourth degree assault, assorted misdemeanors, and for threatening their lives. The local district court ordered that Whitney and Michael be summoned to answer the complaint. This led the Houstons to file their own counter-complaint. By now, the ruckus had become front-page news around the country and the world. Whitney's public relations team attempted damage control, presenting the star and her brother as "victims of an unprovoked attack." Soon John Houston was putting his own spin on the situation, telling the press he was proud of his daughter because, "By exposing herself to potential physical harm, she risked career-threatening injuries." Eventually, the court, upon recommendation from the district attorney for Fayette County, Kentucky, dropped the charges, explaining that with the conflicting evidence the investigation had turned up thus far, winning a conviction would be "impossible."

According to some in Whitney's camp, this nasty episode was a defining moment in the relationship between the artist and her public. Thereafter, the singer became even more reluctant to interact with her fans and maintained an even frostier veneer towards her public offstage than before.

Whitney's road tour in support of *I'm Your Baby Tonight* took her to seventy U.S. and Canadian cities in summer 1991 and was followed by the European leg of the tour that fall. Reviewers and fans alike noted that in this live show Whitney was doing more choreographed moves on stage, but she still was giving no indication of being a dedicated dancer. Her reaction to the topic was, "People love me because I can sing, and that is what I concentrate on." At the time, what seemed more important to Houston than her terpsichorean skills, or even the fact that audience attendance was down everywhere due to the recession, was the frequent proximity of Bobby Brown. Now, he often accompanied her on the tour circuit, and when she had a break from her own schedule, she joined him on his own engagements.

As this romance between two such apparently opposite personalities developed further, some observers claimed to have identified what the duo actually had in common. For example, record producer Teddy Riley, who worked on two of Brown's albums, noted, "Bobby and I were both born in the 'hood and have a little bit of craziness. When I first met [Whitney], I could see she has a little craziness in her too." New Edition impresario Maurice Starr had his own take on the love match: "Bobby Brown fulfilled Whitney Houston's fantasy of a cool, down-to-earth, sexy man. And Bobby Brown played the part to the hilt." Later in the decade, Whitney would offer her own assessment of why she and bad-boy Brown were so compatible, acknowledging, "I'm nobody's angel. I can get raunchy."

Increasingly, segments of the media put forth their own theory, albeit a cynical one, on the connection: that it was largely a publicity strategy on the part of each participant. It was suggested that this match-not-made-in-heaven would give Whitney a more urban black image and further bury recurrent talk about her relationship with Robyn Crawford. As for Brown, who was six years younger than Whitney, the association with Cissy Houston's gospel-singing daughter would diminish his bad-boy status.

☆

While Whitney pondered her romantic future with free-spirited Bobby Brown, she grew more serious about actually starring in a Hollywood movie. This was especially true now that her recording career was no longer at its peak and she was enduring serious competition from Mariah Carey, Toni Braxton, and Celine Dion. In the past, the notions of starring on the big screen in *Dreamgirls* or a biography about legendary singer Josephine Baker had not sufficiently appealed to her. As other cinema offers came in, her mentor Clive Davis cautioned his protégée to be careful about which vehicle she chose. For both her sake and Arista's, he didn't want an artistic misstep to damage her worth in the recording studios.

In 1990, there was talk that Whitney might star in a screen rendition of Terry Macmillan's 1989 novel *Disappearing Acts*. But the hype soon died down and when the film was eventually made, as a 2000 TV movie, it was Sanaa Lathan who starred opposite Wesley Snipes in the tale of a school teacher who wants to become a singing star and, en route, falls in love with a construction worker. For a while, it seemed that Houston might inaugurate her first-look agreement with Twentieth Century-Fox by starring in a remake of the frequently filmed *Daddy Long Legs*. In its last incarnation at Fox, it had been a 1955 musical vehicle for Fred Astaire and Leslie Caron.

While a new and improved *Daddy Long Legs*—one that focused more on the love story and less on the musical aspects—did not materialize, Whitney found herself being courted for yet another screen venture. This time, while she did not say "yes" when first asked, she also did not immediately say a definite "no."

17

A Box-Office Surprise

"The best actors and actresses to me don't have much training. It's about a feeling, it's about that emotion, about putting that emotion into a character."

WHITNEY HOUSTON, 1992

The man who urgently wanted Whitney Houston for his leading lady was Kevin Costner. At the time, he was *the* hot property in Hollywood. Now thirty-five, he had gained box-office clout in the late 1980s with such hits as *The Untouchables*, *Bull Durham*, and *Field of Dreams*. What had really raised his stock was *Dances with Wolves* (1990), an absorbing project about Native Americans in the nineteenth-century West. Told from the Native American point of view, this film had been a difficult sell to a resistant Hollywood, but Costner, who would both direct and star in his cherished vehicle, persisted in pursuing his vision and eventually got the picture financed. Made for $15 million, it grossed $184 million at the American box office alone. Between them, the film and Costner won seven Academy Awards. For some time thereafter, Costner was considered by Tinseltown to have the Midas touch. Voted the "sexiest man in America," his follow-up pictures (1991's *Robin Hood: Prince of Thieves* and *JFK*) solidified his wunderkind status in the business.

Now, Costner was impassioned about launching a new picture. Back when he was making the Western *Silverado* (1985) with filmmaker Lawrence Kasdan, the latter had shown the actor a script he had first drafted more than a decade earlier when he was writing screenplays on spec while working as a copywriter in a Midwestern ad agency. A devotee of movie idol Steve McQueen, Kasdan had conceived the action thriller as a tribute to the actor's hit vehicle *Bullitt* (1968). At one point, there was even talk of McQueen costarring in the project with Diana Ross. When Steve McQueen eventually vetoed the script, there was speculation in the late 1970s that Ross might make the project with Ryan O'Neal, her then boyfriend. That did not come to pass, and the much-rewritten script sat on the shelf until Costner expressed his strong interest in *The Bodyguard* in the mid-1980s and thereafter.

By the time Costner's box-office clout and busy schedule permitted him the luxury of turning seriously to making *The Bodyguard* happen, Diana Ross was approaching her late thirties. She was now considered too mature for the leading role of Rachel Marron, a movie star being stalked by a deadly assailant. As Costner ran down the list of possible contenders for the female lead, he thought of Madonna. However, her acting resumé was littered with box-office misfires. Plus, she had openly poked fun at Costner's "white bread" image in a backstage encounter between the two captured in the 1991 documentary *Truth or Dare: In Bed with Madonna*.

Considering the options available in casting the crucial part, Costner decided it was better to have a singing star who had little or no acting experience than an actor who could not sing. It was at this point around late 1989 that Costner first contacted Whitney Houston. He gave her a strong pitch. As she has recalled, "He used to say to me, 'Whitney, listen. Every once in a blue moon you get this person who just comes around has this *quality*. When you thought about a movie that had music in it, you used to think about Barbra [Streisand] or Diana [Ross]. But now it's *you*.' And I'm like, 'That's what I want. I want it to be *meee*.'"

She was flattered and intrigued that Costner, then king of the box office, should want her as his leading lady. But she had severe reservations about tackling a major part without the benefit of any real acting experience. She certainly had no intention of making a fool of herself in front of millions of moviegoers and becoming the laughing stock of showbusiness. Not only would the humiliation be devastating on a personal level, but it could also, as Clive Davis had so often warned her, ruin her commercial appeal. Getting to the heart of her fears, she would tell *Rolling Stone* in 1993, "You know what I was concerned about? That people would dog me before they gave me the opportunity to do the job. Making the transition from a singer to an actress made me apprehensive. Like 'Can I really do this?'"

Costner was not put off by Houston's initial reluctance, which turned into a ritual of procrastination as she continued to consider the opportunity. Putting all her fears to one side, there were several advantages to the venture. The Rachel Marron character—even in its rough draft form—was one to which she could relate; in fact, in some ways, it was an extension of her real-life persona. Then, too, she was extremely pleased that the film would focus on an interracial romance, which was initially presented as an issue but then accepted as a matter of course. What also appealed to Whitney were Costner's constant reassurances that he would watch over her artistic welfare throughout production and ensure that she did nothing to embarrass herself or the picture.

Now feeling more positive but still scared of jumping into such a major venture, she dragged her feet. She convinced herself that she had enough on her plate, what with her recording career, her concerts, and, of course, the excitement of dating Bobby Brown. More time passed, and periodically Kevin Costner contacted her to see if she had made up her mind. She continued to put him off, perhaps thinking that he would eventually tire of the chase and move on to another candidate; the troublesome matter would then be out of her control. If the part should go to another actress, she could tell herself that conflicting schedules, and not her indecision, had been responsible for the end result.

Late one night in 1991, she received yet another phone plea from Costner. Now he was very insistent. He confided, "OK, I'm telling you, you gotta do this movie, and if you don't do it, I've just decided that I'm just not gonna do it, 'cause I want you to play this part, you're the person to play this part." Finally, giving in to his blandishments—which included helping her with her lines and the rehearsal process—she said, "OK, Kev, I'm gonna do this movie. I think I can."

In further discussions, Whitney expressed her reservations about the female lead, a role that she felt would present her as too hard-edged and icy-cold. Costner agreed to script rewrites. That settled, her representatives entered into negotiations for her to officially join the cast. Later, she would admit another strong reason for her accepting such a challenging screen debut. "It was something a friend of mine said to me that really helped me to decide on this and gave me the final impetus I needed to accept the role. She said, 'Whitney, if you do this, do you realize what it will mean for other black actresses, for other black women, period?' Immediately I was encouraged. She was right. It's a very, very strong role for a black woman."

In preparation for her big-screen debut, Whitney studied old feature films starring Lauren Bacall, one of her favorite actresses. She also watched several of Kevin Costner's pictures to better understand what made him tick on camera. When she suggested to Costner that, perhaps, it would be a good idea for her to taking acting lessons, he vetoed the notion. He reasoned that it might make her too artificial and self-conscious on screen. Again, he promised to always look out for her best interests during the shoot.

By this point, Whitney understood that Costner, who was both starring in and coproducing *The Bodyguard*, would have as much say or more than British filmmaker Mick Jackson, who had been hired to direct. While Jackson had been directing film and TV movies for two decades, he had only recently gained currency in mainstream Hollywood for helming Steve Martin's *L.A. Story* (1989). By Tinseltown standards, he presently had nowhere near the same clout as Costner, especially as the latter's contract afforded him control of the movie's final cut.

Recognizing his own somewhat tenuous position on *The Bodyguard*, Jackson was extremely sensitive to what Houston would be enduring during production. As he explained, "You're making a queen of her genre into a beginner again, and Whitney was aware of the loss of control that would mean. . . . Her life as a pop star means that everything is set to her requirements, which is totally different from what happens when shooting a film."

Not too long before *The Bodyguard* was to begin shooting, Whitney learned that she was pregnant. For the father-to-be, Bobby Brown, it would be his fourth child, and he was pleased. However, when Whitney informed her parents, her mother in particular was upset to the point of hysteria that her daughter was going to have a baby out of wedlock. For a while, Whitney thought about dropping out of the picture, but after all her past indecision about making the film, she felt she could not back out now.

Some of the movie's opening scenes were filmed at Lake Tahoe, Nevada. Houston was not thrilled to be on location, where her strenuous physical activity on the set caused her to perspire and the cool climate simultaneously chilled her. It wore her out and she started to feel not quite right. However, she attributed this to her jitters over making her motion-picture debut. True to his word, Costner was protective and understanding of her nervousness during the first days of the shoot. Most of the time, he was even patient with her deeply engrained diva habits.

By the time the film company flew to Miami in late March to shoot scenes at the Fontainebleau Hilton Hotel, Houston felt worse. She sensed that her pregnancy was going wrong. She phoned her mother and confided her concerns to her. According to Whitney, "She told me to brace myself and to deal with the biological changes that a woman goes through when she's miscarrying, which are very painful." Cissy immediately flew to Florida, only to find that her daughter's premonitions were correct. Said Whitney, "My mother walked in. I am in the bathroom and I am crying incredibly. My mother looked at me and she goes, 'Hey, this is life. This will pass too. You will get this over with and we will move on. Do you hear me girl?' I look at my mother's eyes and reality just hit me. My mother is the reality lady. 'Get up and get it together, girlfriend.'"

Meanwhile, Whitney also alerted Bobby Brown, who was busy commuting back and forth between Atlanta and Los Angeles to record his new album. Whitney remembers, "I called Bobby and said, 'I think I've lost the baby.' He was quiet for a long time. Then he said, 'Well, are you okay? Are you fine? Is everything all right inside? You didn't damage anything, right?' I said, 'Yeah I'm cool.' He said, 'Well, that's all that matters. We can always have another.' He was so compassionate and comforting, that got me through." He came to Miami to be at her side, and the tragedy of the miscarriage brought them closer together.

After much soul-searching over the misfortune, Whitney would come to realize, "My body was not ready to carry a child. I think of it as God's way of saying, 'This is not right this time; let's try it another time.'"

A few days after the tragedy, the news leaked to the tabloids and, in short order, it was announced in the supermarket publications with headlines such as: "Pregnant Whitney Houston Loses Her Love Child!" A few articles inferred in their recap of the events leading up to the star's misfortune that Bobby Brown had purportedly been partying rather than working at the time she suffered the miscarriage.

After recuperating for some days, a still-shaken Whitney returned to the set, with her mother or Bobby (or both) often on hand for emotional support. Before long, Houston settled into the routine of filmmaking. However, what she never became used to was having to be up at such an early hour to start shooting. As she phrased it bluntly, "I'm not a day person!" What also bothered Whitney was the relatively slow process of it all. "It was the hurry up and wait syndrome that was difficult. I'd be there for six, seven, maybe eight hours a day and then suddenly be told that 'We're not getting to your scene today.' And with me that was a bit of a problem, because I hate to be idle and there's always something else I could have been doing." She also discovered that "Acting requires a lot of concentration. While music has a rhythm that comes naturally to me, acting takes concentration. I would compare it with starting my music career and working the clubs. It was like starting all over again, but in a new field." It also required her to be puppet-like, talking when and how the director insisted, moving here or there exactly as the script required, and always keeping in mind never to step outside of the focused lights. Suffering through this alien regimen, Whitney began to understand what Costner had meant when he told her: "Movie business is like drying paint . . . like watching paint dry."

As filming progressed, there were occasions when Whitney grew so nervous and bored simultaneously that she did not think she could last until the picture wrapped. Adding to her mounting stress was the fact that during the day she was making the film, while at night she was frequently recording songs for the picture's soundtrack. At such difficult times, she recalls, "Bobby would say: 'Yes, you can. You can do it. And you're gonna do it.' There were days I'd get up in the morning and say: 'I can't take this anymore.' And he'd say: 'Yes, you can. Come on girl, get up. Come on.' He's a motivator."

During the many weeks of production, the shoot took the troupe from Nevada to Florida and on to Los Angeles, where locations included the Greystone estate, used previously in *The Godfather* (1972) as the home of the moviemaker who finds a horse's head in his bed. For Whitney, one scene in particular proved hardest to accomplish: "I was supposed to be hysterical, and it required a lot of emotions. And I had to slap him [Kevin Costner] several times. I kept saying, 'Oh, God, I don't wanna hit this man 'cause this man didn't do anything to me. And I had to really slap him hard. That was a very difficult scene. Very difficult." Reflecting back on this sequence, she would say, "I just had to reach down inside of me and bring it out. It takes a lot for me to cry, a lot to make me mad, and acting took a lot of concentration." (Ironically, in the final edit of the over-long movie, this sequence was deleted.)

Regarding her costar, Whitney admitted, "It was exciting to work with someone who has such notoriety in Hollywood and experience in doing films. That was more exciting for me than the actual idea that he is this hunk Kevin Costner. Yes, he's a hunk and he's sexy. We all know that, but that's not what I was looking for." What she also was not looking for and refused to do (as per specific terms in her contract) was nude scenes. As she phrased it herself, "Whitney will not be showing any butt!" Being so private a person regarding many things, she could not imagine even pretending to be that intimate with a coworker on a set with many others looking on. As a result, when the script required the leads to roll around naked in bed for a steamy seduction scene, a double was used instead of Whitney. (Later, in the final edit, this footage was excised as being inappropriate to the mood of the overall picture.)

If Whitney felt uncomfortable about her onscreen love scenes, Bobby Brown also had concerns about his woman having a romance—if only on camera—with Hollywood's reigning heartthrob, even though Costner was then married and the father of three children. Whitney admitted that she let Bobby read the script and that he questioned her about how her love scenes were going to be played.

By spring 1992, filming on *The Bodyguard* had wrapped. Executives at Warner Bros. were uncertain about how this story—of a singer-actress stalked by a killer and protected by a top-flight bodyguard with whom she falls in love—would fare at the box office. As the post-production process got underway, there was growing concern on the lot that the resultant picture was simply not all that special. The powers-that-be continued to tinker with the footage for a longer-than-usual time, hoping for a miracle. Because of the uncertainty over each "final" cut, the picture kept being pushed further along in the company's release schedule for the year.

Determined that his latest pet project should have the best possible public reception, Costner eventually stepped in to exercise his right to help with a new final cut. In the prolonged editing phase, what had been a nearly three-hour feature was chopped down to a more manageable 129 minutes. As the tightening-up process continued, it was decided that bits of Whitney's dialogue needed to be re-recorded, so she returned to Hollywood to do the looping.

When the filming of *The Bodyguard* had gotten underway, Whitney was already busy rehearsing and recording the songs that would help to define and accentuate the film's story line. When she signed up to make the picture, it had been negotiated that the soundtrack album would be released by Arista Records and that Whitney would share the executive-producer credit with Clive Davis.

To make the soundtrack disc an important release, it was agreed that she must sing several numbers within the picture, whether on camera or in the background to set the mood. Picking most of the selections proved to be a relatively simple task. Among others, Whitney suggested using an old favorite of hers, Chaka Khan's 1970s hit "I'm Every Woman," which Narada Michael Walden would produce. Whitney and Arista turned to the writer-producer team of L. A. Reid and Babyface for the hard-rocking "Queen of the Night." The spiritual "Jesus Loves Me" provided an opportunity for Houston to work with her friend BeBe Winans in producing, vocal arranging, and singing (Winans appeared on background vocals). David Foster produced the dramatic "Run to You" (written by Allan Rich and Jud Friedman) and "I Have Nothing" (written by Foster and his wife Linda Thompson).

Besides other incidental instrumental and vocal cuts, one key song still needed to be finalized. Costner was a music buff and suggested a 1960s classic: "What Becomes of the Brokenhearted." However, that selection was preempted when another version of the song turned up in the movie *Fried Green Tomatoes* (1991). The search went on until one day Costner excitedly came to Whitney and told her he had found just the right number. It was Dolly Parton's "I Will Always Love You," which Parton had written as the result of a personal romance gone sour. The song had been a top country hit in 1974 and again in 1982. Costner cautioned Whitney to approach the song not in the country style of Parton's original version, but as she could reinterpret it for today's marketplace.

Whitney soon came to agree that "I Will Always Love You" was not only appropriate lyrically, but it also provided solid material to which she could bring her special style. It was also at Costner's insistence that she recorded the song with an opening section sung a cappella to allow a dramatic build-up. This idea initially caused concern at Arista, where executives feared that if the track was executed in such a manner for the album, it would not receive sufficient airplay because radio stations would conclude the song took too long to hook listeners. Whitney recorded five takes of the number in Miami, with her own band accompanying her. The fourth take was the one used for the movie and the soundtrack album.

By the time *The Bodyguard* finally premiered on November 23, 1992 at Mann's Chinese Theater, the industry buzz was that the project was a flop. But at this point, the soundtrack album was already on sale in record stores.

"I Will Always Love You" had been released as the first single and was already on the music charts' Hot 100. By late November, the track had jumped to number one in the U.S. and would remain in that coveted position for a total of fourteen weeks. "I Will Always Love You" also reached the top of the British music charts. Later, in 1993, both "I Have Nothing" and "I'm Every Woman" became relative hits as well.

Because "I Will Always Love You" was already such a popular track when the film opened, this worked to counteract the savaging the picture (and especially Kevin Costner's bizarre hairstyle) received from most movie reviewers. Owen Gleiberman of *Entertainment Weekly* rated it a D, labeling the entry "an outrageous piece of saccharine kitsch—or, at least, it might have been had the movie seemed fully awake. Instead, it's glossy yet slack. . . . To say that Houston and Costner fail to strike sparks would be putting it mildly. . . . Houston, the Olympian pop-soul diva, has moments of quickness and humor; she shows more thespian flair than many musicians. Her presence, though, is defined by the same glassy perfection that makes her singing, for all its virtuosity, seem fundamentally anonymous." Mike Clark in *USA Today* dismissed the thriller as "the year's highest-profile stinker." For *Newsday*'s John Anderson, it was nothing but a "clunky, formulaic thriller about love between a stone-faced bodyguard and his pop-star client." He also noted that "Costner is puffy and sluggish; Houston is sleepy-eyed. Someday, they may even appear in the same film."

Roger Ebert in the *Chicago Sun-Times* was more charitable towards the venture, which used glossy editing to hide the story's many loopholes and plot incongruities: "I thought the basic situation in *The Bodyguard* was intriguing enough to sustain a film all by itself: on the one hand, a star who grows rich through the adulation that fans feel for her, and on the other hand, a working man who, for a salary, agrees to substitute his body as a target instead of hers. Makes you think."

When *The Bodyguard* premiered in the U.K. weeks later, the reviews were equally mixed. While Ian Lyness of the *Daily Express* insisted, "Costner and Houston spark together with a special chemistry," the *Daily Telegraph* rated the proceedings a "a flaccid overweight affair, notable chiefly for the much touted acting debut of singer Whitney Houston." Lizzie Francke in *Sight and Sound* was unimpressed with the end results and thought Houston was "ill served by flimsy characterisation and the total lack of chemistry between herself and Costner."

Between the frenzy over "I Will Always Love You" and the favorable word-of-mouth message that *The Bodyguard* was a good date picture, the picture began building rapidly at the box office. Audience surveys indicated that many people were returning to see the feature a second or third time. When all was said and done, the picture, which earned two Oscar nominations for its songs, grossed $121.9 million in the American marketplace, and a whopping $410.9 million worldwide.

If the commercial success of *The Bodyguard* was staggering, the sales of the film's soundtrack were hardly less so. The "I Will Always Love You" single sold in excess of 4 million copies, making it the biggest-selling track at the time. The album had such a phenomenal shelf life that by 1996, it had racked up sales of over 15 million copies and was still in active distribution. Meanwhile, as 1993 progressed, Whitney Houston and those associated with the soundtrack's production would receive numerous music-industry awards.

Relieved that critical reaction to her feature-film debut had not been too devastating, and relishing the unexpected tremendous popularity *The Bodyguard* was enjoying, Whitney was suddenly the toast of Hollywood. Everyone seemed to be clamoring for her services in their latest projects. When asked what screen venture she'd like to pursue next, she replied to *Premiere* magazine's John H. Richardson: "I want to play a cop. I like the idea of having a gun and hiding behind walls. My brothers and I used to play, when we were young, like we were cops and robbers. It's just fun."

18

The New Family

"When I met . . . [Bobby Brown] I identified with him. We had something in common. It wasn't all about trying to be a star. We wanted to take what we had accomplished and put it together, to share it."

WHITNEY HOUSTON, 1997

By the time Whitney Houston had completed filming *The Bodyguard* in spring 1992, she and Bobby Brown were engaged to be married. He had flown to meet her in Florida and seemed very nervous when she met him at the airport. After a shaky start, he said he had something serious to discuss with her. Realistic enough to know that with Bobby that could mean a host of subjects, she waited for his "confession." It was then that he fumbled in his pocket and pulled out a small gold ring with a petite diamond, one that she found "really cute," and proposed to her.

Jubilant (and relieved) at this positive news, Whitney said "yes" straightaway. Next, he reached into another pocket and extracted a much fancier ring that boasted a ten-karat diamond. He handed it to her, explaining, "This is the real one. I just wanted to see how you'd react." Whitney's response to Brown's jewelry ploy was, "It was really cute. I was like, 'I'm in love with this man and he's going to ask me to marry him. I don't care about the ring.'" She also admitted, "He played me like I was an Atari. He tested my nerve. This ring blew my mind."

When Whitney told her parents the news, they were not surprised, but they had strong reservations about the couple's compatibility. Later, Cissy Houston acknowledged, "There was some trepidation, for sure, but it was her choice and she thought he could make her happy. I did what all mothers do; I sat her down and tried to show her the pros and cons, but ultimately it was her choice. I prayed a lot." As the news of the pending nuptials leaked to the media, there was a resurgence of articles that repeatedly asked the rhetorical question: What can refined Whitney Houston possibly see in rascally Bobby Brown? But there was another slant that some discerning media writers noted. Said one, "Rather than the nice girl seduced by the naughty Bobby from the Boston projects, 'soul aristocracy' Whitney saw Bobby as her ticket to 'ghetto fabulousness.'"

Ignoring continued press probing into the true motives for their coming marriage, Bobby insisted, "I may be a B-boy and she's America's sweetheart, but it's love." The bride-to-be concurred, "I love him and he loves me, and that's what matters."

Following their royal-style honeymoon aboard a swanky yacht in the Mediterranean in July 1992, the unlikely couple of the decade returned to Whitney's New Jersey estate. Very soon, the media were reporting that Whitney was already pregnant and expecting their first child the following March. As a result, although she appeared on stage to fulfill a few commitments (such as at the Desert Inn in Las Vegas in November), she cancelled overseas bookings (including a late-October engagement to perform in Israel).

By now, the groom's new album, entitled *Bobby*, was in the record stores. Its first single ("Humpin' Around") went to number three on the charts, a sign that the record was destined to be a big success. One of the other album tracks, "Something in Common," gave the Browns a forum in which to duet and to suggest reasons why they were a good love match. The couple would make a music video to support the song and would sing the number on several televised music-industry celebrations.

To present the softer side of the megastar to the public, Whitney starred in an hour-long TV special (*This Is My Life*) for the ABC network that aired on May 6, 1992. Devised as a quasi-documentary, the proceedings contained snippets of Houston and entourage on her recent European concert tour, footage of the star in live performance, shots of the luminary sleeping (her favorite occupation), and at work on the set of *The Bodyguard* with Kevin Costner. There were also brief interviews with the celebrity's family. This pleasant, if somewhat innocuous, offering functioned as a low-key vehicle to promote her multi-media activities. Reviewing the program for *Daily Variety*, Bruce Haring reported, "Whitney Houston is just your average multimillionaire international pop star next door. At least, that's the message of this, her first network special, which makes a childhood confrontation with neighborhood bullies seem like the worst obstacle Houston has ever faced. . . . Unless you love, love, love Whitney, there's absolutely no reason to tune in."

As 1992 drew to a close and Whitney was enjoying incredible success with the release of *The Bodyguard* and its soundtrack album, her attention was more focused on becoming a mother. "I want to have children. I've done so much in my career, but the greatest moment in my life will be to have my child. I'd even give up everything and spend the first two years just looking after it. It's very important to me." She also voiced concerns about the problems involved with two working parents: "It is going to be tough keeping a family together—even now it's hard when Bobby and I want to see each other and we can't. We're going to have to fit everything around our careers when the baby comes. I'm not planning to stray too far from home over the next year. I can record here [from home], and make short trips, but that's it."

Things did not exactly work out that way. Despite having gained a sizable amount of weight during her pregnancy, she followed through with recording music videos in support of singles from *The Bodyguard* soundtrack album. Among these music shorts was the buoyant anthem "I'm Every Woman," which concludes with the noticeably expectant Whitney patting her now huge stomach and smiling radiantly.

Meanwhile, Bobby Brown was meeting with a series of career reversals. His *Bobby* album was not selling as well as anticipated; it eventually stalled at 2 million copies. Industry analysts concluded that what had been novel—the New Jack Swing style of his *Don't Be Cruel* album (1988)—had by now been copied or adapted by too many other artists (including Bobby's old New Edition bandmates). Thus, Brown's offering lacked the requisite freshness and inspiration demanded by the ever-changing tastes of the music-buying public.

While he was coping with this disappointment, Bobby had a fresh brush with the law. Three days before Christmas 1992, he was in Atlanta Municipal Court pleading not guilty to two counts of battery. The charges alleged that Brown (and his bodyguards) had beat up two individuals at an Atlanta hotel. Brown had purportedly become incensed when one of the victims had supposedly bothered dancers from his stage show. The case was set for trial that following February but would disappear from the news after a quiet disposition between the parties.

In January 1993, Brown was again in trouble with the police. Although he had added a few gospel songs to his concert act now that he was to become a father once more, his live show still revolved around his sexy image and his suggestive gyrations. Police officers in Augusta, Georgia concluded he had violated a local ordinance about lewd behavior in front of an audience containing any person under eighteen years of age. Brown shrugged his shoulders, bemoaned his fate as a "funk artist," and dealt with this latest legal hassle.

On March 4, 1993, after fourteen hours of labor at St. Barnabas Medical Center in Livingston, New Jersey, Whitney Houston underwent a Caesarean section to give birth to a six-pound, twelve-ounce baby girl, whom she and her husband named Bobbi Kristina Houston Brown. The beaming mother exclaimed, "When they put her in my arms, I thought, 'This has got to be *it*. This is the ultimate.'"

Having been away from the live circuit for many months, it was agreed that Whitney should embark on a new tour to capitalize on the enormous recent success of *The Bodyguard*. Her biggest problem was how to lose the fifty or so pounds she had put on during her pregnancy. Her postpartum efforts to slim down so intrigued the media that they would not let the matter alone. In particular, one New York paper insisted that Whitney had become so hooked on diet pills that she overdosed and had to be admitted to a Miami hospital for emergency treatment. This report so upset the diva that she filed a suit against the publication to show that there was a limit to what she would accept from the media. The publication printed a retraction and an apology to calm Whitney's wrath.

Trying to figure out why so many press people were hell-bent on presenting her unfavorably to the public, Houston concluded, "I can't really be the average pregnant woman. People say, 'God, you got b-i-i-i-g!' For some reason, I'm not supposed to be pregnant. I'm not supposed to be a woman. I'm supposed to be something else. What, I have no idea. . . . A guy who was once my manager told me, 'You're an icon!' I was like, 'What the fuck is an icon?' He said, 'People look up to you and they think you're a god.' Maybe that's what it is, I don't know."

Cissy Houston had her own take on the nasty, often contradictory media rumors that had dogged Whitney for years about subjects such as Nippy's closeness to Robyn Crawford and her relationships with Eddie Murphy and Bobby Brown. Said Mrs. Houston: "It's because Whitney doesn't wear clothes up to her behind with her tits out, excuse my French. Either you're the biggest whore or you're a lesbian."

Such persistent branding led Whitney to admit, "You develop a core, a hard one. People love scandalous shit . . . I think, for the most part, people respect and like me. I really do. But I think [the tabloids] would rather say, 'Oh, she's a nasty old freaky witch.' People go, 'Oh, really? Let's buy it and see.'"

While Whitney was coping with her newly elevated popularity, Bobby Brown was caught up in his own image problem. On the one hand, his career success had been built on being the sexy bad boy. That's what his female fans expected and still wanted from him. However, now that he was married, a father of four, and approaching his mid-twenties, he began thinking seriously about altering the public's perception of the real Bobby Brown. But he soon realized that being a faithful husband and a good parent—which would reflect well on Whitney's own image—was not going to appeal to his enthusiastic fans. They much preferred the old irrepressible, free-spirited Bobby. It was a public relations puzzle that he couldn't seem to win.

As Whitney prepared for her latest nationwide tour, she gave an interview to Anthony DeCurtis of *Rolling Stone* magazine. The cover article, entitled "Whitney Houston Gets Nasty," was published in the June 10, 1993 issue. It was an unvarnished look at the "real" Whitney as she held court in her Mendham Township mansion. By now, the new mother had been transformed from the clean-cut daughter of a noted gospel singer into a regal superstar who now displayed a raucous, no-holds-barred vocabulary when it came to explaining herself to the world. Like any self-respecting diva, she relished the opportunity to discuss herself for the record. However, at the same time, she let it be known that she resented such intrusions into her private life. Moreover, she was deeply suspicious of those who asked her probing questions, just as she was leery of members of the public who would be titillated by reading her reactions to the latest allegations circulating about her in the rumor mill.

As was par for the course, Whitney's ambiguous relationship with Robyn Crawford was a key topic in this *Rolling Stone* piece. Both angry and bored to find the issue being raised once again, the singer said, "There are so many, so many women artists who have women as their confidantes, and nobody questions that. So I realize that it's like 'Whitney Houston—she's popular, let's fuck with her.' I have denied it over and over again, and nobody's accepted it. Or the media hasn't." She argued further, "People out there know I'm a married woman. I mean, what kind of a person am I—to be married and to have another life. First of all my husband wouldn't go for it—let's get that out of the way, okay? He's all boy, and he ain't goin' for it, okay? But I'm so fucking tired of that question, and I'm tired of answering it."

Moving on, she tore into the topic of rival divas. Her pronouncements were, "People who go out and buy me, buy for me. Furthermore, I came out first anyways [laughs]—anybody that's gonna come has definitely got to come after. They don't say I sound like Mariah Carey, they say Mariah Carey sounds like me, you dig what I'm saying? So I don't feel like I'm in competition with these people. Madonna and I certainly aren't in competition. Mary J. Blige—it's her own thing. She is the queen of hip-hop. She's the first girl to come out that's real down, real cool, but can sing. So everybody tries to follow. But I've been out here since 1985, so whoever comes got to come after me."

By July 1993, a trimmed-down Whitney was back on the concert trail, where she had twenty-five sold-out performances lined up, including five in New York City. One of her first stops on this trek was at the James L. Knight Center in Miami. That evening in Florida had more than its share of problems. First of all, the ticketholders were kept outside the arena until just a few minutes before showtime, all the while the crush of the crowd getting larger and more unruly. Then a delayed soundcheck caused nearly an hour's delay in the start time. To the audience's surprise, with the entertainment already two hours late in starting, they were presented with a previously unannounced opening act: two gospel-singing siblings from the Winans clan. Irritated at having been kept waiting so long, the attendees were not kind to the Winans, nor to the second opening act, a saxophonist.

Waiting backstage, Houston was enraged that the crowd was being so discourteous. By the time she marched on stage, she was in a rotten mood and made it evident how displeased she was with the audience.

The volcano exploded when, after her opening song, an overzealous fan rushed up to the stage to ask for an autograph. Instead of dealing diplomatically with the request, Whitney imperiously pointed her finger towards the audience and spat, "Your ticket definitely does say *seat* on it, doesn't it?" The crestfallen, mortified fan quickly hurried out of her sight.

Since this dismissal had been hissed into her microphone, the entire arena had heard Whitney's biting remark. Their response was to boo her. This might have intimidated many another star, but not Whitney Houston. She snapped back at the multitudes, "I've been booed before," adding, "and it really doesn't faze me!"

Whitney was equally undaunted when reports of the incident in the Miami press the following day led the arena management and others to caution the volatile star against any further such behavior. But there was no need to worry. The next evening she was in a harmonious mood towards the new crowd at the Knight Center and the show came off without any hitches. Claiming to be perplexed by the commotion, Whitney would remark later, "I don't know what makes an audience happy, what makes them sad. I don't know what people want. All I want is to sing."

Whitney arranged her schedule so that she would be back at her New Jersey home in mid-July 1993 to celebrate her first wedding anniversary with Bobby. They dined quietly at home, shared a piece of wedding cake that had been frozen, and then danced under the stars.

Throughout 1993 and into 1994, Whitney received an assortment of music-industry and showbusiness awards tied to her great success with *The Bodyguard*. At such events, it was inevitable that she would be required to perform "I Will Always Love You," and she did so to the point where she must have come to abhor the vocal workout it demanded. On the other hand, she never tired of telling the world how wrong everyone had been about her marriage to Bobby Brown. She apparently kept an exact mental count of precisely how many years, months and days they had been wed.

Thus, she could proudly spout forth the latest statistics to confirm that their union was a success.

On one occasion, when the subject of her beloved Bobby came up, regal Whitney told the inquiring reporter, "I want to get something straight. I've heard a lot about my husband being this womanizer. You know: 'He's a womanizer, he's got three illegitimate children, da-da-da-da-da-da'—you know that whole thing? I just want people to understand something: My husband has never, never disrespected any woman. Any woman that he's wanted has wanted him. And I want people to know that my husband's a good person. He's a respectable human being. He was raised with respect." Obviously wound up about the topic, she insisted vehemently, "He loves being married, and he's respectful to his marriage. He respects me, and I respect him. I'm tired of people talking about him like he's this bad guy and he has no respect for me or his marriage. That's bullshit. He does. And anybody who knows him knows that's true."

Bobby Brown also seemed fixated on discussing their marriage with journalists. On one occasion, he confided to the *Los Angeles Times*: "It's love. When it happens, you have to grab it. You can't let it go no matter what anybody else thinks. Whitney is a proud black woman. That's what really drew me to her. She's beautiful, not just outside, but on the inside. When we finish a show, she puts on jeans and we roll."

And sometimes Whitney and Bobby gave a joint performance. In November 1993, the couple were grilled on national TV by veteran interviewer Barbara Walters. After interrogating Whitney on the usual range of subjects (her career achievements, her friendship with Robyn Crawford, and so forth), Walters abruptly turned the conversation to Bobby Brown. Hoping to get a rise out of her skeptical guest, her opening salvo was, "I would've thought he'd be the last person you'd be attracted to!" Not missing a beat, Whitney retorted, "That shows how much you know about people, doesn't it?"

Having failed to bait Whitney, the game Walters next put Brown on the spot. Ever so matter-of-factly, she inquired in her politest manner, "Do you believe in total fidelity, being faithful?" Bobby cooed back, "Oh, I am faithful. That's why I got married."

Taking in this exchange, a gleeful Whitney exclaimed to Walters, "Told ya!"

19

Storm Clouds

"At the beginning it bothered me. It hurt me that people would spread rumors about me or my family—things that weren't true, lies. You want to defend yourself, but you can't. It's like my mother said: 'Don't dignify a lie with an answer.' So my husband and I, we sit there and laugh about it."

WHITNEY HOUSTON, 1994

Back in the late 1960s, Whitney Houston's godmother Aretha Franklin had enjoyed a number-one hit with "Respect." And that's just what Whitney and her husband, Bobby Brown, wanted in the fall of 1993—from the New York Port Authority Police.

It stemmed from an incident on September 29 that year at New York's John F. Kennedy Airport. The Browns' limousine was commanded to stop by nine gun-waving transit police officers searching for drug couriers. (The officers claimed later that they had been given a hot tip that drugs were being smuggled into New York through limos at the airport. Because the vehicle's windows were tinted, they had not been sure if anyone inside was armed.) Once the limo had been halted and the car's windows opened, the officers quickly recognized the passengers. The much-reported incident escalated in news value when, two days later, Olivia McClurkin, one of Houston's backup singers, was forced from her limousine at JFK Airport by armed robbers who tore open her luggage in what police theorized was probably a search for drugs.

On Wednesday, October 13, Charles Knox, superintendent of the Port Authority police, telephoned Whitney's business office to make a personal apology to the celebrity couple. Meanwhile, Knox conducted a personal enquiry into the situation, as a result of which two of the officers involved were docked ten days' pay and a third retired. That appeared to be the end of the matter. However, two years later, Knox (who, it emerged, had known Whitney and her family for two decades) became embroiled in an alleged improper labor practice action by the Port Authority Lieutenants Benevolent Association. It was stated that the initial departmental investigation had found no misconduct and the Association was now claiming that Knox's separate exploration into the matter was, in their view, "seriously flawed."

In contrast, on the other side of the continent, Whitney was getting a *great deal* of respect. Thanks to the surprise success of *The Bodyguard*, *Entertainment Weekly*, in its annual survey of the 100 most powerful people in Hollywood, ranked the diva as number seventy-one—higher than acclaimed director Martin Scorsese or veteran leading man Sylvester Stallone. The magazine explained its decision thus: "America loves that voice. Even when it reflects hollow dialogue or hopeless lyrics."

Now, Warner Bros. wanted Whitney for the latest remake of *A Star Is Born*, which had last been filmed in 1976 with Whitney's idol Barbra Streisand in the lead role. Said a studio executive, "It's a natural for Whitney. We were already talking about doing it, but after *The Bodyguard* it became something specifically tailored to her." It was rumored that Denzel Washington or Wesley Snipes might be Whitney's leading man in the project, to be coproduced by Quincy Jones and Joel Silver. Already, Whitney's team of advisors (that is, John Houston and Robyn Crawford) had rejected an early draft of the script—partly due to its excessive use of profanities—and a new version was in the works. The same studio was also developing *Serenade* as a vehicle for Whitney; the story line would focus on a romance between a singer and a composer.

Meanwhile, Whitney's representative at the prestigious William Morris Agency told the trade press: "We don't have to make shoes fit. We have many options." And it was true. Besides the Warner Bros. film possibilities, Walt Disney wanted Houston to play a small-town church singer in a project teaming her with Wesley Snipes. The Disney executive attached to the property reasoned that Whitney "has proven that people are interested in seeing her—all over the world." Over at Twentieth Century-Fox, the honchos were offering to showcase Houston in a romantic drama about a young singer who comes to Manhattan to launch her career. In touting this vehicle, Fox's president of worldwide production pleaded, "Light a candle for me. A lot of people want to make a movie with Whitney Houston."

There was even industry chatter that Whitney and Kevin Costner might reunite for a sequel to *The Bodyguard*. As time wore on, however, Costner would fixate on having Diana, Princess of Wales play opposite him. But her tragic death in August 1997 put an end to that dream. Thereafter, it was repeatedly suggested that Whitney might, after all, team up with Costner for a follow-up to their joint box-office bonanza, but, to date, the mooted sequel has never gotten off the drafting table.

Yet another big-screen project linked to Whitney—and one which did get made—was Touchstone's Tina Turner biopic *What's Love Got to Do With It* (1993). However, between her indecision about returning to the screen immediately after finishing *The Bodyguard* and her pregnancy with Bobbi Kristina, Houston dropped out of contention. Angela Bassett took on the demanding assignment of playing the lead in Turner's turbulent life story and would be Oscar-nominated for her finely etched work.

While Whitney vacillated about choosing a new film property, she continued to work the live circuit. She appeared in Birmingham, England in early November 1993, accompanied by her seven-piece band and her four background singers, including brother Gary. Wearing a tight-fitting crushed-velvet dress, statuesque Whitney amply demonstrated that she had regained her slim figure. Choosing to sit on a stool much of the time as she delivered her catalogue of hits, she informed the packed arena, "When you've had a baby you tend to sit a lot."

Joy Morgan in the *Weekly Journal* reported, "From the start it became patently obvious that working up a sweat was the furthest thing from her mind. . . . Perhaps she knew only too well that the crowd were firmly in her grasp and there was little attempt to involve them. Unfortunately that was the main problem with the show: it was far too perfunctory, a greatest hits collection, a concert without soul." The reviewer continued, "Despite the tremendous reception she was receiving from the audience, Houston curiously kept them at a distance. Even bringing on baby Bobbi [Kristina] and reporting that she and her husband Bobby [Brown] were 'doing fine' smacked of mere gesture. Not that the audience seemed to mind."

Morgan also observed, "A couple of times her voice failed to touch the high notes even on slow love songs. . . . The mighty roar of recognition which greeted "I Will Always Love You" turned to stunned silence as her voice gave way again. . . . For scant seconds the reigning Queen of Pop had to endure a tirade of whistles and stamping feet, the empress was suddenly naked before her subjects. But then, to the relief of all, out of the darkness, a loyal fan yelled: 'You're doing great Whitney!' Smiling coyly, the superstar continued the song. The Queen of Pop lived to reign another night."

Ensconced once again in her Mendham Township home by late November, Whitney embarked on a crusade to show the world that she and Bobby were just an everyday couple, very much in love with each other and with their daughter Bobbi Kristina. Their forum of choice was *Ebony* magazine, and they met with Joy Duckett Cain for an informal chat in their spacious kitchen. In between answering the journalist's questions, the couple dined on spaghetti with Whitney doing double duty holding her child in her lap. Bobby eventually traipsed off with his dish piled high to consume his pasta in front of the TV.

The obviously enthralled Cain gushed of the Browns: "They act like two high-schoolers with a bad case of the hots for each other. They giggle, they flirt, they tease—at one point, Bobby even gives Whitney a piggyback ride up the stairs. . . . Are they for real? The vibes say yes. Still, Bobby stroking Whitney's bare foot? I don't know. Maybe I'm hanging with the wrong crowd, but the married folks I know just don't act like that. Particularly after they've recently had a baby."

Later, the question-and-answer session adjourned to the lounge area near the games room. As the celebrity pair smoked cigarettes and sipped beers, Whitney explained to the captivated scribe: "You see him onstage, you see him on the video. You see me onstage, you see me on the video but you don't see the people here in this house. . . . You don't see us sitting back watching TV, watching a movie or something, drinking a beer, just coolin' out. You know—talking to each other, being real. But if you really think about it you've got to realize that we've got to get up and brush our teeth. We've got to wash our behinds. There is relativity here."

Briefly, Whitney turned to the subject of their so-called marriage of convenienc:"This ain't about publicity. . . . I've got enough of that on my own. And so does he. You don't have a baby based on that madness." Having dismissed that topic, she moved on to the next item on her agenda—her three stepchildren (Landon, LaPrincia, and Robert Jr.), who often lived with the Browns: "I don't deal with that stepmom madness. I tell them that I love them and they can love me and we can talk and be friends. That's our relationship."

Before long, Whitney shifted to another issue: trust. She asserted, "I don't worry. I know my husband respects me. My husband doesn't carry himself when he walks into a room like, 'Okay, let me see who I can mack [take advantage of] tonight.' He's a married man. So it's not about that." Not wishing to be left out of the limelight, Bobby chimed in with, "When I go out, I can't look at another female in that sense, because I don't feel that anymore. When you love somebody, you love them with everything that you have. Yes, I still hang out. But it's all about beer and hip-hop. So I hope my wife doesn't worry about it. But I don't worry about that, either—because I know me."

At the end of 1993, *Entertainment Weekly* ranked Whitney Houston as number five in a list of "Entertainers of the Year." By then, her husband's singing career was in rapid decline. His 1992 album, *Bobby*, had failed to achieve the huge sales predicted, and his next offering (1993's *Remixes N the Key of B*) was only a modest seller. So, when in 1994 Houston finally rejected the starring role in the new *A Star Is Born*, some industry wags insisted that it was because the scenario, about a man overshadowed by his film-star wife, hit too close to home.

During this period, when Bobby's career was stuck in a rut, his most frequent public appearances were accompanying his wife to music-industry award shows as she collected yet more accolades for *The Bodyguard* soundtrack. At such gatherings, when Whitney rushed to the podium to receive her latest prize, she would typically thank "my heavenly Father and my Lord and Savior Jesus for without I am nothing, with I am everything." Then, in her list of acknowledgments, she would always include her husband. The TV cameras would pan to Bobby Brown in the audience, usually holding a sleeping Bobbi Kristina.

At the American Music Awards held in Los Angeles in February 1994, Houston claimed seven trophies, plus the Award of Merit. In the midst of all the attention focused on her, she did her best to include Brown in her limelight. One journalist there described the scene backstage: "When Whitney arrived in the press room, a wave of camera flashes came first and then the reporters' questions. Bobby was standing trustingly by her side.

As if to seek approval, or gain strength and support, she glanced over at him often while speaking. The media ate it up. She was flawless."

In contrast, on those occasions when Brown was the center of public attention, he revealed an increasingly truculent side. A case in point was his twenty-fifth birthday party, which Whitney hosted for nearly 400 guests in February 1994 at the famed Tavern-on-the-Green in Manhattan's Central Park. As the night wore on, Bobby grew increasingly fractious. At one juncture, he defensively told some of the assembled group, "No matter what anybody thinks, my marriage to Whitney is real. And if you don't respect it, then fuck all of you!" Reportedly, Bobby and a photographer had a face-off when Brown took offense at a comment the cameraman had supposedly made about the singer's mother, who was also at the party. In retaliation, pugnacious Bobby reputedly backhanded the man across the face. Outbursts such as this were a foreshadowing of what would occur in the coming months.

With some of the several millions of dollars that Whitney had accumulated over recent months from recordings, concerts, and so forth, she made a fresh investment to prove that she was now landed gentry. She purchased the property behind her New Jersey compound. Now, she exclaimed, "I have a real 'estate'! It's not considered an estate in Jersey unless you have 11 acres or something, and now I have 11½, so I'm over the limit. I'm building a playground for my daughter. A big basketball court. A lap pool, because I love to swim." She said of her lifestyle: "Now that I can move the studio out of my house and into the new house, I won't hear that doomp, doomp, doomp all night! . . . My husband's a studio man—he stays in there from morning till night, unlike myself. I limit myself to six or eight hours and then I've got to come out of the cave. Bobby can stay in there for days and days."

When the annual Grammy Awards were held at Radio City Music Hall in New York City, Whitney (with Bobby Brown and their daughter in tow) accepted trophies for Best Pop Vocal Performance—Female ("I Will Always Love You"), Record of the Year ("I Will Always Love You"), and cheered on producer David Foster and his team (which had included herself) when *The Bodyguard* was named Album of the Year. Whitney admitted that she was "nervous as hell," when she opened the evening's festivities with a rendition of her signature song. Dolly Parton was also on

Top: Bobby Brown with his children Bobbi Kristina and Robert Jr. at the Hollywood premiere of *The Princess Diaries,* July 2001.

Above: Whitney Houston, Bobby Brown, and their daughter, Bobbi Kristina, meet the public in 1998.

Top: Whitney Houston in the high-tech "Queen of the Night" club sequence from *The Bodyguard* (1992).

Above left: Kevin Costner and Whitney Houston share a joke on the set of *The Bodyguard*.

Above right: Bobby Brown, Whitney, Kevin and Cindy Costner at the Hollywood premiere of *The Bodyguard*.

Top: Loretta Devine, Whitney Houston, Angela Bassett, and Lela Rochon in *Waiting to Exhale* (1995).

Above: Brandy and Whitney Houston star in *Rodgers and Hammerstein's Cinderella* (1997).

Center: Whitney Houston and Denzel Washington go skating in *The Preacher's Wife* (1996).

Above: Whitney and the Georgia Mass Choir sing a gospel number in *The Preacher's Wife*.

The young Whitney Houston holding forth on stage in Houston, Texas, 1991.

The mature diva performing at the Brit Awards at the London Arena, 1999.

On stage in 1993 with Bobbi Kristina.

Whitney Houston and Bobby Brown making music together in 1999.

Top: Mariah Carey and Whitney Houston sing their hit duet "When You Believe" (from *The Prince of Egypt*) at the 71st Academy Awards on March 22, 1999.

Above: Deborah Cox and Whitney Houston performing at Arista's twenty-fifth-anniversary party in Los Angeles, April 10, 2000. Whitney is clutching her trademark white handkerchief.

With her frequent costumers Dolce and Gabbana in 2000.

Performing with Michael Jackson as surprise guests at the *Miracle on 34th Street* concert, December 2000.

Bobby Brown is taken into police custody in Fort Lauderdale, Florida, May 22, 2000.

On July 7, 2000, a jubilant Whitney greets Bobby Brown on his release from jail in Florida.

Top left: With her affectionate husband, Bobby Brown, at a post-Oscars party in Los Angeles, March 2001.

Top right: Looking emaciated at Michael Jackson's thirtieth-anniversary tribute concert, September 7, 2001.

Above: A playful Whitney posing for the cover of her 2002 album, *Just Whitney.*

Beyoncé Knowles, Jewel, Mary J. Blige, Whitney Houston, Stevie Wonder, Chaka Khan, and Queen Latifah performing on VH1's *Divas Duets* in Las Vegas, May 22, 2003.

With Bobby Brown and Bobbi Kristina on "spiritual retreat" in Israel, May 28, 2003.

hand that evening and quipped of the fantastic success that "I Will Always Love You" had enjoyed: "On behalf of the Internal Revenue Service and myself, I want to thank Whitney for making that song such an enormous hit." Parton also noted, "When I wrote that song . . . years ago I had a heartache but it's amazing how healing money can be." Houston subsequently continued the banter at the MTV Movie Awards, where she joked, "I would like to thank Dolly Parton for writing a great song. She made a lot more money than I did, but that's okay."

A few weeks later, at the Soul Train Music Awards at the Shrine Auditorium in Los Angeles, Whitney and Bobby Brown performed live for the first time in public, singing their duet "Something in Common." Again, it was Houston who captured the lion's share of attention that evening.

Meanwhile, Bobby's sprawling home in Atlanta was in danger of going into foreclosure due to hefty back taxes (reputed to be in the millions) owed to the Internal Revenue Service. Whitney stepped in and obtained a second mortgage (over $800,000) on the property to forestall Brown losing his house. Later, the property would be repossessed by the bank, and Houston's Nippy, Inc. would purchase the gone-to-seed estate and sell it in the late 1990s. Reputedly, this was not the first time that affluent Whitney had bailed out her spouse financially. According to one account, around the time of their marriage she had helped to clear Bobby's extensive credit-card debts.

Money, however, was not the only compelling subject that the Browns found time to discuss. There was the ongoing delicate matter of Robyn Crawford, still a strong influence in Whitney's business life. The uneasy truce between this trio was broken by an explosion in Los Angeles in late March 1994 while they were registered at the classy Peninsula Hotel. According to onlookers, some type of verbal (and possibly physical) altercation had occurred between Brown and Robyn. The ruckus led to the hotel's security staff, Whitney's own bodyguards, and the police being summoned to the scene. Full details of what transpired have never come to light.

As 1994 progressed, Whitney and Bobby's relationship turned increasingly abrasive. One of the problems was that Brown, apparently with too much time on his hands, was unable to resist partying—with or without his wife. Despite the couple's strong denials that anything was amiss in their marriage, there were recurrent rumors that they were separating, reconciling, splitting apart again, and then making up once more. It became such a persistent pattern that the intrigued press finally developed a "What's next?" attitude in their coverage of the supposed spats.

By the time Whitney hit the concert trail again in mid-1994, the status of her marriage was again up in the air. The tabloids recorded that when she had returned from Europe in May, she had immediately rushed from New Jersey to Los Angeles to surprise her beloved. Instead, Whitney was the one in for a bombshell. Reputedly, Brown was entertaining a young lady at the time. An extremely upset Whitney flew back to the East Coast that same night. Now that she was performing around the country, Brown was doing his best to win over his angered wife. On those occasions when he was back in her good graces, he would appear on stage with her, as he did at a concert in mid-June 1994 at the Nassau Coliseum in New York, where the couple sang "Something in Common."

During Whitney's twenty-two-city tour, there were frequent reports of her being late for showtime, having a hoarse voice on stage, or canceling the program due to ill health. When she did perform, reviewers noted a new maturity to her styling, but observed that her stage presentation was still too mechanical. On the other hand, her show at the Omni in Atlanta, Georgia on July 5, 1994 was decidedly spontaneous. That evening, she brought Bobby on stage and sang him a verse or two of "You Give Good Love." She told the several thousands in attendance that Brown is "all the man I need," and then she pressed his head to her stomach and said to him: "There's a lot of love inside." Originally, Houston had planned to keep her pregnancy to herself and surprise Bobby on the couple's upcoming second anniversary. However, she impulsively decided to tell the crowd that she was expecting their new baby in December.

Sadly, a few days later, while in Houston, Texas for another concert stopover, Whitney noticed blood spotting while in her hotel room; she had suffered another miscarriage. Bobby had been with her at the time, helping her prepare for the show. After a few days of coming to terms with this loss, Whitney went on with her tour schedule. This included singing at the final World Cup Game on Sunday, July 17, 1994 at the Rose Bowl in Pasadena, California. There, suffering from a cold, she sounded hoarse and gave a rather perfunctory performance, which was televised worldwide.

By the time Houston's tour ended in late summer, the show had turned into a family act. Sometimes Bobby Brown would be on stage for the entire performance, acting as his wife's emcee, even saying to the audience, "Let's hear it for my wife, y'all, Whitney Houston!" Frequently, the diva would bring out young Bobbi Kristina to take a bow or have her stand in adoration as mama sang. At other times, some of Brown's other children would join Whitney on stage and she would make a show of kissing and hugging them. At one performance, Brown's mother came on stage to be serenaded by Whitney; another time, the star took care to remind the concertgoers that another of her relatives (besides Gary Houston) was part of the proceedings. By far the strangest were those times when the Browns would sing a finale number to the crowd, after which a pleased-as-punch Bobby would inform the audience with a wink, "I'm taking my wife home with me, y'all."

Whitney had been engaged as the headline act for seven performances at Radio City Music Hall in early September 1994. It should have been a jubilant occasion. However, her father had just suffered from congestive heart failure, shortly after his seventy-sixth birthday, and he was currently in critical condition in hospital. Adding to her emotional stress, she was again being stalked by an obsessed fan who insisted he was the singer's lover, not to mention the father of her daughter and a make-believe son. The disturbed individual had even gone so far as to join the Houstons' church in Newark, New Jersey, where he got into a confrontation with Cissy. In short order, the offender was barred from New Hope Baptist Church and he agreed to leave the star alone. Now, reneging on the promise, he was sending an increasing number of notes as well as constantly making calls to Whitney's business office. This led to the artist obtaining a restraining order against him, but, so far, it seemed to have had little effect. As a result of all this tension, Whitney was distracted and frequently had problems performing to her usual high standards at Radio City.

On October 4, 1994, Whitney was invited to an elaborate dinner hosted at the White House for South African President Nelson Mandela. She had been asked to appear as the featured performer at the gala. When the big night came, there was no Whitney Houston on hand to entertain Mandela and 200 other dignitaries. Two hours or more after the official start of the event, she and Bobby Brown breezed into the East Room of the White House. Casually and dismissively, she mentioned that she was tardy because "I just got off tour." The only problem was, her tour had concluded four days earlier in New York.

This widely reported incident seemed a strange preamble for Houston's upcoming South African tour, scheduled for the following month. However, by now, the world was coming to expect the unexpected and the unexplained from Whitney Houston.

As Houston's trouble-filled year wound down, she, along with Bobby Brown, Bobbi Kristina, Cissy Houston, and other family members and friends as part of her hefty entourage, flew to South Africa. She was contracted to give three concerts there, one of which would be broadcast live throughout the world by the HBO cable channel. Increasingly anxious about the press, stalkers, her own shaky marriage, her miscarriage, and her father's poor health, Whitney was in an extremely defensive mood when she made this pilgrimage. At her first concert, she referred to Mandela's controversial wife, Winnie, as "your queen." This led members of the audience to boo her. In now typical fashion, the artist retorted coldly, "I don't care what you think!" Commenting on her daughter displaying such hauteur in public, Cissy said, "Whitney's a human being. There's a grown-up side and a little-kid side, but she is human, and if you push the wrong button. . . ."

After a warm-up concert in Durban, the much-promoted televised event was held on Saturday, November 12 at 9 P.M. at the 70,000-seat Ellis Stadium in Johannesburg. Advertised with the tagline "One voice . . . one concert . . . one place to see it," it was the first-ever stereo broadcast to be transmitted from South Africa. Between the television and tour crews, more than 200 staff were required to travel to South Africa for this big event. All proceeds raised from the evening were earmarked for South African children's charities.

As well as her repertoire of hits—from "I Wanna Dance with Somebody (Who Loves Me)" to "I Will Always Love You" and "I'm Every Woman"—Whitney also included "Amazing Grace" and "Master Blaster" in the set list. Dressed regally for the occasion, she opened the event wearing a skintight gold evening gown with jewelry dangling from her neck and ears. During the evening, a multi-ethnic group joined her on stage for "We Can Touch the World," with Cissy Houston performing on this number as well as "Let's Make It Love." The show ended with

Whitney telling the throng, "I hope you have all you ever dreamed of." Next, a burst of fireworks lit up the sky over the stage. With the concert over, Bobby Brown emerged from the wings to give Whitney a big hug.

Finally, Whitney performed at Cape Town's Green Point Stadium on November 19, where she was late starting the show, was reportedly hoarse on several numbers, and ended the program early. Afterwards, the Browns took time out for a second honeymoon at the luxurious Palace Hotel in Sun City. Obviously they had patched up their differences from their visit to Indonesia the month before, when the couple had been sighted feuding and fussing. These clashes were supposedly triggered by Bobby's spiraling financial problems and his ever-roving eye.

When Whitney and company left South Africa, media accounts of her visit were filled with new examples and old rehashes of her unappealing diva-like behavior, her undiplomatic remarks in public, and so forth. There was a recurring thread of jealousy and anger from some of the country's press (duly reported in the black media in the U.S.) about Houston's enormous wealth and her frequent gaffes in interacting diplomatically with dignitaries and fans.

Back in the United States and reviewing her difficult year, Houston would wonder aloud if fame was worth its tremendously exacting price. She pondered, "How famous can you be? How many number-one songs can you have? Having all these things, having money and all that, didn't make me happy and nobody understands that. It's always, 'Oh, girl, to be in your shoes!' but they have no idea! They are clueless."

20

Waiting to Exhale

"I don't take shit as I used to and if that makes me a bitch, then so be it."

WHITNEY HOUSTON, 1995

Being in the international limelight for a decade is a very long run in the mercurial world of showbusiness. So far, Whitney was maintaining her position as leader of the pack in the music industry. However, besides Mariah Carey and a few others, Toni Braxton, in particular, seemed poised to make a grab for Houston's crown. How did the reigning diva feel about this "threat"? Talking to *Ebony* magazine, Whitney insisted, "What do I have to be jealous of? God has blessed me so. If I coveted somebody else's stuff, God would take it away from me just like that."

Then, taking another tack, Houston commented on Braxton's fast-rising popularity: "I think it's wonderful. In some ways it kind of takes the pressure off me, the weight off me. I can share it. For a while there, it was just me. And talk about being lonely at the top. Man, you're lonely up there. I certainly wouldn't want Toni to be—but she is going to be—subjected to a lot of media madness. But I hope she never has to deal with it at the height that I've had to deal with it. I don't wish that on anybody." Leave it to Whitney Houston to turn a statement about the merits of a rival into a comment about herself—one in which she congratulates herself for possessing the unique ability to handle the huge degree of success (and the accompanying pressure) that she has personally experienced.

☆

As with her recording career, Whitney's laid-back nature (and her healthy bank account) combined to assure her reluctance to rush into a new screen venture. She explained, "I don't do movies back to back. I don't run like that. I don't want to do movies like that. It's not about doing movies for the sake of doing movies and because it's Hollywood and it's beautiful and glamorous. I want to do great work with great people and that takes time. I'll pick and choose carefully what I do."

Having procrastinated for so long about what film project to tackle next, if any, Whitney finally made a decision. She agreed to star in a remake of *Rodgers and Hammerstein's Cinderella* for CBS-TV. Originally touted to begin production after she completed her summer 1994 world tour, the made-for-television musical had now been pushed back to 1995. Whitney had also agreed to costar with Denzel Washington in a remake of 1947's *The Bishop's Wife*, a Yuletide classic. In addition, she had expressed an interest in joining forces with Harrison Ford for a new version of 1954's *Sabrina*, taking the role once played by Audrey Hepburn. However, when the romantic comedy went into production in early 1995, director Sydney Pollack cast British-born Julia Ormond in the title part. Although disappointed, Whitney was consoled by her involvement in another feature film scheduled to begin shooting in winter 1995.

Whitney had consented to a costarring role in *Waiting to Exhale*, based on the 1992 best-selling novel by Terry McMillan. (Previously, Whitney had been in negotiations to star in a screen version of McMillan's 1989 book *Disappearing Acts*, but the adaptation never got off the ground and she had moved on to other professional activities.) Once Twentieth Century-Fox had acquired the screen rights to *Waiting to Exhale* soon after publication, the studio persuaded the author to collaborate with Ron Bass on a film version. By 1994, a satisfactory script had been drafted and the casting process had begun. The spicy story concerned four contrasting African-American women who invariably choose the wrong mate and wind up in volatile romantic situations. By story's end, the female quartet has found great solace and joy in their growing friendships with one another as they prepare, once again, to pursue their search for Mr. Right.

Initially, McMillan had expressed interest in having Angela Bassett play the role of Savannah Jackson, a public relations executive who moves from Denver, Colorado to Phoenix, Arizona in search of a fresh life. However, Bassett much preferred the highly dramatic part of Bernadine Harris, the self-sacrificing wife and mother whose selfish husband abandons her for his white bookkeeper. With Bassett penciled in as Bernadine, the producers and McMillan turned to Whitney to take on the role of Savannah, who has a seesawing relationship with her interfering mother. The singer was excited by the project. "Savannah is me. She's very straightforward, she knows what she wants, and she goes for it." The differences between the artist's wealthy background and that of her middle-class character did not intimidate her. "I have to believe this role is me," she said (although she would later admit she never finished reading the novel). "Like Barbra Streisand, when Barbra did *Funny Girl* [1968], we knew she was Barbra Streisand, but we thought she was Fanny Brice because she was so herself. You know what I'm saying?'" Whitney signed up for the picture, glad to be part of an ensemble cast, which would allow her to draw support and counsel from her female costars.

Before long, Lela Rochon was cast as Robin Stokes, a very competent insurance broker who is recuperating from her latest dead-end love affair. Loretta Devine signed on to play Gloria Matthews, the plump owner of a stylish beauty salon for black women. Gloria is a single parent raising her teenage son and is about to meet an appealing new next-door neighbor, played by dancer Gregory Hines. McMillan insisted that a black director helm the project. When her original choice of Julie Dash did not work out, the novelist suggested actor Forest Whitaker (*Platoon, Bird, The Crying Game*), who had already directed a TV movie. He was successfully brought aboard the production, which was budgeted at a relatively modest $15 million.

Initially, Whitney regarded this vehicle as an opportunity exclusively to showcase her acting abilities. She planned neither to sing within the film nor on its soundtrack album. However, Twentieth Century-Fox and Whitaker soon convinced her otherwise. Her interest was piqued when her friend Kenneth "Babyface" Edmonds was hired to produce the soundtrack album and to write and arrange many of its tracks. With a further push from Arista Records, who had not had a new disc from their moneymaker in three years, Whitney finally agreed to perform on the album, which would be released by Arista.

In February 1995, *Waiting to Exhale* began its ten-week shoot in Greater Phoenix, with auxiliary filming in Arizona's Fountain Hills and Paradise Valley, and Utah's Monument Valley. Of the four female leads, there was no question that Loretta Devine and Lela Rochon were subordinate in the pecking order. While Bassett had been acting on camera for over a decade and had a recent Academy Award nomination to her credit, Whitney had top billing—thanks to her startling success in *The Bodyguard*, her track record in the music business, and her visibility in the media (for assorted personal reasons).

While the female foursome developed a camaraderie during the filmmaking, they were all well aware that the picture's best chance for box-office success depended on Whitney Houston's pulling power with the public. As a consequence, the deferential tone that permeated the set—from the director down to the lowly grips—was an unspoken part of the protocol of these women in their time out from filming. In the coming months, Whitney would relish relating to the media how she had invited her costars to dinner at her rented home in Phoenix so that they could chat over mounds of soul food and become better acquainted. However, what was diplomatically left unsaid by any of the lead actresses or the rest of the troupe was that the star could often be problematic.

To begin with, early on in production she became ill with symptoms that seemed remarkably similar to morning sickness. She flew back to New Jersey to regain her strength. A few of the tabloids insisted that Whitney was pregnant again, but those rumours proved unfounded. Back in Arizona, Whitney had her usual problems with early-morning calls for filming. When she did arrive on the set, she was accompanied by her entourage, which included young Bobbi Kristina, a nanny, her British bodyguard, and other staff. When her daughter turned two years old in early March, Whitney hosted a party for her on the set. Both Cissy and John Houston attended the celebration, and Bobby Brown, away recording a new album, also made an appearance for his daughter's big day. However, because he and Whitney were experiencing such difficult domestic times, seldom was he asked onto, or seen on, the *Waiting to Exhale* shoot. Disgruntled at being mostly on the outside looking in, he began to refer to his wife's picture as *Waiting to Cough*.

During filming, Whitney would gush to the media, "In just two weeks, Forest [Whitaker] has taught me a lot about acting." She also professed to be enthralled to "have three other beautiful ladies who are all great actresses and whom I can play off." In particular, the star said of Bassett: "That girl is amazing. I don't sing a song the same way every night; different emotions come into play. Watching Angela do that in acting with words helped me a lot."

During the shoot, Whitney spent much of her time in the company of Robyn Crawford. Frequently, when the star was not in her trailer chain-smoking cigarettes or nibbling on her favorite sandwich (bologna and cheese), she appeared lost in private thoughts on the set. Some attributed this to her ongoing problems with her husband. However, when one or two individuals dared to suggest that she should not let Brown control her outlook on life so much, she withdrew into an even more standoffish attitude towards them.

When *New York* magazine was preparing a piece on the making of *Waiting to Exhale* for its August 10, 1995 issue, an unnamed source close to the project was asked to remark on Whitney Houston's behavior during filming. That unspecified person backed off quickly with a timid, "It would be inappropriate of me to discuss Whitney's personal life." Another unidentified individual on the shoot observed of the mercurial star: "The people that she surrounds herself with are not as cultured as she is. They're kind of gruff. And I think that's her interior. There's something cold about her. She's tough."

When published, the *New York* article ("Whitney Houston's Unfriendly Skies") suggested that the artist proved to be less than a joy to work with during production. The magazine gave as an example that, at the end of the shoot, Whitney and Forest Whitaker were scheduled to share a rented plane that would fly them back to Los Angeles. The feature quoted an onlooker who stated that, "Forest asked her to wait with the plane and said he'd be right along. But when he pulled up on the tarmac, the plane was taking off."

Waiting to Exhale was scheduled for a late-1995 release and Houston was persuaded to embark on her first-ever promotional tour. One of those who chatted with Whitney during a San Francisco stopover was the *New York Post's* Stephen Schaefer. He reported, "Unlike a lot of celebrities, Houston isn't exactly dressing down for her meet-the-press duties. Though casual in a pants suit, one ring finger sports a diamond the size of a golf ball and the other hand bears a rock not quite half that size." He also noted, "She has the usual army of handlers and her agent following her around a hotel ballroom in San Fran, but they might as well be invisible—Whitney Houston doesn't need anyone to run interference, much less protect her. . . . She's perfected the look. It's a face, an attitude, a tone that says 'Be careful.'"

Like the original book, the film version of *Waiting to Exhale* had three major hurdles to overcome with mainstream moviegoers: that it focused on a quartet of African-American women; that it could be accused of (black) male bashing; and the preconception that this was, perhaps, just another ghetto story of unhappy lower-class characters. To help counteract such perceptions, the movie was given a special glossy look in its sets, costumes, and lighting so it could be marketed as a slick soap opera.

After viewing the new release, Roger Ebert in the *Chicago Sun-Times* admitted he was "never bored" but wished the movie had "more sharpness, harder edges and bitter satire instead of bemused observation." *Boxoffice* magazine, in its two-and-a-half-star review, suggested that "the characters seem mired in situations within their control, and it's a slow-paced process to see them through to their respective epiphanies." Barry Walters of the *San Francisco Examiner* had problems with "four main female characters trudging through a movie's worth of similar repeated blunders" which he felt "adds up to one scary truckload of drama."

As for the cast, Bassett came in for the lion's share of positive attention, especially for her showy scene in which she gains revenge on her adulterous spouse by burning his cherished wardrobe and fancy car. But Whitney's highly promoted presence in the film did not go unnoticed. Barry Walters judged that "Houston's tangible toughness is put to good use." Applauding the film for "the women's acerbic outlook on the sexual predilections of the men they become entangled with," Kenneth Turan of the *Los Angeles Times* cited, among other pluses in the picture, those scenes between Whitney's character and the egocentric figure played by Jeffrey D. Sams. In *Variety*, Godfrey Cheshire remarked that Houston was following up *The Bodyguard* with "another glamorous turn."

On the other hand, Amanda Lipman of the British film magazine *Sight and Sound* had mixed feelings. While complimenting Whitney for being "far more lively here than she was in *The Bodyguard*" and even seeming "often cutely raunchy," Lipman concluded that "just like the film itself, she can also be unbearably sanctimonious—tenderly chiding her friends for their lack of insight." Edward Guthmann in the *San Francisco Chronicle* felt that Houston "underplays so much that she comes off bored and removed, as though she had better fish to fry." Novelist and screenwriter Terry McMillan provided an oblique critique of Whitney's performance in the picture when she commented to a national magazine: "She's going to be a really better actress when she starts seeing herself as an actress and not a singer who acts."

With such mixed reviews, as well as the aforementioned hurdles with the plot, Twentieth Century-Fox were understandably worried about the picture's commercial fate. However, a surprising thing happened at theaters showing the picture. Women (both black and white) came out in droves—often in groups—to see it, not once but two or three times. At many showings, the audience talked back to the lead female characters, cheering them on for their resiliency, and chiding them for falling into their battle-of-the-sexes traps. With such highly favorable word-of-mouth, *Waiting to Exhale* went on to gross over $66 million in the U.S. alone.

Part of what helped to sell *Waiting to Exhale* to the moviegoing public was its score and the soundtrack album, which was already enjoying brisk sales. The soundtrack would eventually sell over 10 million copies worldwide. The creative forces behind the album had decided to surround Whitney's three agreed-upon songs with a roster of leading black artists interpreting the other thirteen numbers. The lineup included, among others, Aretha Franklin ("It Hurts Like Hell"), Brandy ("Sittin' Up in My Room"), Patti LaBelle ("My Love Sweet Love"), Toni Braxton ("Let It Flow"), and Chaka Khan ("My Funny Valentine").

Needless to say, the lynchpins of the *Waiting to Exhale* album were Whitney's three songs. In particular, "Exhale (Shoop, Shoop)" was a winning selection within the film, on the album, and as a music video. Written and produced by Babyface, the title cut puzzled many fans initially—as it had Whitney—regarding its use of the words "shoop, shoop." Said the songwriter, "When Whitney first heard the song, she figured I'd lost it—I couldn't come up with words anymore. And actually, she's right. I couldn't think of anything for that particular part. It felt like it should groove there. But I knew it couldn't groove without any vocals, so I started humming along with it and that's what happened. The 'shoops' came. But they felt so good, I thought, 'Why not?' It doesn't have to mean anything."

A few weeks before *Waiting to Exhale* premiered, "Exhale (Shoop, Shoop)" rose to the top of the music charts, giving Houston her eleventh number one. Her second song for the film was "Why Does It Hurt So Bad." It had been written by Babyface for Whitney a few years previously, but she had not felt in the right mood to record it at that time. Now, events in her domestic life had given the lyrics special resonance. This track would reach number twenty-six on the American charts. The third offering ("Count on Me") was a collaboration between Babyface, Whitney, and her brother Michael. On record, it became a duet for Whitney and her good friend CeCe Winans, and reached number eight on the charts.

In the liner notes to the *Waiting to Exhale* album, Whitney thanks God, Bobbi Kristina, her parents, her personal staff (including Robyn

Crawford), her agent, her publicist, her Arista family, and even her travel agent. However, *not one word* is said about her errant husband.

Throughout 1995, the status of the Browns' marriage went through more fluctuations and public speculation than the stock market. The couple's domestic tensions were not helped by the fact that Whitney's recording and film careers were flying high as she worked on *Waiting to Exhale*, while, in contrast, Bobby Brown was adrift, trying to redefine himself professionally. Hoping to get a film career moving, he had taken a supporting role in Mario Van Peebles's *Panther* (1995). This account of militant black activists had failed to captivate moviegoers, and it would be months before Bobby landed another film assignment (as Martin Lawrence's pal in 1996's *A Thin Line Between Love and Hate*).

Neither MCA nor Brown were certain how to shape his next album. There were rumors that he would reunite with his former group, New Edition, for the MCA label. The individual artists, along with Johnny Gill (who had not been part of the original group), would go back into the recording studio to turn out *Home Again* (1996), which would spawn the number-one single "Hit Me Off." In the meantime, Brown was at a loose end professionally and personally.

During 1995, there were Bobby Brown sightings all over the United States. For example, in March, Bobby and a few of his posse were in Minneapolis, Minnesota and stopped by a barbecue restaurant which was already closing for the night. Once the staff recognized Brown, they refired the grills and cooked the group's special order. When the after-hours patrons finally departed, the obliging servers found that they had been left only a twenty-dollar tip on a $152 bill.

In late April, Bobby and two cronies were in Orlando, Florida at the Mannequins Dance Palace, a nightclub at Disney World's Pleasure Island complex. Early in the morning of the twenty-fifth, Bobby and his companions were arrested and charged with the alleged beating of a club patron. The victim had supposedly made a pass at an attractive woman that Brown was paying close attention to, prompting a violent altercation. The injured man—whose ear was torn off and had to be reattached with stitches at the hospital—claimed to have been repeatedly kicked and punched by the trio, a fact confirmed by witnesses.

The Disney security squad caught up with the three men before they could escape Pleasure Island and the police were summoned. Asked to sit on the street curb while the matter was sorted out, two of the detained men obeyed, but Brown refused, claiming it would soil his clothes. He kept shouting, "Don't you know who I am? I could buy each and every one of you." Reportedly, when forced into the back seat of the police cruiser to be taken to the station, Bobby became belligerent. He shouted profanities, banged his head against the back seat, carved a curse word into the seat with a ballpoint pen, and urinated in the patrol car. At this point, officers handcuffed him.

After questioning at the precinct, the three accused men were released on bail of $5,000 each. They faced more than three years in prison if convicted. While preparations for the criminal case were proceeding, the victim filed a $6.6 million lawsuit against Brown and his friends. However, before the case came to trial in January 1996, an out-of-court settlement was reached, which put an end to the high-profile caper, since the plaintiff was no longer willing to pursue the matter with the prosecutor's office.

Whitney had been overseas performing in concert when news of this raucous incident reached her. On her return to the U.S., the scandal was still blazing. She, meanwhile, had flown on to Los Angeles for further work on *Waiting to Exhale*. Brown called her from Atlanta and he must have said the right things, for a few days later he was shopping with his famous wife at a chic Beverly Hills menswear shop, where she spent a reported $32,000 on apparel for him. One onlooker noted, "He was acting like the perfect husband. A well-trained puppy dog couldn't have behaved better. . . . Whatever Whitney liked, he tried on. He was hell-bent on making her happy. They were holding hands and hanging all over each other, acting like newlyweds."

This honeymoon period was, however, short-lived; Whitney had more pressing problems to resolve. In summer 1995, she had to deal with another stalker, one who had been following her around the country to concert venues, calling her business office, and sending her flowers. He had also been claiming to be her brother. With these latest actions, he was violating a restraining order instructing him to stay far away from the celebrity. Now, the man, a sometime carpenter, had been arrested by the police, who found an arsenal of weapons in his trucks, including knives, fuses, blasting caps, and electrical wiring. Eventually, the man was sentenced to prison, where he served two months on weapons' charges. Along with the previous offender (against whom a Morristown, New Jersey judge had just issued a permanent restraining order), this new incident brought the total of Whitney stalkers to date to around twenty. With such nerve-wracking incidents, it seemed that Whitney's real life was imitating art—her role as the stalked diva in *The Bodyguard*.

Hardly had Whitney finished dealing with this new menace than the irrepressible Brown was back doing his thing once again. In late August 1995, while hosting a late-night party in his accommodations at the Le Montrose Suite Hotel in West Hollywood, the feisty singer was alleged to have kicked a facility security guard in the backside. (The employee had been dispatched to ask Brown to keep the noise down at his gathering.) Police deputies called to the Hammond Street scene issued a citation for battery which required Brown to appear in court at a later unspecified date. The officers described Brown as being cooperative throughout the process. Once again, the legal matter was settled out of court. Word had it that a fuming but eventually compliant Whitney once again paid the attorney fees.

After all this summer madness, one might have hoped for a calmer fall, but that was not to be. That September, Bobby Brown was seen in several New York nightspots, including the trendy China Club, where he made a point of showing patrons that he was not wearing his wedding ring. He told listeners that he needed "freedom to be himself." The supermarket tabloids latched onto the situation, speculating on this latest turn of events. According to them, a particular bone of contention in the Brown–Houston household was, "They've been fighting over the amount of control she has over Bobby's life. Whitney gives him an allowance to live on while he's waiting for a record deal to come together. And her lawyers are the ones defending him in all his legal battles."

By now, the "single" Mr. Brown was telling associates he was thinking of relocating back to Boston and opening a business there. On September 28, he was back in his hometown, where he narrowly escaped death. That Thursday evening, Brown visited the Biarritz Lounge in Roxbury, about a block from the tough neighborhood where he had grown up. He had driven there in Whitney's $300,000 cream-colored Bentley, a gift to her from Arista Records. Brown was accompanied in the vehicle by his boyhood pal and now bodyguard, Steven "Shot" Sealey. The latter, engaged to wed Brown's younger sister, had recently been released from prison after serving a two-year sentence on a weapons charge, but was already wanted on a parole violation. After partying with pals at the Biarritz Lounge, the two men left the bar at around 12:45 A.M.

Sealey got into the front passenger seat of the Bentley. Brown was about to get behind the wheel when a gunman appeared out of nowhere. The armed man used two guns to shoot at Sealey through the front windshield. Meanwhile, a panicked Brown ran into the bar he had just vacated. A gun battle ensued between the man and Brown's bodyguards. In the skirmish, two shots smashed through the bar window, presumably aimed at Brown. While Sealey was being pulled from the blood-stained car and rushed by ambulance to Boston City Hospital, where he died at 6:20 A.M., Brown was being questioned by the police. During the interrogation, he showed officers where he had been grazed on the hip by a bullet. Brown kept repeating to the police, "They shot my boy. They shot my boy." Thereafter, the badly shaken star left the scene and soon retreated into seclusion down in Atlanta. The unsolved homicide was said by some to have resulted from Steven Sealey's involvement in the drug trade.

When Whitney learned of this near-fatal escapade, her immediate concerns over her estranged husband's welfare were overshadowed by a more pressing fear. What if her beloved Bobbi Kristina had been with her dad when he got into such a deadly scrape? Chilled at the thought of her innocent child being put at risk, Whitney was haunted by this scary notion for months to come.

A few weeks after the slaying, Bobby Brown entered a rehab program at the Betty Ford Center in Rancho Mirage, California. This sudden action surprised many because, over the years, he had always vehemently denied that he had a substance-abuse problem. His enrollment at the high-profile facility gave the media carte blanche to review his dossier of legal scrapes over recent years. These included arrests for public lewdness at concert venues in Georgia, as well as some unsavory occurrences in Atlanta in the early 1990s: once when he was charged with disorderly conduct after arguing with a police officer outside an eatery, and then, in 1992, he and his bodyguards were accused of beating up a man in an Atlanta club.

In rehab, it was expected that the patient would share an account of his past substance abuse with others in his treatment group. This quickly became a problem for Brown, because his confessions of bad behavior and so forth brought into the discussion his relationship with high-profile Whitney. Details of some of these private sessions leaked to the outside world and became tabloid fodder. Meanwhile, Brown, who was being treated for alcohol dependency, was becoming frustrated because the rules at Betty Ford required that he have no contact with his loved ones, Whitney and Bobbi Kristina, until he had kicked his addiction. Bridling at the facility's stringent dictates, Brown soon left the Ford Center and transferred to the more liberal Charter Peachford Hospital in Atlanta, which charged $1,000 a day for its treatment program.

During this period, in November 1995, Whitney flew to Atlanta with

Bobbi Kristina and an assistant and checked into the posh Nikko Hotel (at $750 a night). Brown arranged a pass from Charter Peachford so he and his wife could discuss their badly faltering marriage. Their chat turned into a twelve-hour talkathon. Later, the couple dined with their child in the establishment's exclusive Japanese restaurant. Brown still had at least another week to go at the hospital, and it was suggested that since Whitney was now in town she might wish to sit in on his group counseling sessions. She declined, not wishing to air their problems in public.

Around the end of that month, Whitney joined her *Waiting to Exhale* costars on an episode of Oprah Winfrey's national TV talk show to promote the film's upcoming release. The hostess began asking Houston leading personal questions. The star retorted, "It's none of your business." Then she added, "Bobby is fine. That's all I want to say [on the subject]." During a commercial break, Whitney reached for a white handkerchief and dabbed at her teary eyes. Actress Angela Bassett clasped her hand, while Winfrey tried to comfort her upset guest. By the time the show resumed, Whitney had recovered her composure and perked up considerably for the rest of the televised hour.

As her traumatic year came to a close, Whitney was saluted at New York City Center for her accomplishments in music and film. When she addressed the audience, she made no mention of Bobby Brown, but looked out at his daughter seated in a front-row seat and said to her emotionally, "You are my reason for being."

Not too long afterwards, the diva was vacationing at her getaway home in Miami. When she met with the press at a beach near her condo, she arrived in a form-fitting purple dress walking hand-in-hand with Bobby Brown! When not gazing romantically at her mate, she insisted to the reporters, "People think I'm Miss Prissy Pooh-Pooh, but I'm not; I like to have fun. I can get down, really freakin' dirty with you. I was born in Newark, New Jersey, with two brothers and a very strong father. It made me tough—perhaps too tough."

During this same period of readjustment, Whitney and Bobby showed up at Bar None, a trendy nightspot in Miami's South Beach. They were later seen in an upstairs VIP room. There, Whitney sipped Cristal champagne while her husband drank two Bud Light beers. (This was the same Bobby Brown who had recently told a national magazine, "The bottle's out of my life now, so everything is all good.") Later, while the Browns were dancing, a young female asked Bobby for his autograph. He declined politely, but Whitney uttered a vehement, "Please *leave* him alone!"

In rounding up 1995, *People* magazine said of Whitney Houston and Bobby Brown: "Stories about the trials and tribulations of her three-and-a-half-year-old marriage to Brown have been as familiar as the strains of 'I Will Always Love You,' Houston's monster single from her first film, *The Bodyguard*. In the three years since that blockbuster movie secured Houston's superstar status, her once-perfect Prom Queen of Soul façade has begun to crack as her marriage has become increasingly strained and she seems, at times, to be losing touch with her audience."

In the midst of all of this unsolicited media advice, Houston gamely—and sharply—told *TV Guide*: "We'll work our problems out, not we and the world."

21

I Believe in You and Me

*"I'm a singer turned actress, not the other way around. I haven't lost any
enthusiasm for music. I have lost enthusiasm for the music industry, because
it sucks. It's unfair. There are some real crappy people looking to screw you.
Industry people are nosy, and they talk about you behind your back."*

WHITNEY HOUSTON, 1996

As 1996 got underway, thirty-two-year-old Whitney Houston was in a
flurry of filmmaking activity. Perhaps she was making up for all that
professional downtime in recent years. Maybe it was prompted by a
growing awareness that her years as a screen ingénue were fast evaporating.
Or, possibly, Houston simply wished to distract herself from her
increasingly complex personal life.

In any event, Whitney's production company had lately acquired screen
rights to Donald Bogle's recent biography of Dorothy Dandridge. The
latter was the beautiful, talented black actress and singer who had endured
a tragic life and died a (possible) suicide in 1965. News of Whitney's
plans upset Janet Jackson, who had already announced she wanted to star
in a Dandridge biopic. Tensions between the two camps mounted, with the
press providing updates on the progress of each competing project.
(Adding a bit of personal fuel to the rivalry between the two singing stars
was the fact that Jackson had dated Bobby Brown before Houston came
on the scene.) At first, Whitney considered starring in the film herself, and
then at other times she professed that she would only produce the venture.
Eventually, neither Whitney nor Jackson would play Dandridge on screen.
Instead, it would be non-singer Halle Berry who headlined the 1999

made-for-cable feature, entitled *Introducing Dorothy Dandridge*. Halle would win an Emmy for her striking performance, for which she lip-synched the songs to the recordings of ghost singer Wendi Williams.

Meanwhile, Whitney's Houston Productions had signed a two-year, non-exclusive, first-look development and production pact with Touchstone Pictures. The terms provided that the singer's firm would produce theatrical features and TV programs for the Walt Disney Company under the Touchstone banner. One of these upcoming projects would be Whitney's long-planned made-for-television musical *Rodgers and Hammerstein's Cinderella*. Providing the day-to-day stewardship of Houston Productions would be Debra Martin Chase, who had come to Houston Productions the previous October as executive vice president and producing partner. Formerly, Chase had been senior vice president and head of Denzel Washington's production company.

Even as these new deals were being structured, several of the participating parties were already doing business together. In January 1996, Whitney began shooting *The Preacher's Wife*, to be released by Touchstone Pictures and teaming Houston with Denzel Washington, whose production firm (Mundy Lane Entertainment) was one of those involved.

A few years earlier, Whitney and Denzel had been spoken of as possible costars in *A Star Is Born*. While that particular project did not come to pass, the notion of teaming up two of Hollywood's most attractive African-American stars in the same picture lingered. Later, the concept of remaking *The Bishop's Wife* (1947), the Loretta Young–Cary Grant–David Niven Christmas whimsy, was suggested as a replacement vehicle. Houston recalls, "Denzel and his wife, Pauletta, and myself met in a restaurant in Los Angeles last year and we sat for hours talking about the [black] community. You look around you, and you see our brothers and sisters going down. It seems like our young generation has no fear anymore, and surely no fear of dying. They don't realize they are useless in death. So we felt that this [screen project] was about the community taking charge again and raising our children."

Another factor that appealed to Whitney about the film was that it would give her "the opportunity to sing a kind of music that I love most and to sing to the Creator that I love most." She was referring to gospel songs, which had been and were still so much a part of her life. Unlike *Waiting to Exhale*, for which she had to be persuaded to participate in singing onscreen and on the soundtrack album, this time she required no such convincing. She relished the notion of being an executive producer (billed ahead of Arista's Clive Davis) on the album and having a major say about the choice and execution of the music, along with the artists that were to participate.

Yet another factor bringing pleasure to Whitney on this assignment was her fee. She was to be paid $10 million, making her Hollywood's highest-paid black actress. It was certainly a sweet revenge on all those naysayers who had said—before *The Bodyguard* made its impressive bow—that Whitney Houston would never become a force to be reckoned with in Tinseltown.

As restructured for the 1990s and given a black point of view, *The Preacher's Wife* now focused on an African-American clergyman in an unspecified part of New York having a crisis of faith about how best to serve his inner-city community. He is also conflicted about whether he should go along with the scheme of a grasping real-estate tycoon who wants to raze the neighborhood church (to make way for a business enterprise) and rebuild it in the suburbs. Simultaneously, the preacher is having difficulties in his marriage because he too often ignores his loving wife (the choir director; this was the role intended for Whitney Houston) to pursue his secular work in the community. In the process, he has become a pedantic workaholic.

Sent from above to resolve the preacher's dual dilemma is a chipper angel (to be played by Denzel Washington) who has not yet adjusted to his ethereal posting and sorely misses earthly pleasures. Before the angel's complex assignment on Earth is completed, he falls in love with the beautiful preacher's wife (which reawakens the preacher's love for his spouse). Eventually, the heavenly visitor accepts that this hoped-for romance can never be realized. With his job accomplished, he wistfully returns to paradise. Before vanishing, he arranges that none of the interested parties will remember him per se—they will only have the feeling and spirit of wellbeing and joy that he has inspired.

To costar with Whitney and Denzel, Courtney B. Vance was cast as the Reverend Henry Biggs. The established actor (*Hamburger Hill, The Tuskegee Airmen*) would marry Whitney's *Waiting to Exhale* costar Angela Bassett in the coming year. A few alumnae from the latter feature also joined the cast of *The Preacher's Wife*. Gregory Hines was hired to play the scheming real-estate huckster and Loretta Devine was brought on board as the husband-hunting church secretary. Jenifer Lewis, noted for her broad comedy roles, was contracted to appear as the sassy, interfering mother of Whitney's character. Houston's real-life mom, Cissy, joined the proceedings as Mrs.

Havergal, one of the choir members at St. Matthew's Baptist Church. This casting would provide a reversal of real life, as Whitney played the choir master instructing Cissy and the other church singers on how their song numbers should be performed.

As director of this family-oriented picture, the studio selected Penny Marshall. The former comedian, best known for her TV sitcom *Laverne & Shirley* (1976–1983), had become a film director and had made a number of successful features such as *Big* (1988) and *A League of Their Own* (1992). (She had also had her share of box-office disappointments, such as 1994's *The Renaissance Man*, starring Danny DeVito.)

On the surface, Marshall seemed a strange choice to helm this black project, but she professed to have great appreciation for spiritual music. In addition, she had directed Madonna in *A League of Their Own* and it was reasoned that if she could handle one diva effectively on camera she could do equally well with another. When asked if she felt Whitney Houston was appropriate for the female lead, Marshall quipped, "She was right for the part. I mean, not a million people come to mind."

After a few days of working together, Whitney and Marshall came to an understanding about the star's habit of arriving late on the set and other difficult matters. Marshall learned to schedule around the self-focused star, who kept insisting that she did not abide by filmmaking rules: "I'm music. I'm *not* film." Marshall would later acknowledge that Whitney was "very directable. You ask her to do something, and she does it. With Whitney, there were certain things she couldn't do, like with Madonna, but she was very eager. Because they're larger than life, people are afraid to tell them to do things. People are afraid to say to them, 'It's not so good.' They're not intimidating; [it's just that] people are afraid of them."

In capturing Whitney in the title role, Penny had a creative hurdle to overcome: "Here's a girl who's a business, a conglomerate. I had to make her more passive." Fortunately, Houston understood and accepted the need to tone down her actual personality on camera. She reasoned, "I grew up in the church. . . . I knew the elements. I saw the preachers' wives. I don't know firsthand what it takes, but I truly believe that just being a woman you have to submit to certain things. As a preacher's wife, one of the rules is to be submissive. . . . I have been that in real life. Although I couldn't be that submissive. The role of the wife, it takes . . . diplomacy."

The Preacher's Wife was shot on location on the East Coast in areas of New York, New Jersey, and Maine. One of the first sequences to be filmed was the ice-skating scene, which was executed at Deering Oaks, Maine.

Unfortunately, there had been a recent "warm" spell, which made the pond's frozen top layers of water somewhat unstable. Stunt doubles were used for the fancy footwork the lead characters undertake in this sequence, while Houston and Washington did the close-up work.

The skating scene was key to establishing the beginning of the emotional chemistry between the couple, with Denzel Washington's angel flirting with Whitney's married woman and her being flattered by this burst of attention after being ignored so much lately by her overworked spouse. From the start, Whitney and Washington had a good working rapport. She was extremely impressed by his acting talents and would enthuse, "You have to watch Denzel because it's all in his eyes. And in his movement and the way he stands. He doesn't have to say a word. Charisma and charm exude from Denzel." With this handsome star, she felt like she was working with an "older brother," having absorbed his "flavor and character" from several of his prior screen performances. She found him "a gentleman, very funny, silly like me" and "very easy to work with. He's an old pro."

One on-set observer was particularly suspicious about the growing camaraderie between Whitney and Washington. That was Bobby Brown, who had come to visit his wife on location in Maine. Knowing that longtime family man Washington and his wife, Pauletta, were going through a marital adjustment, Bobby was extra-sensitive to the obvious affinity between the two costars. One evening, when cast and crew dined at DiMillo's restaurant in Portland, Maine, Brown was sulky, and after a few drinks he let everyone know the reasons for his unhappiness. It put a distinct damper on the lighthearted tone of the get-together. Almost everyone was relieved when Bobby departed a few days later.

Actually, throughout production Washington proved to be very supportive of Whitney in their scenes together and did his best to be a good listener when she confided in him about some of her domestic concerns. Regarding the media-touted "romance" between Whitney and himself, Washington would counter, "I read that Whitney and I hated each other's guts. The newspapers printed so many lies. One day I'm reading that we're tearing each other apart, and the next the rags are saying that Whitney and I are both leaving our families because we've fallen in love and plan to get married. It's all such garbage."

For Whitney, the highlights of making this movie were the gospel interludes on screen and recording the numbers to be used for the soundtrack album. She enthused, "When I come onto the set of this movie, it's very spiritual. Last week we had the choir here. We were doing our scenes together. I'm singing and the choir is singing, and all of a sudden it got out of hand where we couldn't control the spirit that took us over. And we just kept going and going. It wasn't part of the movie, but it was part of our feeling." She continued, "We were all affected spiritually by this film. When you deal with the Spirit of God, you're truly calling upon it to enter you and it touches everyone. When we were doing the church scenes and were singing, the Holy Spirit came down and took over. I saw people crying, people were inspired who might not normally be moved. But the Spirit has a way of loving and arousing everyone. You cry, and you shout, and you give thanks."

As the filming drew to a close in spring 1996, Whitney was happy to return to her regular lifestyle in familiar surroundings. She explained, "I'm not what [the press] makes me out to be . . . I'm not Hollywood. I'm not industry. I don't have dinner with them. People I've known for years I'm still friends with. I like to be with the people I know."

Obviously geared towards Yuletide filmgoers, *The Preacher's Wife* had its special premiere at the Ziegfeld Theater in New York City on December 12, 1996. After the gala screening, the guests adjourned to the Roseland Theater, which had been converted into a chic supper club for the night. Celebrities in attendance ranged from Michael Ovitz, head of Disney, to the Artist Formerly Known as Prince. For entertainment, the Georgia Mass Choir performed three songs, and then Whitney came on stage to sing various numbers from the picture. Before she finished, she was joined first by castmates Shirley Caesar, Jenifer Lewis, and Loretta Divine, and, for the finale, by the rest of the available *Preacher's Wife* ensemble. Excerpts from the premiere and party were aired on VH1.

The following day, Friday the thirteenth, the PG-rated feature debuted across North America. *Boxoffice* magazine suggested that "criticizing a film like *The Preacher's Wife* seems a little like criticizing a useless Christmas gift. In both cases, it's the thought that counts." Roger Ebert in the *Chicago Sun-Times* rated the effort a "sweet and good-hearted comedy" but admitted he would have preferred it to have "more punch and bite." In the *San Francisco Chronicle*, Peter Stack warned readers that "the story is so predictable and the setting so romanticized that it's a wonder this film can hold the interest it does." Joan H. Allen of the African-American newspaper *New York Amsterdam News* insisted, "Gospel is the music that keeps this film together which sometimes plays like a music video." *Time* magazine judged the lengthy release "noble sludge."

As to the cast, reviewers and public alike were most taken with young Justin Pierre Edmund, who so winningly portrayed the preacher's son. There was general disappointment at the lack of chemistry that came across on screen between handsome Denzel and beautiful Whitney and that too much of the film was played (by the supporting characters) for broad comedy or cardboard villainy.

Regarding Whitney's participation in the lightweight picture, Peter Stack concluded that she displays a "divine talent for being virtuous and flirtatious at the same time." Roger Ebert was appreciative of "the way Houston sings." For Leonard Klady in *Variety*, "Houston remains more a presence than an actress, but she is extremely commanding all the same. She's stellar at the microphone and, flanked by Washington and Vance, a credible dramatic foil."

Robin Givhan of the *Washington Post* was on the mark when, after complimenting Whitney for playing her assignment with warmth, she observed, "Her challenge in this movie is to rise above a stupendously ill-fitting wig that in some scenes pooches out in back like a ducktail and in others looks to have landed accidentally and haphazardly on her noggin. The thing has a life of its own. She tries valiantly to upstage that rug by emoting with wrinkled brow, rolling eyes and singing with a voice that could blow the roof off St. Matthew's Baptist Church, the fictional site of this Christmas tale." It should also be noted that Whitney wore a most unflattering wardrobe throughout the picture.

Liese Spencer of *Sight and Sound* felt that converting *The Preacher's Wife* into a starring singing platform for Houston had distorted the overall film. As she explained, "The story becomes a kind of pop-gospel musical, its whole structure fitted around Houston's show-stoppers." Spencer allowed, though, that "this showcasing of Houston may be the reason the rest of the film feels so thin, but the moments when she sings are also the only time that the picture come alive."

For many of the reasons cited above, the expensive-to-mount *The Preacher's Wife* did not fare well at the box office, grossing only $44.09 million in its domestic release. (This was $10 million less than *The Bodyguard* had earned in video rentals alone.) Some months later, when Penny Marshall was asked to name the biggest box-office turkey of her career, she cited not *Jumpin' Jack Flash* (the 1986 flop comedy with Whoopi Goldberg), but *The Preacher's Wife*. Said the filmmaker in her trademark nasal whine, "I made the movie because I like gospel music. I'm not sure why Whitney Houston or Denzel Washington made it."

Fortunately, the popularity of the soundtrack album of *The Preacher's Wife* helped to compensate Whitney creatively for the artistic disappointments of her new picture. In devoting herself wholeheartedly to the project, she gushed, "Gospel taught me a wide range of things: how to sing fast, how to sing slow, how to sing when the tempo changes in the middle of a song. How to sing four-part harmony without thinking about it. And how to sing without music, which is how you learn everything there is to learn about music—in terms of your voice being the instrument, your feet being the drum, your hands [and she begins clapping] being the tambourine." Warming to her subject, she pointed out, "I make great records that transcend the barriers between white and black, fat and skinny, gay and straight. With pop records, you have to be restrained because you're making songs for the Top 40. With gospel, you're singing to the spirit of God, so everything comes out."

Of the disc's fifteen tracks, Whitney is heard on fourteen. "I Believe in You and Me," written by David Wolfert and Sandy Linzer, reached number four on the music charts. Her rendition of Annie Lennox's "Step by Step" leveled off at number fifteen, but it was accompanied by a very high-energy music video (again with a supporting cast of dancers doing all the impressive steps) and, in its remix formats (of which there were several), got much airplay.

Entertainment Weekly rated the soundtrack to *The Preacher's Wife* an A, while *USA Today* complimented Whitney's voice, which "soars." Chris Dickinson of the *St. Louis Post-Dispatch* commented, "She fuses her current pop impulses with her gospel roots. Many of these pop-gospel numbers swing with bright melody, aided frequently by a mighty back-up assistance from the Georgia Mass Choir. . . . To winning effect, Houston layers a good deal of vocal grit against the smooth strains of the Babyface-produced cut 'My Heart Is Calling.' With the accompaniment of husband Bobby Brown, Faith Evans, Johnny Gill, Monica, and Ralph Tresvant, she enters contemporary funk-land with 'Somebody Bigger Than You and I.'"

Adding to the chorus of approval was *Newsday's* Martin Johnson: "It sounds like the recording Houston has wanted to make for a long time. It is mostly a roots recording. . . . The giggle in her voice that animated her early work is back. Often she has sounded as if singing was her investment in a lucrative career; here it sounds like she's singing for the pure joy of making music."

The Preacher's Wife album would peak on American music charts at number three. With sales of over 3 million copies in the U.S. alone, the disc was one of the biggest-selling gospel albums of all time. It was nominated for a Grammy in the R&B category (which upset Houston, who felt it should have been judged as a gospel entry) and for an American Music Award in the Favorite Soundtrack category.

Unlike the *Waiting to Exhale* soundtrack album, which had contained no mention of Bobby Brown, on *The Preacher's Wife* disc Whitney's husband was asked to perform with her and others on one track ("Somebody Bigger Than You and I"). Whitney was also clearly in good spirits about her man when she wrote in the liner notes: "To my husband Bobby—what God has put together, let no man put asunder. Honey, I am blessed to have you. You've been my strength and my shield in so many ways. I can't count them. I love you."

It was amazing that Houston could express such high praise about her spouse at the end of 1996, given the amount of chaos that characterized their past year together *and* apart. For example, one item on their agenda of domestic dissension was the matter of the Boston woman who was claiming that her newborn baby girl was the result of a get-together with Bobby Brown that purportedly had occurred *after* his marriage to Whitney. Now involved in a paternity case over the matter, defendant Brown told *Sister 2 Sister* magazine: "It's bullshit. Women just do that. I'm going to give my blood and show that the baby is not mine." The delicate situation, however, soon disappeared from the media's radar.

On the matter of his financial assets, Bobby confided to the same publication: "I've had some financial difficulties but all that is taken care of. And no, I'm not being supported by my wife. I am a writer-producer who has a string of hits and receives checks weekly. I don't think I could ever be broke with the gifts that God gave me. You never say never but I don't think I'll ever be broke as long as I have God in my life." As to the ongoing Robyn Crawford situation, Brown insisted the two had no serious disagreement. In fact, the New Jack Swinger revealed, "Me and Robyn are tight. We have problems because of the fact that she handles my wife's business. . . . There are some things that I see could be handled differently. . . . As far as anything else, no."

Regarding the matter of substance abuse, Bobby's position was that liquor was his only stumbling block. "I did have a problem with drinking. I was drinking to get drunk. I would go wild and drink and try to wash away what was being said about me, my wife, my family. . . . But I recognized that you can't drink those problems away." This was the same "reformed" individual who, in early 1996, had been involved in a ruckus at Los Angeles' chic Bel Age Hotel. He'd been in the lobby one morning at about 3 A.M., reputedly inebriated. He got into a dispute with a rocker there. Apparently, in the altercation that followed, Brown had been hit and was bleeding. Now further riled, he was screaming angry threats at his opponent. When the police arrived, Bobby was given the choice of returning to his room upstairs or being taken to jail. Growing truculent, he refused to yield ground until his brother Tommy led him forcibly into an elevator.

While Whitney, then still making *The Preacher's Wife*, was absorbing news of this latest embarrassment, her brother Gary was arrested for alleged possession of drugs on March 7, 1996. Her older sibling lived in Kingstown, North Carolina, where he had apparently happened on a police stakeout. He had grown suddenly fearful and had attempted to flee. Reportedly, the police found in his possession a crack pipe and five rocks of cocaine. After being charged at the police station with alleged felony drug possession, possession of drug paraphernalia, and resisting arrest, he was released after posting bail of $11,000. Gary, who worked at his wife's gift shop in the area, had been charged with a similar offense in 1989. After being freed, he told reporters, "I made a mistake." Weeks later, the tabloids were publishing accounts that Whitney had offered to complete payments for the new house that Gary and Patricia were building in North Carolina if her brother would enter a rehab program.

But still worse events lay ahead.

At around 3 A.M. on April 23, 1996, Atlanta police stopped and arrested Bobby Brown on the outskirts of town for reportedly driving his red Mercedes-Benz over the posted speed limit and for weaving in and out of the traffic. At the time of the arrest, he was accompanied in the car by a young woman whom he said he had met earlier in a bar. Brown had no insurance papers with him. When asked to take a sobriety test on the spot, he proved to be unsteady on his feet and it took him three tries to recite the alphabet in full and in order. After refusing to take a breathalyzer test—because he said he'd already admitted he had been drinking—he was placed under arrest. (Bobby's female companion was not arrested.) By now, he had become quarrelsome. After being taken to jail, Brown was released later that same day on bail of $1,260. A court date to hear the case was eventually set for 1997, an appointment the defendant would fail to keep, leading to further complications for him.

It must have been a relief from the ongoing drama in her life for Whitney to cohost the 9th Annual Kids' Choice Awards on May 11, 1996. Asked why she was taking on this chore for the Nickelodeon cable network, Houston explained that kids "read a lot of crap printed about me. It's just crap. And I don't want them to believe that that is me." Demonstrating that she still had a sense of humor, she indicated that a bonus of her emceeing duties was, "I can just wear jeans and sneakers and no one will tee off on my wardrobe." Furthermore, she confided, "For once I can just not worry about satisfying everyone's expectations."

In mid-1996, Whitney had troubles with Robyn Crawford, if the supermarket newspapers were to be believed. Purportedly, the two longtime friends argued over the career path of a young would-be singer they were both guiding professionally. According to the *Globe*, an irate Whitney worked off her anger by destroying hundreds of copies of a photo of herself and Crawford.

Next, it was John Houston who caused fresh concerns for the beleaguered Whitney. During the summer, he and his thirty-four-year-old wife had a spat at their Fort Lee, New Jersey home which led to the police intervening, and a court hearing was scheduled to resolve matters. When the singer's publicist was asked how her client felt about this turn of events, she said, "Of course Whitney was distressed. Her father suffers from heart problems and is a diabetic."

Thereafter, it was trouble-prone Bobby, having finished recording tracks for his reunion album with New Edition, who was back in the news yet again. In mid-August 1996, he was driving Whitney's black Porsche on a residential street just south of Fort Lauderdale in Florida. The car smacked into a street sign and also damaged shrubbery. The impact caused the vehicle's airbag to open. Brown maneuvered himself out of the wreck and crawled to the curb, where he sat nursing injuries to his leg and neck. According to a bystander, Brown cried out, "It's my legs, my legs, they're all messed up. For God's sake somebody get me help." The singer was taken to Hollywood Memorial Hospital, where he was treated for whiplash, bruised ribs, and a broken anklebone. The police report claimed Brown's blood alcohol level was above 0.2 percent—more than double Florida's 0.08 percent limit—and blood tests detected the presence of drugs. With Bobby out on bail once again, the case began its slow progress through the court system. Meanwhile, according to one media report, a few days after his Florida car accident, Brown was spotted carousing with pals at a Miami restaurant, flirting with women, and partying at a South Beach hotel.

Weeks later, when Bobby and the other members of New Edition were guests on Oprah Winfrey's TV chat show, he was still using a cane. He mentioned the car accident but carefully stated the mishap was not his fault and that he had lost control of the vehicle. He said, "I have the blood of Jesus all over me." On the same program, Brown referred to his stay at the Betty Ford Clinic, stressing that it was just for alcohol abuse. He claimed that part of the reason he drank heavily was in reaction to the bad press he was enduring and how unhappy it made him feel. Then, in what had to be the understatement of the year—or decade—he offered his own opinion on himself: "It's not that I'm bad, it's just that I'm outgoing and a very different type of person."

In late November 1996, Whitney Houston and the Georgia Mass Choir sang a medley of songs ("I Love the Lord" and "Joy to the World") from *The Preacher's Wife* to open a TV special entitled *Celebrate the Dream: 50 Years of Ebony* (the black U.S. magazine).

By that time, Whitney had confirmed to the world that she was indeed pregnant again, and that her and Bobby's baby was due in July of the following year. As a result, she planned to take life easy over the coming months, except, perhaps, for a two-week concert trip to Japan and a few additional appearances to promote the forthcoming *The Preacher's Wife*. In her new earth-mother mode, she informed E! TV's *News Gossip* show: "Me and Bobby protect each other. He watches out for me and I watch out for him. You try to hurt Bobby and I'll go for your throat."

As Whitney looked ahead to the holidays, she must have sighed with relief. She admitted, "I thought I would lose my mind . . . [a few months] ago, but the 'too much' part is over now. Movie's done, album's done, baby's on the way, husband and daughter are in place, everyone is healthy and strong. It's a very happy time."

22

Walking the Tightrope

"I've grown. I think the changes come when you finally realize you've stopped living for yourself and you're living for someone else. And that you can't eat by yourself anymore, and you can't go to the bathroom by yourself anymore; 'Mo-om!' You know, the whole thing. But it's great."

WHITNEY HOUSTON, 1997

In late 1996, Whitney had reasoned to *USA Today*, "Maybe people think I'm a bitch because I know how to say no. As you get older, you find out how to take care of yourself in this business. I watched Gladys [Knight] and Dionne [Warwick] and Aretha [Franklin] say, 'This is the cut-off. I'll do this much and no more.' I've learned from them."

One of those who felt Houston was a walking tornado was Kevin Ammons, a singer who had been romantically involved with Whitney's publicist, Regina Brown, in the early 1990s. In November 1996, his book (written with Nancy Bacon) *Good Girl, Bad Girl: An Insider's Biography of Whitney Houston* was published. This unauthorized tome dealt with such topics as "Why Whitney really married Bobby Brown," "Why her close childhood friend Robyn Crawford threatened suicide," and "Why Whitney refused to heed doctors' warnings that she will ruin her voice." The book presented Houston's family as highly dysfunctional, claimed that Whitney constantly reminded her cowed staff (known as the Royal Family) to "Remember who the goose is that lays the golden egg," and alleged that the world-famous singer had a growing penchant for drug abuse. At the time of its release, many of Whitney's fans around the world refused to accept this bleak, possibly biased, account as the truth. However, a few years later, as new facts about Houston's personal life came to light, Ammons's graphic account acquired some credibility.

In early 1997, Houston was making further new adjustments to her ever-turbulent life. Of primary concern was her recent miscarriage—her third.

In mid-December 1996, Bobby Brown had been in Los Angeles recording the New Edition reunion album. He and Whitney were once again battling, this time because she'd heard fresh rumors that her husband was partying heavily and that he'd been seen flirting with various women while on the West Coast. Furious with her spouse, who was 3,000 miles away, Whitney, back at her New Jersey estate, tried to remain calm because of her pregnancy. When she began spotting and having stomach pains, her physician prescribed total bed rest. By the next day, she had developed flu, and her doctor had her hospitalized at Saint Barnabas Medical Center in Livingston, New Jersey (where she had given birth nearly four years earlier to Bobbi Kristina). On December 19, Houston suffered a miscarriage. It was difficult enough for her to deal with this loss, but she particularly dreaded telling her daughter that she would not be gaining the little baby brother or sister she had expected. When Whitney phoned Bobby in Beverly Hills, he was so upset by the bad news that he reportedly trashed his hotel room. Thereafter, when he arrived late at the recording studios in Burbank, he was in an explosive mood. After arguing with the New Edition crew over this and that, he left the facility and flew back east to be with Whitney.

In early January 1997, Bobby set off on tour with New Edition. When they performed at Manhattan's Madison Square Garden, Whitney was in good enough spirits to come on stage during a break in the lengthy show to say hello to the audience.

The next month, the tabloids were packed with headlines about the latest escapades of the battling Browns. The *National Enquirer*'s account was emblazoned with the title "Bad Boy Bobby Beats Whitney . . . Twice!" The story recounted that, in early January, the couple had fought with one another—both verbally and physically—at an Atlanta hotel. A similar scenario was played out when the couple moved on to Los Angeles later that month for a music-industry awards show. The topic of contention was again the question of Bobby's fidelity. Their ongoing argument was temporarily adjourned when Bobby left to board one of New Edition's tour buses, but then Whitney came on board and the feuding resumed. Before their bus reached its destination of Salt Lake City, Utah, Bobby had fixated on the notion that Whitney had taken out a life-insurance policy on him recently because she was thinking of having him liquidated. Hopping mad, he made an unscheduled stop in Moab, Utah, where he trotted down the deserted road until he happened upon a junkyard. There he begged its bewildered owners to sell him a firearm for self-protection. According to the *National Enquirer* report, the police were hastily summoned. To resolve the argument, Whitney was ordered onto a separate bus from Bobby. When everyone arrived in Salt Lake City, a fuming Whitney flew back to New Jersey, while Bobby undertook the scheduled shows with his bandmates.

In early February, Brown was scheduled to appear in a DeKalb County, Georgia courtroom to deal with his April 1996 arrest for allegedly driving under the influence of alcohol, having no proof of insurance, failing to maintain his car in the lane, and speeding. The media was present in force that day hoping to videotape Bobby's special appearance. However, when his attorney told the court that he would be making Brown's plea *in absentia*, state court judge Wayne Purdom adjourned proceedings until February 14. When the singer failed to appear in court a second time, Purdom issued a bench warrant and Bobby forfeited his $1,260 bond.

While Brown was avoiding courtrooms, Whitney appeared at the 28th Annual Image Awards held on February 8 in Pasadena, California. She won three trophies that evening for *The Preacher's Wife*: Best Motion Picture Actress, Best Gospel Artist, and Best Soundtrack Album. Later that spring, Whitney would do her own no-show when she was awarded the Triumphant Spirit Award by *Essence* magazine at their annual celebration. She was cited for this honor because her "consummate professionalism has been matched by empowering philanthropy." When Houston announced she could not attend the function—she was supposedly busy in Florida— her mother accepted the prestigious award on her behalf.

By mid-1997, Bobby Brown and New Edition had once again gone their separate ways, while he and Whitney were once more enmeshed in their nightmarish cycle of codependency. The two jetted off to Hawaii in June in search of rest and relaxation. However, once there, they soon provided fresh fodder for the media. While in Honolulu, they went on a shopping expedition to a local mall. The pair began arguing in the parking lot and, supposedly, Brown slapped Whitney in the face. Reportedly, Whitney refused to cooperate with a subsequent police investigation. Later, her publicist put a media spin on the negative episode, insisting that the reported encounter had actually involved someone who looked like Whitney Houston.

The following month, the couple joined a few friends and relatives—including Whitney's brother Michael and his wife, Donna—aboard the 120-foot luxury yacht *Aquasitium* in the Mediterranean. What was supposed to be a joyful second honeymoon turned into a publicity debacle. During their voyage, Houston suffered a small but deep cut to her face while the yacht was anchored off Capri. She was brought to the island's Giuseppe Capilupi Hospital, where she received two stitches to close the two-inch gash on her left cheek. The attending physician reported that the patient had been crying profusely and seemed concerned that the sutures might leave a permanent scar. Local police were brought in to investigate the matter because of the conflicting accounts of what had caused the injury. The singer told authorities that she had hurt herself when she scraped against a razor-sharp rock while swimming. On the other hand, a crew member aboard the yacht insisted that Whitney had been injured while on the boat. Later, Bobby Brown provided his own recollection of the incident. The couple had been eating lunch on the yacht. Whitney had arisen too quickly and her hands slipped, causing plates to fly. One of the dishes broke and a fragment had hit her cheek, causing the cut.

The controversy around Whitney's injury became the news story of the moment and it simply would not fade away. Although the police eventually dropped their enquiry due to the lack of any hard facts, the incident became a standard part of the Browns' biographical résumé whenever the press recited the past history of their relationship. By the time Whitney made her next public appearance at the dedication of the new 23,547-seat Arthur Ashe Stadium in Flushing Meadows, New York in late August 1997, her infamous scar was hardly noticeable. She admitted that she was unsure now if she would bother to have cosmetic surgery to fix it. Brown did not accompany his wife at the event.

That October, there were fresh rumors of Whitney and Bobby clashing in public. This time he was reported to have slapped her face as she stepped out of a limousine. However, despite all these rumored incidents, Whitney remained unshakably faithful to her husband. She seemed to gain strength and satisfaction each time she defended him anew to the press. For example, she informed *Sister 2 Sister* magazine in their October 1997 issue: "I feel secure that this man loves me. I know that. We're friends. . . . I'm in love with him and he's in love with me and ain't no funny stuff going on. It's real. I have no doubts about that. We got a good thing going." She continued, "Bobby fights men. Bobby don't beat on women. To him, that's really beneath a man's standards as far as he's concerned. . . . That's how he feels about it . . . He likes to fight men. . . . He likes a challenge. My husband is all boy."

Meanwhile, Bobby was maintaining to the world that his union to Whitney would last forever—perhaps: "We are together today and we are going to be together tomorrow and we plan on being together on the day after that." But he then qualified his prediction with, "You know you can only plan on being together as long as you are together. . . . We are going to be together as long as we can be, as long as we want to be together."

While Brown was hedging his bets, his new solo album, entitled *Forever*, was released, but it received scant attention from record-buyers, who had already moved on to new favorites. Bobby's plan to appear in the Miramax screen comedy *Ride* (1998), featuring Cedric the Entertainer, went awry. So did another film project—to be shot in Miami—in which Brown was, ironically, to have played a court-appointed attorney trying to get local street gangs to make peace.

With too much time on his hands, Bobby now had ample opportunity to speak to the press. He acknowledged, "I have a really bad temper, but I think it takes folks to ignite me. I've calmed it down as much as I can. I was born with a temper. My kids have quick tempers. I won't disrespect someone unless they disrespect me first." On the subject of himself and his wife, he admitted he had his sensitive points, especially when someone called him Mr. Houston or if they referred to Whitney as Mrs. Houston in his presence. Said Bobby, "That's like slapping me in the face." As to his reputation as a cheat, his comments managed to blend thoughts on bigotry and adultery into the same discussion: "I'm not a prejudiced person. But if I'm going to cheat on my wife or doing anything, it's [going] to be a sister. Believe me!" That certainly must have made Whitney feel much better.

While Whitney's marital problems and personal misfortunes were being served up for public consumption, her professional life moved forward in small bursts. It was announced that Danny DeVito's Jersey Films was developing a feature version of the 1970s TV series *Get Christie Love!* as a project for Whitney at Universal Pictures. The star would play Detective Christie Love of the Los Angeles Police Department's special investigations unit. The project has yet to materialize on screen.

Then there was the disturbing matter of her two-hour concert (*Classic Whitney*) aired by HBO on October 5, 1997. (Obviously the cable network had chosen to overlook an earlier occasion when the artist had been invited to breakfast with top company executives: Whitney had dispatched a message to them indicating she was being paid to sing for them, *not* to dine with them.) The performance was taped live at Constitution Hall in Washington D.C. At the time, the singer claimed to be suffering from a cold, worrying about family concerns, and coping with assorted other personal problems.

When the program was broadcast, a dismayed *Entertainment Weekly* commented, "Clearly something was wrong during Houston's Oct. 5 live HBO concert, in which she strained to sing her tunes, reeled off a random, bewildering medley of tributes to dead celebrities—including the Notorious B.I.G. and Princess Diana—and dripped more flop sweat than [President Richard] Nixon. The *Washington Post* suggested that Whitney had had a "very public meltdown, physically and emotionally" during the performance, which they termed "a tape-delayed near-death experience." Those who attended both the taped dress rehearsal and the actual performance two days later claimed Whitney was far superior in tone and much more in control of her voice at the Friday-night run-through. On the other hand, everyone rated her spangled white gown "smashing."

As the press, music industry, and public wondered afresh about Whitney's welfare—professionally and personally—the star had yet another difficult encounter. This time, her adversary was popular TV talk show host Rosie O'Donnell, then known as the Queen of Nice.

Whitney was set to appear on O'Donnell's October 30, 1997 program, recorded in New York City, to promote her latest venture. This was *Rodgers and Hammerstein's Cinderella*, which was to air on Sunday, November 2 as part of ABC-TV's *The Wonderful World of Disney*. Houston was executive producer of the eighty-eight-minute musical and also played the role of the Fairy Godmother. (She had decided that at thirty-four years old, she was too mature to tackle the title role, which went to eighteen-year-old pop singer Brandy.) Rosie O'Donnell had generously earmarked an entire one-hour episode of her daily program to showcase Whitney and the cast of

Cinderella. About 9:15 A.M. that day, forty-five minutes before the show was to air live in front of a studio audience, Whitney's representatives phoned O'Donnell's office to say that she had been suddenly taken ill with stomach flu and was too indisposed to appear that morning.

The TV industry thrives on the unexpected and overcoming such last-minute obstacles, but this extremely late cancellation left O'Donnell badly frustrated and upset. Always one to speak her mind in public, the host was in rare form when she advised her audience that the singing star would not be appearing after all. Said the sarcastic comedian, "Whitney is not here. She's ill. I hope she's *very* ill." Refusing to let go of the issue, O'Donnell suggested during her interview with a perplexed Brandy, "If you could do Whitney Houston, we could pretend she was here." Later in the episode, O'Donnell looked into the camera with a devilish glint in her eye and mockingly proposed, "We should do a Whitney Houston song to bring a little of her essence here. . . . She'd probably have sung it if she showed up." At the end of the hour, Rosie improvised her own lyrics to "I Will Always Love You," singing "You didn't show up, but we love you." Finally, the *Cinderella* cast members joined the host for a rendition of the hit song from *The Bodyguard*. As the song came to an end, Rosie mouthed into the camera to an imaginary Whitney, "I'm going to call up. You'd better be sick."

What made a bad situation worse was that the same evening Bobby Brown was scheduled to appear on TV's *Late Night with David Letterman*. Who should turn up for the Manhattan taping but Whitney Houston, a fact duly reported back to Rosie O'Donnell. This turn of events made the gossip columns nationwide, with many sarcastic remarks about Whitney's strange behavior towards the much-loved O'Donnell. Days later, after O'Donnell had calmed down over the slight and the hassle caused by Whitney's absence, she commented publicly, "I'm sure that one day, when Whitney has another album, she will come back on the show. I'm not mad at her personally, [but] I did find it a little startling."

Eventually, the two personalities "made nice," and in the coming months Whitney would appear on O'Donnell's show to promote other new projects. But while the two joked on air about their past misunderstanding, Whitney continued to harbor bad feelings about what had happened. In late 1998, while talking to *Newsweek* magazine, Whitney brought up the unfortunate incident again. "I was very ill around that time, and my father was very sick. [There was] a lot of stress coming down on me at that point in time. The morning I was supposed to do *Rosie* I wasn't fit to do *Rosie*. And I figured that if I'm not presentable and if I'm not feeling it from here [points to her heart], then I'm going to do worse damage to myself by appearing. Rosie and I had a conversation about it, 'cause Rosie was mouthing off about a lot of stuff that we straightened out. But I don't hang with Rosie, and Rosie doesn't hang with me. I haven't been to her house for dinner, and she hasn't been to my house for dinner. Rosie knows nothing about me, and I don't know nothing about Rosie, so nobody can talk anything about me that ain't in my house. I was sick—it happens—forget what you heard. We've straightened it out fine now."

Rodgers and Hammerstein's Cinderella had first aired as a TV special in 1957 with Julie Andrews in the lead role. Tremendously popular at the time, it was restaged in 1965 with Lesley Ann Warren in the title part. In the new edition, coproduced by Whitney's company (now called BrownHouse Productions), the show had a multi-ethnic cast. Among the leads were several African Americans: Whitney Houston as the sassy Fairy Godmother, Whoopi Goldberg as the Queen, and Brandy as the doe-eyed young Cinderella. Her Prince Charming was played by Pablo Montalban from the Philippines. The roles of the wicked stepmother, the King, and Buttons, the royal aide and joker, were handled by Caucasian actors: Bernadette Peters, Victor Garber, and Jason Alexander. A few songs were borrowed from the extensive Rodgers and Hammerstein canon to round out the existing score and to balance the numbers allotted to the assorted characters.

Costing $12 million in all—a huge budget for a TV movie at the time—it was one of the most elaborate productions ever staged for the small screen, with a great deal of expense devoted to the colorful costumes, fanciful sets, and special effects such as the pumpkin turning into a carriage. For all that she had pushed so long and hard for the project to become a reality, Whitney often arrived late on the set and there were reports of tensions between the star and other members of the cast and crew. Later, in early July 1997, when the Disney studio gave the press a sneak preview of excerpts from the upcoming spectacular, Whitney was strangely absent. Having already completed her scenes for the project, she had chosen to fly to Europe to join her husband on a Mediterranean cruise (on which the cut-cheek incident had taken place).

When *Cinderella* was aired, it proved to be a light-hearted, low-key entertainment, buoyed up particularly by strong performances from brassy Bernadette Peters and earnest Pablo Montalban. Brandy had not yet attained the poise and refined figure that she would soon acquire. As to Whitney, she was encased in an unbecoming gown which accentuated both her protruding stomach and her bust line—the latter enhanced by breast implants which were inserted sometime after making *Waiting to Exhale*. She rather overplays her part as the hip, funky maker of dreams-come-true. (When she makes her entrance, she wisecracks to a bewildered Cinderella, "You'd rather have some old lady in a tutu?") Much more appealing is Houston's singing of "Impossible," in which her voice soars delightfully and is clear as a bell, as in years gone by.

Marilyn Moss of *Hollywood Reporter* noted, "There's something off about this musical *Cinderella*. . . . It has to do with the crawl of the whole affair; it moves at a snail's pace, and between production numbers it displays wide gaps of nothing going on. And when we get to the good stuff—the touching songs of Rodgers and Hammerstein—we're almost too petered out to care." As for Whitney, Moss reported, "As Cinderella's fairy godmother, Whitney Houston . . . revamps (almost to vamphood) the sweet and dowdy woman we're used to seeing. This fairy mom is feisty and forthright yet hardly a match in the chutzpah department for Bernadette Peters' riveting take on the wicked stepmother."

People magazine rated the show a B+. Its critic remarked, "Wishes do come true, insists this new production of the timeless fairy tale. Okay, we wish Brandy could sing like Whitney Houston." As to Whitney, the publication concluded, "Houston has too little to do, although she does get to exercise her pipes on the closing 'There's Music in You.'" *USA Today* was fairly positive in its assessment: "It's gaudy and garishly overproduced, but erring on the side of excess pays off in an exquisitely romantic ball sequence as the dreamiest of Cinderellas is led through the most lilting of waltz tunes ('Ten Minutes Ago') by the most dashing of young princes." The paper also pointed out, "Adding star presence: Whitney Houston as the glittery and slightly funky fairy godmother, who way overdoes her final number, overshadowing the kingdom like SuperDiva."

On the other hand, the public at large adored this musical movie. Over 60 million viewers in the U.S. alone watched the show, giving ABC-TV its best Sunday-night ratings in ten years. *Cinderella* would later be nominated for several Emmy Awards, winning one in the category of Outstanding Art Direction in a Variety, Musical, or Special. The huge commercial triumph of the show (and the home-entertainment versions released later) did a great deal to restore Whitney's luster in Hollywood. Items began popping up with regularity about new Whitney Houston projects such as *How to Marry a Black Man*, based on the book of the same name, which was to be made for Touchstone Films on the Disney studio lot.

Sometimes celebrities (or their representatives) get involved in sticky situations that they dearly wish they could have avoided. Whitney Houston had agreed to perform at "Blessing '97," which was to be a mass wedding performed on Saturday, November 29, 1997 at a Washington D.C. stadium by Reverend Sun Myung Moon as part of his World Culture and Sports Festival III. Reportedly, her salary for the unusual event was to be over $1 million. As the momentous day approached when over 2,500 couples would take their marriage vows at the stadium, Whitney had a change of heart and was a no-show. The event's promoters said she was "unable to perform due to a sudden illness." More to the point was that the singer and her staff had suddenly become aware that the ceremony was being sponsored by Moon's highly controversial Unification Church, and she now wanted no part in the rite (especially as the press was pointing up the bizarreness of the occasion and mocking her for wanting to perform at it). She returned her fee and pop star Jon Secada went on to entertain the newlyweds instead.

As 1997 snapped to an end, Whitney and Bobby were recovering from their latest trip to Hawaii, a location that seemed to stimulate unbridled behavior in the couple. Their most recent escapade had occurred in November, when they were visiting a club on the island of Maui. There were reports of raucous behavior among the Brown–Houston party, including suggestions of substance abuse. There was also a purported altercation between the party and a patron who had, he claimed, innocently passed by where Whitney was standing and accidentally brushed against her shoulder. This encounter had led to an unpleasant exchange and police were summoned to the scene before the situation calmed down.

Back on the mainland, Whitney received more unfavorable scrutiny in

December when the *New York Post* reported, "Pop diva Whitney Houston has stunned entertainment circles by severing her ties to longtime publicist Lois Smith. Neither side will comment on the split—but sources close to the action suspect Houston's hot-tempered hubby Bobby Brown could be behind it. As *The Post* reported last month, Brown has reportedly fired most of his wife's entourage and is pulling the strings himself. Other insiders speculate that Smith may at last have tired of running interference for the embattled Houston and dropped her."

Losing Smith, a chief buffer with the media and the public during this period of Whitney's increasingly bizarre behavior, was a misfortune indeed for the tumultuous Brown–Houston camp.

When not attending awards ceremonies in January 1998 (she picked up trophies at the People's Choice Awards and the TBS Trumpet Awards), Whitney was playing the dutiful wife. On January 29, she was in a courtroom in Broward County, Florida with Bobby when he was convicted of drunken driving (for his 1996 misadventure). According to prosecutors, Brown had rejected a standard offer to first-time offenders that carried no jail time but entailed mandatory drug treatment. Brown was ordered to spend five days in jail, undergo treatment for substance abuse, "star" in public service messages, pay a $500 fine, do 100 hours of community service, and be on probation for a year. The defendant burst into tears when the verdict was read out, while Whitney, who was seated behind him in the courtroom, cried as well.

When Brown was led out of the courtroom in handcuffs, he said, "It ain't justice." As Whitney, at her most demure, departed the building, she signed a few autographs and advised one concerned fan, "I'm fine, baby. Don't believe everything you read." Meanwhile, Brown's attorney immediately arranged for bail and said that they would appeal against the verdict. If the sentence were to stand, Brown would have to serve five days in jail. However, the terms of the judgment allowed that he could undergo rehab and perform community service back in New Jersey. The requirements for his public service announcements were that they should be aired at least once on each of the four major American TV networks.

As for the put-upon Bobby, he had the comfort of his wife having given him, a few months earlier, a $150,000 pearl-white Rolls-Royce as a replacement for the Porsche Carrera that he had written off in Fort

Lauderdale. A few nights later, the "free" man was spotted at a hip-hop club in Miami's South Beach district with a posse of guys and gals. Reportedly, it was not until the early hours of the morning that he returned home to the Williams Island condo he shared with Whitney.

When interviewed on a British TV chat show in 1998, Whitney was asked, "Do you feel Hollywood has accepted you as an actress?" She replied, "I don't think they have a choice. I really don't. *The Bodyguard*, even if the critics didn't like it, the people did. People think the color of Hollywood is black or white. The color of Hollywood is green. It's called money, it's what they bank on." (Here, the artist was right on the mark as, even in the late 1990s, it was still difficult for a woman of color to have many options regarding lead roles in major studio movies in Hollywood.)

Now that Hollywood was again beckoning Whitney, it was announced that she and box-office magnet Will Smith were to star in *Anything for Love*, a romantic comedy then in development at Universal Pictures. The lighthearted script by Tom Flynn told the story of a man who has broken off with his girlfriend and then, eight months later, realizes that he will do anything to win back the love of his life.

While this screen vehicle was moving forward, Whitney attended the 29th Annual Dove Awards, Christian music's top event, in Nashville, Tennessee. "I Go to the Rock" from *The Preacher's Wife* won an award, and during the televised show, hosted by Naomi Judd and John Tesh, Houston performed the winning song.

Flying back and forth across the country for such events gave the public ample opportunity to observe Whitney up close and personal—no matter how hard she tried to retain her privacy. During one flight in this period, Whitney suddenly had an urge to smoke a cigarette, even though it was prohibited to do so on board the plane. She adjourned to the rest room hoping to sneak a few puffs, but was caught in the act of trying to light up. In a showdown between the VIP passenger and flight attendants, the captain was summoned. He reminded the star that there was a $2,000 fine for breaking the no-smoking rule. Whitney insisted she'd write a check on the spot if she could have her cigarette, but the captain refused.

In early May, Cissy Houston hit the promotional trail to generate reader interest in her just-published autobiography, *How Sweet the Sound: My Life with God and Gospel*. Accompanied by Whitney, she appeared on TV's *Today* show, where the pair were interviewed by Katie Couric. On her best behavior, Whitney allowed the question-and-answer session to revolve mostly around Cissy. The sixty-four-year-old matriarch was in sharp form, even managing to mention how unfairly she thought the media was in perpetually hounding her beloved daughter. At this point, as Cissy explained how such gossip hurt everyone in the Houston family (including little Bobbi Kristina), Whitney seemed to be close to tears.

A few days later, Cissy gave an interview to *USA Today*, and in between publicizing her tome, she resignedly fielded questions about her famous daughter. When Mrs. Houston was asked about a new rumor that Whitney's erratic behavior over recent months might be attributable to drug usage, Cissy responded, "Are you kidding me?" Then, after making a fist as one would do before punching someone, she added, "She's fine." As further explanation, Cissy added, "For twelve years Whitney was constantly doing touring, recording and touring. She was just tired, and she wanted to take a rest. And she has problems like normal people. They're just normal people. You have to realize that." When the interviewer inquired whether she thought that Whitney's volatile marriage to Bobby Brown would last the course, Cissy answered, "Who knows? I think they love one another."

When Cissy Houston's book tour took her to Atlanta in mid-May, she met with a journalist from the local *Journal-Constitution*. Once again, she found herself in the position of interpreting her daughter's off-kilter actions to the world. The gospel singer admitted, "It becomes a bit annoying at times. Sometimes I just don't feel like answering the questions, and sometimes I just don't feel like it's anybody's business." Then, turning to a more upbeat topic, she explained why the younger Houston had not been recording much in recent years. "Whitney's a singer. She doesn't do all of this yip-yap rap stuff. But that's what the people have been wanting to hear. Now, she feels it's time for her kind of music again."

Cissy then confirmed that it was indeed true that her daughter was returning to the studios. She would be recording her first album of new material since 1990.

23

It's Not Right,
But It's Okay

*"Bobby [Brown] is a party guy. He likes to go out, and he likes to hang with
his friends. He likes to dance with different people. When people saw him
without me doing that, they figured, 'Oh, he's out cheating.' Now I'm a smart
girl, okay? I follow up. I have checked my husband out and he was nothing
like they say he was—nothing. I checked him out when he wasn't even looking,
so I can say that truthfully."*

WHITNEY HOUSTON, 1999

Celebrated athlete Earvin "Magic" Johnson, once a star of the Los Angeles
Lakers basketball team, was taking the plunge into showbusiness by
hosting a syndicated TV talk show. *The Magic Hour* debuted on Monday,
June 8, 1998. His first-night guests were Arnold Schwarzenegger and
Whitney Houston. Magic had once known Whitney's brother Gary when
they were both young professional basketball players; later, Magic and
Whitney had become friends. When the singer came on stage in a pleasing
gray-and-black pantsuit, she seemed relaxed (no sweating this time) and
down-to-earth—unlike many of her earlier TV talk-show appearances
in which she was stiff, awkward, and often distant.

An inexperienced but amiable emcee, Johnson asked Whitney, "What
is something normal you like to do that most people don't know about
you?" She responded good-naturedly that besides eating with a fork, "I'm

a good vacuumer." In a flash, an assistant brought out a vacuum cleaner and Houston began cleaning the stage set, accompanied by a cool beat and with the star jiving along to the rhythm of the music. It was a wonderful bit of TV, revealing again that Whitney could be a delightful physical comedian when given the chance. Later in the program she sang a cappella a ditty about Johnson's new show and, later, joined the show's percussionist, Sheila E, in rapping out a cheer to Magic. Whitney mentioned that her daughter, Bobbi Kristina, was at home in Florida with a fever and, on air, the singer took the opportunity to remind her youngster (who was watching the show) to take her medicine.

In mid-1998, the international press claimed that Whitney Houston would soon be announcing her pending divorce from her husband of nearly six years. One British publication suggested that a likely reason for the breakup was that Houston had supposedly discovered that Bobby had been secretly videotaping their bedroom lovemaking. Within months, the tabloids would change their tune. For example, one supermarket publication would report later—with due skepticism—that there had been a dramatic domestic turnabout in the Brown household: "Apparently their brief separation was a failure and they've worked out their differences. . . . She plans to renew their vows at an all-night chapel in Las Vegas followed by a gigantic blow-out party. What she has to celebrate remains a mystery." The ceremony never took place, but the mercurial couple remained man and wife—at least, for the moment.

In the summer of 1998, Whitney Houston embarked on a new European tour that began in Halle, Germany on June 20, then moved on to other German cities, and included later stopovers in France, Italy, the United Kingdom, and other European cities. Her set list included songs from *The Preacher's Wife* ("I Go to the Rock" and "I Love the Lord"), as well as many of her previous hits and a Diana Ross medley.

When Whitney went abroad to begin her tour, she and Bobby Brown were again in troubled waters. He was currently in Los Angeles registered at the Beverly Hills Hotel. Gossip-column items mentioned that recently he'd grown fond of Louana Rawls, the daughter of singer Lou and the sister of Bobby's pal Lou Rawls Jr. (Louana had previously dated Eddie Murphy in 1990, after he had broken up with Whitney.)

Whatever the reality of Bobby's extracurricular love life, he was soon front-page news once more, on this occasion for a supposed act of randy behavior. At about 4:15 P.M. on June 21, he was placed under citizen's arrest and then taken into custody by the Beverly Hills police, who booked him on sexual misdemeanor charges. According to accounts gathered after the fact, the singer had been in the Polo Lounge at the Beverly Hills Hotel, drinking and chatting with several attractive women. Later, he had returned to his $695-a-night bungalow. A "mystery" woman had purportedly visited him very early on Sunday morning. A few hours later, she fled the bungalow after Brown allegedly attempted to force himself on her. The aggrieved female went to the police and filed a complaint, accusing Brown of touching her (specifically, slapping her on the backside) against her will. Thereafter, she accompanied officers to the hotel, where Bobby was arrested. As he was taken into custody, he was heard saying, "I swear I didn't do it!"

Around 8 P.M. that night, he was released on $2,778 bail. A court hearing was scheduled for July 17, 1998. The day before the hearing, local prosecutors dropped the case against Brown, citing a lack of sufficient evidence.

After this latest escapade, Brown made several highly emotional calls to Whitney in Europe. Somehow, he convinced her both to forgive his recent indiscretions and to patch up their latest spat. As so often before, she caved in to his blandishments, and Brown flew to the Continent to be with her, joining her in Paris. Later, they journeyed on to England together for Whitney's Manchester concert. In London, Brown was seen with Whitney and her bodyguard at an upscale shoe boutique, where he purchased $4,000 worth of footwear. According to one observer, Bobby seemed a bit intoxicated that day and ended the buying spree with a brief snooze on a couch in the shop.

Sometimes, Whitney and Bobby even made news when incidents occurred and they were nowhere near the scene. For example, back on July 13, while Whitney was in Europe and Bobby was still in Los Angeles awaiting disposition of his most recent brush with the law, a nineteen-year-old female reported to New Jersey police that she had been raped at Whitney's Mendham Township home over the past weekend. It was revealed that the victim was unaware of her alleged attacker's identity, but the police were investigating. The spokesperson for Morris County prosecutor's office would not comment on what the woman had been doing at Whitney's estate that weekend, although it was revealed later that the man accused was a "rap singer" using the estate's studio to make a recording.

Whitney Houston's representatives released a response from the star, which included the statement: "She is hopeful that anyone with pertinent information will cooperate with local authorities, and is concerned for any who may have been injured." The case later evaporated.

Once back on home turf, and with her marriage momentarily stabilized, Whitney girded herself to do battle of another kind. DreamWorks Pictures had contracted the artist to sing a duet as a theme song for their forthcoming animated feature *The Prince of Egypt* (1998). For this retelling of the biblical story of Moses in the land of the Pharaohs, the artist would interpret Stephen Schwartz's ballad "When You Believe." What made the assignment such exciting news was that Whitney was to team up with rival diva Mariah Carey for the number. The track was to be produced by Houston's good friend Babyface.

The media played up the pending duet with all the hype usually reserved for a top-level summit meeting between high-ranking diplomats from opposing countries. Contrary to expectations, the meeting of soprano Whitney and coloratura Mariah (seven years younger than Houston) came off without any of the expected high-voltage fireworks. Nevertheless, journalists did their best to provide an eager public with a moment-by-moment account of the "dueling divas" and any tangible undercurrents of tension. The duet was recorded in August 1998, and the video was shot two months later at the Brooklyn Academy of Music. According to both camps, the two competing artists, although a bit wary of each other's reputation, put on a good show most of the time and got along relatively harmoniously (at least when the press was on hand). After the supposed "ordeal," Whitney commented to *Ebony* magazine: "Mariah and I got along great. . . . We had never talked and never sang together before. . . . We just laughed and talked and laughed and talked, and sang in between that. It was a good feeling. . . . She's a smart lady. I really like Mariah."

The tremendous buildup for "When You Believe" was a great asset in getting moviegoers interested in *The Prince of Egypt* by the time it opened in

December 1998. And the film needed all the help it could get. Made at a cost of over $60 million, it grossed only $101 million on domestic release. On the other hand, the theme song rose to number fifteen on the American music charts. "When You Believe" went on to be nominated for an Academy Award in the Best Song category. Whitney and Mariah performed the song at the March 21, 1999 Academy Awards ceremony, and later that evening it won the Oscar. The track would also turn up on both Whitney's and Mariah's upcoming albums.

Whitney celebrated her thirty-fifth birthday in August 1998 with a star-studded celebration at the China Club on Manhattan's West 47th Street. The guest list included her parents, brother Michael, Dionne Warwick, Penny Marshall, Clive Davis, and other notables such as singer Lil' Kim and the group Destiny's Child. Bobby Brown, who had turned twenty-nine the previous February, was also present, and the couple seemed in a particularly compatible mood that evening.

By now, Whitney was actually back in the recording studios preparing her first studio album since 1990's *I'm Your Baby Tonight*. Keenly aware that hip-hop was currently the favorite musical idiom, Whitney and Arista chief Clive Davis corralled a group of top hip-hop artists including Wyclef Jean, Faith Evans, Rodney Jerkins, and rapper Missy "Misdemeanor" Elliott to contribute to the new disc.

Whitney applied herself to lauding the new project to the press. For instance, she told *Newsweek* magazine, "Well, I've gone from singing too white to R&B diva, and now I'm hip-hop. I guess it's flattering to know that I can sing it all. My mother always said if you can sing you can sing. Having a church background has allowed me to be able to sing every note, every lyric. I'm not a hip-hop buyer. But I love Mary J. Blige—I love the best of hip-hop. To me, Wyclef [Jean] is not hip-hop—Faith [Evans] is not hip-hop. Music is a wide range. My husband can rap, sing and dance. He can do it all, and that's what I think of all these artists—they can do it all."

However, despite Whitney's enthusiasm for her refreshingly gritty urban project, she continued to display her trademark diva-like traits. Missy Elliott described the difficult process of making the new album: "Some days you got a call in the studio saying that 'Whitney wasn't feeling it' today and that she wasn't coming in." Other participants noted a similar lack of discipline on the part of the star during the recording of this crucial comeback release. As a result, there was a huge rush to meet the project's announced shipping date. The finished product, entitled *My Love Is Your Love*, was released on November 17, 1998, preceded by an eight-minute promotional movie short that was marketed to every conceivable outlet.

The album's cover photo immediately conveyed the sense that this was a "new" Whitney. Wearing a coppery-blond wig and a black Dolce and Gabbana dress, with stiletto-heel black boots and leather gloves, the artist appeared relaxed in her striking outfit. The predominant theme of the album's eleven new cuts (the twelfth was "When You Believe," her duet with Mariah Carey) was troubled romance and dealing with men in a streetwise fashion. More so than *I'm Your Baby Tonight*, the new disc revealed the tough urban-soul side of Whitney Houston.

"Heartbreak Hotel," featuring Faith Evans and Kelly Price on vocals, would become a number one R&B hit for seven weeks, rising to number two on the pop listings for three weeks. "It's Not Right But It's Okay," produced and cowritten by Rodney Jerkins, would land at number four on the Billboard Hot 100 music chart and remain in the top twenty for fifteen weeks. The third of the album's successful new tracks was the catchy title song, written and produced by Wyclef Jean and Jerry "Wonder" Duplessis. It remained on the charts for twenty-four weeks, peaking at number four. "My Love Is Your Love" also marked the recording debut of Houston's five-year-old daughter: Bobbi Kristina can be heard saying, "Sing, Mommy!"

As to the overall album, *Time* magazine concluded, "The CD tries to update Houston's soul-lite formula . . . you've got to give Houston credit for stretching herself on at least part of this disc; the first song, 'It's Not Right But It's Okay,' is one of her best." *Rolling Stone* concurred, "The former ingénue has some grown-up scars now, singing the marital blues with a bite in her voice that she's never come close to before. . . . Check out *My Love*, pal, and hear Houston prove beyond a doubt that she will survive." *Newsweek* enthused, "Her new album has all the 'flava' a fan could want. Houston's voice is a treasure."

The *Washington Times* was more qualified in its praise of Whitney's new work. While it felt the disc "proves she can handle any style she wants," it pointed out that the artist "plays follow the leader on *My Love Is Your Love*, rising and falling to the level of her producers." In Canada, the *Windsor Star* complained, "Erratic doesn't begin to describe *My Love Is Your Love*. It contains some of the most touching ballads Houston has ever recorded, but it also includes electronic, R&B drivel that amounts to little more than simplistic riffing . . . The most substantial entry here is 'Until You Come Back,' a torch song for the millennium. It's the desert rose in a wasteland of music, the only song that challenges Houston."

My Love Is Your Love peaked on the U.S. album charts at number thirteen (in the Hot 200) and number seven (in the R&B/Hip-Hop listing). It was considered a commercial disappointment by some in the industry, but nevertheless it sold over 3 million copies on domestic release. (By 2003, the total was up several more million worldwide.) At the February 2000 Grammy Awards, Houston would receive an award for "It's Not Right But It's Okay" in the category of Best R&B Vocal Performance—Female. The memorable number became her new anthem and a major set piece in her concerts.

Increasingly, as in the case of *My Love Is Your Love*, it would be the remixes of her album tracks that would win Houston expanded popularity in the dance clubs and boost her stock with a wide range of music listeners. Whitney approved of the situation: "I like when my remixes surprise my fans. I think it's exciting to see this pop princess embrace dance music and create music that's on the edge. I know me and what I like. With the remixes, the world can experience me in all my various colors." She added, "The remixes give people other options and show that I can do more than one form of music. I don't ever want to be locked into one groove. For *My Love Is Your Love*, the original versions have such bad groove, which made the record. That's the vibe I wanted for the album. But I always knew the remixes would come later. The remix is usually what creates the anthem. Will I include dance songs on upcoming albums? Of course it's all about timing."

On the liner notes for *My Love Is Your Love*, Whitney provided a special tribute to her husband. "You were meant for me. Nothing can come between this love. I know 'cause I'll never let you go."

But Whitney had to let go in September 1998, when Bobby Brown surrendered to Florida authorities to serve his five-day sentence for the prior drunken-driving arrest in Fort Lauderdale. That December, Bobby appeared in front of Judge Leonard Feiner in Broward County court regarding an arrest warrant issued after Brown advised his probation officer that he had smoked marijuana just before beginning his jail term in

September. Feiner released Brown on $2,500 bail but he was clearly annoyed. "I'm no longer inclined to give him any more consideration and to treat him any differently than any other defendant that walks through these courthouse doors," the judge declared. As Bobby left the courthouse on December 3, he informed reporters he wanted to enjoy a sober life: "I'm making efforts to clean up my record. I'm sorry for the disrespect I caused anybody."

To ballyhoo *My Love Is Your Love*, Whitney made a promotional tour of Europe in winter 1999. She met with the British magazine *O-Zone*, whose interviewer inquired of the new Whitney Houston, "What's changed?" She replied, "Nothing. It's just growth. Nothing's changed, I'm the same person. I feel the same things, have the same morals, same standards, same thoughts, same ethics. I still feel the same way about the media as I do, I still feel the same way about God as I do. I have some things that don't change. The growth period is cooler, because I get to work with a lot of younger people. Much younger then myself, who are just brilliant, and who know music, all that's new."

In March, the diva was back in the U.S. to perform at the Grammys and then at the Soul Train Music Awards, on both occasions giving an impressive rendition of "It's Not Right But It's Okay" before collecting her latest prizes. At the Soul Train event she enthused, "Whew! It's a whole lot of fun, you get to see a lot of friends, comrades, it's a lot of fun."

Continuing her new streak of success, Whitney was a key participant in VH1's *Divas Live 99*, broadcast from the Beacon Theater on Upper Broadway in New York City. For a change, Whitney (who dueted on "Ain't No Way" with Mary J. Blige and sang solo on "I Will Always Love You") was *not* the cause of controversy that night. Rather, gossip centered on the clash between Tina Turner and Sir Elton John during their rehearsal for "Proud Mary" and what the proper tempo should be for the duet. There was also some controversy over whether Cher had lip-synched on the show to her hit "Believe." (Later, her representatives acknowledged that her effects-laden performance had been accompanied by a prerecorded "reinforcement track.") A highlight of the high-energy evening was the finale: an ensemble rendition of the pulsating "I'm Every Woman," featuring Whitney, LeAnn Rimes, Chaka Khan, Faith Hill, Brandy, and Mary J. Blige.

The next day, when Whitney and Bobby Brown were interviewed on TV's *Good Morning America* about the previous evening's star-studded concert, Brown was asked his definition of a diva. His answer was, "It's a bunch of things all rolled up in one. A diva to me is talented, beautiful, mean, bitchy at times. You know, so I know my wife can be all of those things, and I'm afraid—well, you all don't know, but I do."

A diva can also be vulnerable and accept the blame for relationships that have gone off track. In May 1999, Whitney was the subject of a much-discussed major interview with *Redbook* magazine. The veteran singer told reporter Jeanne Wolf of her roller-coaster domestic life with her husband: "I don't know anybody who hasn't gone through ups and downs in a marriage. It just so happens that Bobby and I have done it in public. The first five years of marriage are rough—if you can get past them, you're doing good. . . . I had my own money and my own career. It can be tough on a very strong male who has his own success to be with a woman who has hers, too." On the topic of domestic physical abuse, Whitney insisted, "Contrary to belief, I do the hitting, he doesn't. . . . He has never put his hands on me. He is not a woman-beater. We are crazy for one another. I mean crazy in love, love, love, love, love. When we're fighting, it's like that's love for us. We're fighting for our love."

During this soul-baring exchange, the artist revealed her own agenda. She wanted *Redbook* readers to know that her life was *not* all high drama. "If you go back through my life, I will show you a lot of laughing. I think people don't see me as being a fun person. They miss all of that. I wish I could just bring them all up with me and go through the memories with me so they'll all know how Whitney really is, that Whitney has a good time, Whitney is a character, Whitney likes to have fun."

When it was announced that Whitney would undertake a U.S. tour in summer 1999—her first in five years in North America—she declared that this time she would perform at more intimate venues. Wanting to "reach out and touch" the audience, she explained that she had deliberately vetoed gargantuan stadiums because she had already done the "big-arena thing." According to the legend, "Now I want to do something where people can feel me and I can feel them. This show is going to have a jam-session kind of feel." Some industry insiders insisted that this was merely a face-saving gesture, because Whitney's diminished standing in the youth-oriented music business meant she no longer commanded such large crowds as she had a decade ago. Nevertheless, the diva was not downsizing her support staff. Her tour contracts carried a rider clause that warned, "This show carries a large entourage. . . . We will need all available rooms in the building."

The tour was to kick off in Chicago on June 22 and conclude in Concord on August 1. Thereafter, Houston would go abroad for additional performances. The schedule had been built around Bobbi Kristina's school vacations, so that she could accompany her mother on several legs of the trek, even to two weeks of the European jaunt. When Whitney was asked if she would sing her old hits this time around, she responded, "Those songs brought me here. I'll do them forever."

Her tour, which featured the group 112 as her opening act, got off to a good start in the Windy City. As *USA Today* reported, "Whitney Houston wasn't onstage 10 minutes before she had the crowd at Aire Crown Theatre trying to raise the roof. The cause: two pulsating jams sandwiched around her gritty hit 'Heartbreak Hotel.' . . . A relaxed and playful Houston took the audience . . . through a full range of emotions during her 20-song performance."

When Whitney moved on to Detroit's Fox Theater a few days later, the local *Free Press* observed, "Houston plunged right into the hot material off her latest album, *My Love Is Your Love*, the slinky, hip-hop-tinged stuff that represents her most ambitiously trendy effort. There was no doubt, however, that 'luxurious' was the key word for the night, which found Houston in a green fur coat that had the star sweating two songs into the set." The newspaper did, however, express some reservations: "You got the impression that her latest creative moves—revealed again with new, funky tunes like 'In My Business' and bass-heavy renditions of 'How Will I Know' and 'I Wanna Dance with Somebody (Who Loves Me)'—are less artistic gestures than manifestations of a creative identity crisis. Houston often tried to come off loose, imploring the crowd to get its hands in the air and mocking her diva image by saying she hit the tour trail at long last 'because I wanted to.'"

By early July, the strain of the tour was already catching up with the artist, and she missed shows in Newark, New Jersey and Washington D.C. She had an off night during the first of two performances at Manhattan's Madison Square Garden and apologized to concertgoers for her hoarse voice. During the presentation, she took time to introduce family members: Cissy Houston was in the audience, brother Gary was one of her background singers, Bobbi Kristina made her small contribution to the performance of "My Love Is Your Love." Finally, the star brought husband Bobby Brown out from the wings and he bestowed a big kiss on his wife to reflect the couple's new harmony. The *New York Times* reported: "She had more eccentric mannerisms than a talk-show host. Often she seemed to be deliberately lingering vocally as the band tried to push her forward through the set. Perhaps as a result of time constraints, the hits at the end of the show, particularly 'I Will Always Love You' and her latest break-up hit, 'It's Not Right But It's Okay,' were curt and abridged.

"Perspiring profusely from the first song, Ms. Houston often walked to the table filled with towels, sprays, glasses, and other containers to freshen up. Over the course of the night, she descended three times from a stage-set balcony (a true diva must always descend), each time wearing a different shiny or glittering Dolce & Gabbana outfit."

Time magazine reviewed the performance in Philadelphia, noting that Whitney "was not the singer you've come to know from her recorded work; this Houston was deeper, tougher, feistier. Her voice is not as bottled-water pure as it once was, but it's more real now, breaking on the high notes, letting emotion spill out. She belted out her hits, of course. . . . But she also soared through a gospel medley that took the crowd higher than mere pop and confirmed her status as one of today's most accomplished live entertainers."

When the diva reached Atlanta, her concert at the Fox Theater offered some of its best seats at $125 each. One upset fan complained, "We all like Whitney, but we were like, $125! We're not trying to support Bobby Brown's kids." After Atlanta, there were cancelled shows in the Midwest. This led the *St. Louis Post-Dispatch* to assert, "She's no longer America's sweetheart, not with a rabble-rousing headline-magnet of a husband like Bobby Brown, or persistent, image-damaging rumors we won't spell out here (although it doesn't take much sniffing around to catch the worst of them)." Increasingly, major publications were suggesting that Whitney's erratic behavior, despite her vehement denials, might well be drug-related.

At the end of July, Whitney arrived in Los Angeles to perform at the cavernous Universal Amphitheater. She received a general endorsement from the *Los Angeles Times*: "It was all the more surprising when Houston— a marvelous singer whose cold demeanor on stage over the years and melodramatic approach to generally light pop material reduced her to a caricature to much of the pop world—suddenly seemed to break free of her diva chains.

"As she descended the stairs, it was noticeable that her six-piece band was playing with a funky, gritty edge not felt on her earlier tours—and Houston's vocals and spunky manner matched the musical textures, instead of the mere vocal gymnastics of old, she injected personality and character into the songs."

Following her two-night stand in Los Angeles, Houston was booked to end the U.S. tour with a date in Concord, California. She seemed well at around 5 P.M. the night of the concert and sounded fine, but somehow she got "sick" between 5 and 7 P.M. Thus, fifteen minutes before the show was to start, it was called off. By then, about half the 9,000 fans expected were already in their seats. Not only were her fans disappointed—some of them voicing their frustration and anger—but the venue's managers were so incensed that they demanded the recalcitrant star pay as much as $100,000 in damages. The requested reparations never materialized.

While the widespread puzzlement—and furor—over Whitney's increasingly bizarre and seemingly unprofessional behavior accelerated, there was also controversy in some quarters as to whether she was being a good mother (or an exploitive performer) by making young Bobbi Kristina a part of her show and thus taking her away from normal everyday life. The artist scoffed at such allegations. In fact, she countered, she was definitely *not* pushing her daughter to be in showbusiness; rather, it was Bobbi Kristina who had asked to appear on stage and was already showing an inclination for performing.

Leaving behind her the debates about her professionalism, her alleged substance-abuse problems, and so forth, Houston embarked on a European tour in support of *My Love Is Your Love*, opening in Poland. The itinerary concluded on November 8, 1999, with extra dates added in several countries to meet audience demand. While on the Continent, the diva collected prizes at the MTV Europe Music Awards and at the Bambi Awards. At the latter event, she received the award for Lifetime Achievement as Best International Act.

From such highs, Whitney Houston would fall to fresh lows as the new millennium began.

24

The Year of Living Dangerously

"We all need to exhale sometime."

WHITNEY HOUSTON, 2000

As the world celebrated the dawning of the new millennium, Whitney Houston was in Asia. For a fee of well over $1 million, she had been hired by the Pacific Century CyberWorks Ltd., a huge Internet company, to perform for an hour at a New Years' party for 3,000 guests that the company was hosting in Hong Kong.

Back in America, there were growing industry rumblings that Clive Davis, now sixty-five years old, would soon be let go as Arista boss because BMG, Arista's giant European-based parent corporation, wanted younger blood to direct the label. While Whitney's mentor battled with the management, Houston issued a public statement defending Davis: "It hurts me to think he's being treated with disrespect. He deserves total honor and respect from everyone including BMG. And as far as his age is concerned, he's younger than me, so maybe I should be retired."

Meanwhile, Whitney's BrownHouse Productions was piling up potential new projects for coproduction. Besides *Get Christy Love* and *Anything for You* at Universal, the firm had added *Thirty Years to Life* at Twentieth Century-Fox, and *The Princess Diaries* (about a feisty sixteen-year-old; not a star vehicle for Whitney) at Disney. BrownHouse had also teamed up with the makers of the movie and TV series *Soul Food* to develop and produce a feature adaptation of Eric Jerome Dickey's novel *Friends and Lovers*. And the production company had cast R&B artist Monica to star as an aspiring singer in the musical story *Angel of Mine*, geared for the ABC network's *Wonderful World of Disney* teleseries.

Meanwhile, Bobby Brown's music career had reached a stalemate once again and his acting assignments remained patchy. However, his police file was growing. Back in mid-1999, Bobby's Florida probation officer had reported that the performer had tested positive for drugs (cocaine) in April, that the next month he refused to take another urine test, and that he then missed a Broward County court appearance after not returning in time from a trip to the West Coast. As a result, the judge issued an arrest warrant for the entertainer. Because the warrant was for a misdemeanor, Brown would not be taken into custody unless he returned to Florida. Should the police learn that Bobby was in Florida again, he faced up to ninety days in jail.

In January 2000, the Browns were on holiday in the Aloha state once again. As their stay drew to a close, they entertained guests at the Four Seasons Hotel in Honolulu. During the meal, something set Bobby off and he flew into a rage. Eventually, Whitney calmed him down by, among other things, patting the back of his head as one would soothe a child.

On Tuesday, January 11, the Browns were driven to the Keahole-Kona International Airport on the island of Hawaii to board United Airlines flight number forty to San Francisco. As Whitney passed through the security checkpoint, a guard asked her to open her floral tote bag—he thought he had spied contraband when the bag passed through his X-ray machine. The search reportedly revealed 15.2 grams of marijuana (including two plastic bags of the substance and three partially smoked joints). When Houston demanded the return of her personal things, she was informed she must wait in the airport's executive lounge until the police arrived to settle the matter.

Instead of doing as directed by the security guards, the star became irate, reputedly yelling, "I wish people would just stay out of my business and leave me alone." She fumed, "I've been framed. This is a terrible mistake. Someone must have put the drugs in my bag. . . . It was definitely not there when I left for the airport." Abandoning the bag, she walked away imperiously, with Bobby tagging along beside her. They boarded the plane and flew first class to San Francisco.

Because the airport's checkpoint staff were not police officers, they had no jurisdiction to arrest individuals unless it was a security matter. (As one airport employee explained afterwards, "Our job is to keep weapons off the plane, not hassle people about a little bit of pot.") Thus there was no choice but to let Houston depart. The police arrived on the scene forty-five minutes after Whitney and Bobby's hasty departure. By 2.28 P.M. that day, officers had in their possession the confiscated 15.2 grams of marijuana from the airport. The alleged offense carried a penalty of up to thirty days in jail and a $1,000 fine. It was announced that the matter was being referred to the office of Hawaii county prosecutor Jay Kimura.

Later, Kimura stated that he would await the results of a police investigation before deciding whether or not to prosecute the case, and that the process might take up to a month. If the prosecution went forward, Houston could be charged *in absentia* and ordered to appear in the Hawaiian court. If she should fail to show up, the state would not try to extradite the celebrity from the mainland. However, she risked being served with a summons if she should ever return to the island state and could be arrested for possession and contempt of court if she should then ignore the summons. It was also mentioned that Whitney's bag would eventually be returned to her—minus the contraband.

The airport incident quickly became major news around the globe, leading many reliable press sources to openly connect this "discovery" with all the past rumors and accusations of Whitney Houston's substance abuse (which she had previously chosen to ignore, deny, or sweep under the carpet). It was bandied about that the revelations from this Hawaii episode might perhaps explain her escalating strange behavior over recent years: extreme mood swings, missed concerts, frequent loss of her trademark high notes in performance, a seeming lack of career motivation, constant sweats, and so forth. Because so many media outlets and industry sources had previously hinted at Whitney's substance abuse, it was not much of a stretch for them to jump to outright speculation. Then, too, the artist was suspect due to her links with "Bad Boy" Bobby Brown. He was cited as a negative influence on her, with his wild lifestyle, his unconvincing denials of his own attraction to drugs, and his on-the-record treatment for and admissions of problems with alcohol.

If any moment was a life-defining one for thirty-six-year-old Whitney, it was this incident in Hawaii. Thereafter, all her actions—no matter how innocent they seemed—would be interpreted in the light of this illuminating event. For her part, she apparently thought she could continue to deny the substance-abuse allegations and that the negative publicity would somehow evaporate. But she failed to take into account the tenacity of investigating reporters, the emergence of eyewitness accounts of her past activities, and, most of all, her own inability to curb bad habits.

Talk-show hosts, standup comedians, and columnists had a field day making Houston the butt of marijuana-related jokes. (One national magazine entitled their account of the airport debacle: "Waiting to Exhale: Houston, we have a problem.") Assorted celebrities were polled as to their reaction to the "drug bust." Amid all the smarmy remarks, pompous righteousness, and evasive responses, one noteworthy voice—that of country-music superstar Garth Brooks—spoke up in Houston's defense: "Whitney is a classy lady and is always very nice to me. She is innocent until proven guilty."

Over the coming months, the press would publish details as the Hawaii county prosecutor prepared to go ahead with the case, with Whitney's people jockeying to hire a dream team of attorneys to fight it. However, in November 2000, Whitney pleaded no contest to the charges. As part of the plea, she had to meet court-ordered requirements: to pay $4,025 in contributions, court fees, and donations to an anti-drug group, as well as undergo a substance-abuse assessment test by a court-determined deadline. If these conditions were met satisfactorily, the Kona District Court would consider dismissing the charges.

Later, when Whitney's legal team failed to submit proof of the demanded assessment by the court's imposed deadline, the prosecutor threw out the deferred "no contest" plea and sought to have the defendant resentenced. The Hawaii court, however, reconsidered the situation after the full and proper evaluation finally arrived in February 2001. One of Whitney's lawyers took the blame for the delay, claiming that his client had taken the demanded drug test on time. He explained that he thought that was all the court required, rather than an official copy of the report along with an evaluation by a substance-abuse counselor. On March 5, 2001, after reviewing the assessment documents, District Judge Joseph Florendo dismissed the charges against Whitney Houston.

While the world was digesting, reacting to, and judging Whitney's Hawaii fiasco, she carried on with her life. On January 15, 2000, Houston appeared at Radio City Music Hall to sing "God Bless America" before a light-heavyweight boxing match. The following Monday was the 27th Annual American Music Awards in Los Angeles. While Whitney had received nominations from the AMA, she did not attend. An AMA spokesperson said the artist's planned departure for Europe conflicted with the telecast and that her absence was unrelated to the recent Hawaii incident.

In Hollywood, it was business as usual in an industry, which, like the music business, was well acquainted with drug usage. Will Smith's production company announced that it had secured the remake rights to the French thriller *Diva* (1981) and they were talking to Whitney about taking on the title role. On February 11, 2000, Whitney appeared briefly as an interviewee in the documentary *It's Black Entertainment*, which aired on the Showtime cable network.

Later in February, Whitney made a queenly appearance at Arista Records' smashing Grammy party, hosted by Clive Davis. He presented his protégée with a plaque signifying the 110 million albums she had sold worldwide to date. At the 42nd Annual Grammy Awards, Whitney, wearing a long leather coat and a black leather hat with spangles, performed "It's Not Right But It's Okay." She admitted beforehand that she still became nervous before each performance. "I do because I want things to go right. I'm a perfectionist, when it comes to things like that. That means from the monitors to the dance steps, to the little intricate things. I'm like that." She won her sixth Grammy that evening, in the category of Best R&B Vocal Performance—Female for "It's Not Right But It's Okay." Her lengthy acceptance speech included a special dedication to her husband: "Honey, this one is for you—the original R&B king. I love you." Basking in his wife's reflected glory, Bobby Brown enthused later, "What she said to me sent chills through my body, and I'm walking around with this energy that I didn't have before. I'm feeling really good about it."

Less appealing to the couple that night were the wisecracks of the show's emcee, Rosie O'Donnell. Pouncing on the issue of Whitney's recent difficulties in Hawaii, O'Donnell referred to the singing star, seated in the audience next to Bobby Brown and Cissy Houston, as a "big fan of the Doobies." She also remarked, "Whitney was in the news a lot this year. What can we say? Aloha! We'll just leave it at that!"

In early March, as if enough people in the world were not already harassing Whitney, her lawyers were in a New Jersey court to get a restraining order against yet another stalker. The disturbed woman in question claimed to be the singer's "supernatural reincarnated mother" and had been sending the celebrity gifts (ranging from a four-tier cake to underwear) and rambling letters. The restraining order was approved. On a happier note, on March 4, Whitney received the Artist of the Decade Award at the 14th Annual Soul Train Music Awards held in Los Angeles. Since that day was also her daughter's birthday, Whitney sang a few bars of "Happy Birthday" to the beaming seven-year-old Bobbi Kristina in the audience.

Two days later, however, Houston was back to her unreliable self. She was scheduled to participate in the New York ceremony to induct Clive Davis into the Rock 'n' Roll Hall of Fame. Ten minutes before showtime, Houston bowed out of the appearance, citing "voice problems." This apparent slight to her mentor won Whitney no points in the industry.

Then came the Academy Awards debacle. Whitney had agreed to sing "The Way We Were" and "Over the Rainbow" in a medley of classic movie songs. The musical segment would also include performances by country singer Garth Brooks and rapper Queen Latifah, as well as offerings from veteran musicians Ray Charles and Isaac Hayes. With the Oscar ceremony set for March 26, 2000 at the Shrine Auditorium in Los Angeles, Whitney flew to the West Coast in time for rehearsals on the Thursday evening prior to the Sunday telecast. When she arrived (accompanied by Bobby Brown and Bobbi Kristina) at the home of Burt Bacharach, the musical director for the segment, she was supposedly not in the mood for the run-through. After about fifteen minutes of practice, she and her people left Bacharach's house. According to a source on the scene, Houston looked "totally out of it."

The following day, Whitney, never a gracious early riser, vetoed a morning practice session. That evening, she arrived fifteen minutes early at the rehearsal at the Shrine Auditorium. However, she still seemed off kilter to several of those present. As an onlooker observed, "She came in on cue for one number, but missed her cue for the second and sang the wrong song." While Whitney was struggling through her two numbers, Bobby Brown was acting up in the auditorium, including sitting with a coat over his head.

Bewildered and angered by Whitney's peculiar behavior, Bacharach conferred with the show's producers and then met with the artist herself. It was decided that she would have to be replaced. At a cost of $60,000, the show flew in singer Faith Hill as a last-minute substitute. This switch did not please Garth Brooks, since he had been assured that he would be the only country performer in the musical interlude. Trying to put a more favorable spin on this embarrassing turn of events, Arista Records announced, "Whitney Houston arrived in Los Angeles with a sore throat. After participation in rehearsals for the 72nd Academy Awards show both Thursday and Friday night, she was unsure that she would be better by Sunday. She therefore regretfully withdrew from the performance."

Nevertheless, the rumor mills went into overdrive, claiming that Whitney had been dismissed by an angry Bacharach for having messed up so badly in rehearsals. While the telecast, hosted by Billy Crystal, eventually went off without significant hitches, Whitney Houston's Oscars no-show became the latest in a spiraling number of mishaps. The incident gave rise to postmortems from several different perspectives. For example, Jane LaBonte, spokesperson for the Academy of Motion Picture Arts and Science, said of the vocalist, "She was having dreadful problems singing and she didn't have her usual range [at the Friday, March 24 rehearsal]. The poor woman was in trouble."

A backstage source at the Academy Awards run-through commented, "She [Whitney] was anxious and agitated from the first time she showed up for rehearsal. She was twitching and acting funny. She was extremely dehydrated and kept asking for water. She wasn't in a good mood and wasn't ready to be bossed around by [Burt] Bacharach. She's used to calling the shots." *Newsweek* stated that, "According to people who were there, the thirty-six-year-old singer seemed to be in her own world, humming tunes (not the ones being practiced) and playing an invisible keyboard as she walked in circles."

Another onlooker claimed that an agitated Bacharach had finally ordered the beleaguered singer: "Just leave. It's not going to work out." Meanwhile, Whitney's publicist issued a brief statement, maintaining that it was the artist who had chosen to bow out of the major event due to throat problems and because "she was unsure that she would be better by Sunday." Entertainer Garth Brooks chimed in with, "Um, I can only say this about Whitney: she came in, she rehearsed, she tried her best, but she was so sick, and we'll just leave it at that." Gossip maven Ted Casablanca reflected: "My, that gal is really getting to be the Elizabeth Taylor of the music biz. One very public, physical malady after another. How many more spectacles can she create?"

The one thing all observers agreed upon was that Whitney's humiliation would go down as one of the most unique chapters in

Academy Awards history. By now, members of the media were frequently editorializing about what had happened to the once-golden career of Whitney Houston. A TV producer who had worked with her previously said, "When this Oscar thing happened, it did not surprise me. She has a reputation for being a flake and no-showing, and it's dangerous to book her because until she walks on that stage, there's no guarantee she's going to show up."

A publicist, who knew Whitney professionally, pointed out, "Whitney has always looked to strong men to take control in her life. She had her father who was a very powerful personality, then Clive Davis who launched her career. She let him make many decisions for her—and they were very wise ones, most of them—and now there's Bobby Brown. . . . I can't say that he brings the same wisdom or objectivity to the situation as Clive Davis did." An unidentified individual said to be close to the artist offered, "There's a lot of denial from the people around Whitney. They just chalk up her behavior to being a diva." He went on to suggest that no one reads the riot act to her because "she's a financial source for all of them. They don't want to cross her."

Hardly had this calamity simmered down than news spread about a highly controversial Whitney Houston interview and photo shoot, due to appear in the May 2000 issue of *Jane* magazine. According to the magazine's editor, who was at the notorious shoot, Whitney "was acting really strange" when she finally arrived after keeping everyone waiting for four hours. "She was singing to herself. Then she would pretend to play the piano, like an air piano. Her eyes were very heavy-lidded." Houston's camp would insist that her lateness was due to a cracked tooth and an emergency visit to the dentist. To this, the editor retorted, "Novocain doesn't make you act that way. Everyone there thought she was on something." The *Jane* chief did allow that "in the midst of all this really bizarre behavior . . . [Houston] gave one of the best cover shots ever. She's a consummate performer." When the much-discussed piece was published, Whitney was quoted making several off-the-wall observations. For example, when asked if she had ever been introduced to a U.S. president or had hung out with a junkie, she acknowledged she had done both and that the experience was "just the same. The president gets off on the country. The junkie gets off on a couple of hits. They're the same, both cut from the same cloth, they're just men, you dig?"

Two weeks after her Oscar non-appearance, Whitney returned to the site of her embarrassment. She was to be the key entertainer at Arista

Records' twenty-fifth-anniversary concert, to be held at the Shrine Auditorium. The evening was a tribute to Clive Davis, who was about to exit his longtime post to form his own new record label. There was much speculation as to whether Whitney would actually appear that special night and, if she did, how she would fare.

At the six-hour marathon concert (taped and edited down for a later TV special), Whitney took center stage well into the evening. Wearing a chic champagne-colored long dress, the diva received a standing ovation from the audience, which included, besides Davis and other top industry executives, Arista label mates such as Carlos Santana, Sarah McLachlan, Alan Jackson, and Patti Smith. As Houston walked on stage, she tripped on an object lying in her path, and there was momentary concern among some members of the audience that a disaster was about to occur.

During her twenty-minute set, the star seemed upbeat and sang renditions of several of her hits, including "How Will I Know." Carrying her trademark white handkerchief, she frequently mopped at the sweat on her face and chest. At times during her performance she talk-sang some of the lyrics as she struggled noticeably with her voice, often relying on her background singers (including brother Gary) to carry the song forward. Partway through "I Will Always Love You," she stopped to ask Bobby Brown to bring her a glass of water on stage. He promptly did so, dabbed at the sweat on her face, then kissed her on the lips. Whitney then completed the number. For "My Love Is Your Love," she was joined by Brown, Deborah Cox, Monica, Faith Evans, and Angie Stone. Before leaving the stage to much applause, she said cryptically, "The record's not over yet. Remember." Then with a "God bless you, I love you," she disappeared from the spotlight.

Earlier in the eventful evening, when Clive Davis was asked backstage if it were true, as *Newsweek* magazine had suggested, that he had contacted Houston's family to stage a drug intervention, he skirted the issue, saying, "She and I have a professional relationship." He then went on to enthusiastically endorse the singing abilities of his famous "discovery."

For several years, it had been touted that Arista would release a greatest-hits package of Whitney's most celebrated recordings. In fact, that had been the plan when the artist was coaxed back into the recording studios two years earlier. Instead, those sessions had developed into her *My Love Is*

Your Love album. Now, in spring 2000, a few weeks before Clive Davis's contract expired at Arista—and L. A. Reid was installed as the new head of the label—the greatest-hits concept became a reality.

The release was a two-disc album. The first, labeled "Cool Down," featured past hits such as "You Give Good Love," "I Will Always Love You," "Exhale (Shoop, Shoop)," and "My Love Is Your Love." It also contained two new duets, "Same Script, Different Cast" with Canada's Deborah Cox, and "Could I Have This Kiss Forever" with Enrique Iglesias. The second disc, entitled "Throw Down," was heavy on remixes (such as the Junior Vasquez mix of "Greatest Love of All"), but it also contained a new duet ("If I Told You That" with George Michael), as well as two vintage tracks ("One Moment in Time" and "The Star Spangled Banner.")

Whitney had acted in her usual diva-like manner when laying down the tracks for this album. For example, when it came time to do the duet with George Michael, the latter flew over from England expressly to record the song. However, Whitney was preoccupied with a birthday party for her daughter and couldn't make the sessions. The two recorded their vocal tracks separately. The same thing happened when she was to join Enrique Iglesias for their joint number, "Could I Have This Kiss Forever." When the recording was finally made, Whitney was in Hamburg, Germany and Enrique was in Los Angeles. Thus, they recorded their vocals separately, as they did when they made the music video to support the duet.

On its release, critics generally endorsed the album. The *New York Daily News* approved. "She exudes an erotic dynamism that no one else has the power to match. This isn't just an ecstatic piece of party music—it utterly redefines Houston as an artist." *Vibe* magazine agreed: "Timeless tunes and remixed classics . . . pure pop-soul magic. . . . Houston remains an invincible artist." *Ebony* reported that the double album "reminds listeners of the enormous talent this artist demonstrated on "You Give Good Love" 15 years ago, how she has grown, and the fact she has a long career road ahead." E! Online rated the offering an A, explaining, "Houston, you may be in trouble now, but we have no problems with this smartly arranged compilation."

A few months after its release, when the double album had sold just under 500,000 copies, a record-industry insider commented, "That's good, but if she were on tour, it would be doing better." (Houston either could not or would not tour to support the album.) Another concern about marketing *The Greatest Hits* (which was collaterally promoted with a DVD and video compilation of her music videos, interviews, and so forth) was that it was being released during the transition at Arista from the regime of Clive Davis to that of L. A. Reid.

When Reid first arrived at the label in his new capacity, he said to Whitney, his old friend and collaborator: "Are you okay? Is there anything I can do to help you?" She replied, "Yes, I'm okay. Just make sure my record's a hit." Later, Reid would recall in a *New York* magazine interview that shortly after taking charge at Arista, he studied the sales progress of *The Greatest Hits.* "I realized that this thing was headed nowhere, and we were going to spend a fucking fortune." In his estimation, "This whole project was just botched up, from the very beginning." He felt, after the fact, that the entry's release date should have been geared to later in the year when most superstars' albums typically appeared. He also disagreed with key decisions that had been made regarding the releases of its singles and music videos. Nevertheless, the album package would eventually go triple platinum and, in subsequent years, sell an estimated 7 million copies worldwide.

While *The Greatest Hits* package was being shipped to record stores, another Whitney showcase failed to occur. She was scheduled to headline a CBS-TV special during the second week of May. It was to have been an intimate presentation of her songs to a gathering of celebrity friends at her New Jersey home. Suddenly, the program was a no-go. While no official reasons were offered, some sources insisted the cancellation was prompted by the proximity of and conflict with the upcoming NBC telecast of the Arista anniversary concert in mid-May. Other commentators suggested that Whitney's general health and frame of mind prevented the concert from going ahead.

A revealing insight into the artist's current state of mind was provided in early May by veteran syndicated columnist Liz Smith. She reported of Whitney that "at least three, possibly four, 'helpers' [are] with her at all times these days, watching out for the singing star, making sure she stays on the straight and narrow. (These Arista employees take it in shifts.)" The gossip maven pondered, "I wonder just how long Houston and her volatile hubby, Bobby Brown, will accept such stringent tabs on their comings and goings. I suppose I should say her *equally* volatile hubby. As an ex-press rep of Houston's told me shortly before bowing out of the star's professional life: 'She is no delicate flower, Liz. She gives as good as she gets.' Which means: don't assume Brown is a villain. There are no villains. Only human beings with human frailties."

As such tantalizing tidbits continued to pepper the media along with Whitney's controversial interviews in *Jane* and *Out* magazines in May 2000, further revelations appeared in print which shed light on the artist's recent erratic actions. *Us Weekly* and several other major publications presented accounts of events that occurred at the end of July 1999 and might explain some of the pressures that led to Houston's sudden canceling of her Concord, California concert. It seemed that during her stay in Los Angeles for her end-of-July concerts at Universal Amphitheater, she had gotten into another heated argument with Bobby Brown at their Beverly Hills hotel. Subsequently, in the early hours of the next morning, Cissy Houston, accompanied by two drug counselors as well as friends and family, appeared at Whitney's suite. (Bobby had been "ranting and raving" down in the lobby but had then been taken away for medical assistance.)

When Cissy reached her daughter's room, the diva was sitting on her bed, apparently in a daze, surrounded by the wreckage (including broken beer bottles) from a recent altercation. The group talked to Whitney for several hours, begging her to enter an exclusive substance-abuse clinic. Said one unnamed source, "There was nothing her mother could say that night to make her pay attention. It was very sad." Later, in her notoriously candid December 2002 interview with Diane Sawyer, Houston would refer to this confrontation, suggesting that no one—not even her mother—was going to march into her life and tell her what to do. Little wonder then that the distraught artist had been unable to summon the energy to carry on with her Concord Pavilion engagement on August 1, 1999.

Seeking a degree of tranquility away from the madness around them, Whitney and Bobby vacationed down in the American South in early May 2000. However, when they flew back to New Jersey, Brown was detained by police at Newark International Airport. They had been dispatched to return him to Florida to appear before Judge Leonard Feiner for having violated his probation (on three counts) regarding the August 1996 car smash in Fort Lauderdale. By the next morning, Brown had been flown back to Florida. He was incarcerated at Broward County Jail in Fort Lauderdale, where he would remain until the May 22 hearing with Feiner.

On that date, it was decided that Brown must remain in jail until a final determination could be made. The defendant was refused bail because he was considered a flight risk. When this fifteen-minute session ended, Brown complained to his attorney, "It's not fair, man, it's not fair."

On June 12, it was ruled that Bobby would have to spend seventy-five days behind bars because of his parole violations. (The prosecutors had agreed to drop the more serious of the three charges, if the singer pled guilty to the lesser ones.) Brown now insisted, "I want to get it over with, I've had it, I'm spent on this thing." After the ruling, the downhearted defendant told the gathered reporters, "I have a disease. I am an addict. I am an alcoholic. I just want to continue with my sobriety and get back home." Whitney Houston had deliberately remained away from the court proceedings, fearful that if she were present it would turn into even more of a media circus. She had already made two visits to meet with Brown privately during his incarceration.

The good news for Whitney was that since Bobby had already served thirty-nine days of his sentence, he would be released on July 8. Thus, if all went well, she and Brown could spend their eighth wedding anniversary together. The bad news was that Robyn Crawford, after years of friendship and a strong working relationship, had just resigned from Nippy, Inc. and relocated to Los Angeles. As an associate observed of Houston's "personal damage-control center," "It's hard to imagine [Whitney] functioning without her."

25

Just Whitney

'I love you, Bobby! I love you, baby!'

WHITNEY HOUSTON, 2002

At the end of June 2000, Whitney began a three-concert stretch at Caesars Palace in Atlantic City. When press reports suggested that the artist had had a difficult time performing (forgetting lyrics, missing notes, and so forth) at these gigs, her camp loudly cried unfair. Among those countering the negative claims was the Caesars Palace director of entertainment. He commented, "I was surprised and disturbed. . . . These statements were false and fabricated. . . . We were pleased with the extremely high level of professionalism exhibited by Whitney Houston throughout her stay with us."

Whitney was certainly very focused when she was reunited with Bobby Brown on his release from Broward County's Joseph Conte Center. He had served his time in the medium-security facility sharing a two-bed cell. Just after midnight on July 7, Brown was freed and Houston was thrilled to greet her man. Emerging from her white stretch limousine, a jubilant (and barefoot) Whitney jumped into Bobby's arms and wrapped her legs about his middle. The couple hastily left the media-crowded scene and retreated to their Williams Island condo for five days of getting reacquainted.

☆

By summer 2000, Clive Davis had departed Arista to form J-Records. In the final negotiations he took several artists with him (including Deborah Cox, Monica, and Angie Stone), but Whitney Houston and Carlos Santana, among others, remained at Arista. Thus, within several weeks of one another, two of Whitney's key advisors (Clive Davis and Robyn Crawford, now in California) were no longer directly on hand to advise and console her.

Meanwhile, the *National Enquirer* published an extensive article on Whitney in their July 7 issue. In "Whitney's Drug Hell," reporter Don Gentile interviewed a fifty-three-year-old drug dealer—referred to as "Uncle Bob"—who outlined a long history of supplying the artist with assorted drugs as her addiction increased. The following month, the *Star*, another supermarket publication, reported that anonymous callers concerned about the wellbeing of Bobbi Kristina—living in a supposedly drug-filled environment—had contacted New Jersey child-protection agencies. They wanted social workers to intervene on the child's behalf. Such investigations led to no direct action being taken at that time.

That fall, while Whitney was still dealing with Hawaii's court system regarding her airport misadventure, her father, John, contracted with a licensing agent to make merchandizing deals on products (such as jewelry, cosmetics, and clothing) that could be tied to the Whitney Houston name. A percentage of all potential sales would go to the Whitney Houston Foundation for Children, Inc. Also at this time, Sunday, a R&B quintet of five young black women, a New Jersey group mentored by Whitney (and Robyn Crawford), released their first album on the Capitol label.

When John Houston celebrated his eightieth birthday in October 2000, Bobby Brown was among the guests at the party hosted at Justin's, a Manhattan supper club. However, Whitney was a no-show. On the other hand, Whitney did appear at the Aladdin Hotel in Las Vegas on November 10. She and Bobby Brown performed before a crowd of 6,000 people. Brown did a forty-minute solo set, followed by Houston's ninety-minute turn. For their finale, they dueted on "My Love Is Your Love" with daughter Bobbi Kristina standing between them.

Mike Weatherford of the *Las Vegas Review Journal* reported, "Houston rose to the drama, and came roaring back with the cocksure bravado of a jail-sprung Mike Tyson. Brown, the real jailbird of the marriage, was more like Buster Douglas. But then, judging from the crowd, he had the raw deal going in." Weatherford also noted, "Though marriage united them, Bobby and Whitney never had exactly the same audience. And the situation was even more extreme on Friday; the number of retirement-age folks in jackets and ties suggested the Aladdin invited a lot of its high-rollers to the event after initially slow ticket sales." The Browns claimed they so enjoyed appearing on stage together that they planned to tour in concert the following year. The joint tour never materialized.

Back in New Jersey at the end of the month, Houston made another rare public appearance when she sang at a tribute to Paul Robeson at the New Jersey Performing Arts Center in Newark. Wearing a form-fitting olive-green evening dress, Whitney acknowledged her debt to the groundbreaking black entertainer who died in 1976: "Why I stand here today is because of Paul Robeson." She sang a cappella "I Loves You Porgy" (from *Porgy and Bess*) and the inspirational number "You'll Never Stand Alone." When Bobby Brown performed "Every Little Step," Whitney provided backup vocals for him. Cissy Houston closed the program with a gospel song. At an end-of-the-year charity fundraiser at Madison Square Garden, a host of music stars were on the bill. Two surprise guests were Whitney Houston and Michael Jackson, who each made brief appearances.

Whitney next turned up at Carnegie Hall in January 2001. Her friend Wyclef Jean, the hip-hop artist and producer, was making his debut at the Manhattan concert hall. Whitney offered an energetic version of "I Go to the Rock" (backed by brother Gary and her female group Sunday). However, there was a noticeable strain in Houston's voice when she undertook "My Love Is Your Love."

Meanwhile, a female stalker who had previously hounded Houston escaped from a Bronx psychiatric facility. Because the woman had threatened to kill Whitney's daughter, the manhunt to find her was intensive. After an eleven-hour search, the patient was located and returned to custody. With that situation under control, Houston focused on her Hawaii case. By early March 2001, it had been dismissed. As one journalist quipped, "Whitney Houston can now feel free to travel to Hawaii for vacation, not court hearings."

With this much-hyped incident put to rest, the media suddenly became fascinated by rumors that Whitney would return to filmmaking as a James Bond girl in the secret agent's next big-screen adventure. However, the enticing speculation proved to be chaff in the wind, as it was Halle Berry who eventually gained the coveted lead female role opposite Pierce Brosnan as Agent 007 in *Die Another Day* (2002). In the meantime, there were tabloid allegations that in March 2001 Bobby Brown and Whitney had

had yet another domestic spat. It was claimed that while registered at a swanky Los Angeles hotel, the couple had left their suite in great disarray. Their representatives, of course, denied the assertions.

On a more pleasant note, Whitney received a Lifetime Achievement Award at the First Annual BET Awards, held at the Paris Hotel in Las Vegas in June. At the gala, the artist, looking elegant in her sophisticated gown and stylish wig (along with her ever-present handkerchief to mop her brow), performed "I Have Nothing" and "I Will Always Love You." But her voice seemed a bit rough, and for the latter number, she called on Shakira, from girl group Sunday, to handle the difficult passages.

After being presented with the trophy by Babyface, while Cissy Houston and Bobbi Kristina stood proudly by, Whitney launched into her thank-you speech: "To my new Arista family, the best is yet to come. . . . To L. A. Reid . . . my brother, it's gonna be fine. To Clive Davis . . . it really does seem like yesterday . . . I love you, I do." When she came to register appreciation of her staff at Nippy, Inc., Whitney went into a delightful jive mode as she cutely rattled off the names of her in-house helpers. Turning to family members, the artist continued, "Mommy, you're one of the greatest singers I know. I love you with all my heart. To my daddy, who's watching from a sickbed, I wish you were here, but I know you're here, because you're in my heart." Then, after acknowledging her siblings, she said, "Lastly, the love of my life. That little girl is the love of my life. That's my life. Thank you for loving mommy unselfishly. She's a doll baby." When members of the audience shouted out, "What about Bobby?" she added, "Now let's give it up to the R&B king, Bobby Brown. There are a lot of copies, but there's only one original. Bobby Brown, I love you, honey. You are my heart."

In the new millennium, many announcements had been made about possible new film projects for Whitney to star in or produce, including most recently *Friends and Lovers*, to be adapted from the Eric Jerome Dickey novel. There was also talk of a remake of the 1976 film *Sparkle*, starring the young singer Aaliyah. Tragically, Aaliyah died in a plane crash in August 2001, and plans for that picture evaporated.

One venture that did come to fruition for Whitney was *The Princess Diaries* (2001). Coproduced by the artist's BrownHouse Productions, the Disney release was directed by Garry Marshall (brother of *The Preacher's Wife* director, Penny). It starred Anne Hathaway as an awkward San Francisco teenager who discovers that she is a princess and is trained for royal duties by her grandmother (Julie Andrews). Shot on a $30 million budget, it grossed over $108 million on domestic release and earned another $24 million in Europe.

Whitney was but one of the comedy's three listed producers and reportedly rarely appeared on the film set, although she did visit the sound stage one day to join Julie Andrews in singing "Happy Birthday" to director Garry Marshall. However, in Hollywood terms, because of her producing credits on the film, this was considered a success for Whitney. It buoyed up her stock in Hollywood, especially when plans were set in motion for a sequel. In addition, BrownHouse pushed forward with a made-for-cable movie entitled *Cheetah Girls* (2003). It was based on Deborah Gregory's series of books about a multi-ethnic group of girls seeking fame in the music business.

When *The Princess Diaries* premiered at the El Capitan Theater in Hollywood at the end of July, Bobby Brown, Bobbi Kristina and two of Brown's other children attended the gala. But producer Whitney was not on hand, claiming her private plane had developed last-minute engine trouble. However, she was present at her Mendham Township home on August 8 when Brown suffered a medical crisis. At about 3 A.M., he had to be rushed to nearby Morristown Memorial Hospital after an unspecified seizure. He was treated for approximately ninety minutes in the emergency room.

Although the patient agreed to a CAT scan, when the hospital staff asked him to provide blood and urine samples, he declined. Bobby insisted he was now feeling better and that he would seek any further treatment from a private physician. With that pronouncement, he checked himself out of the hospital. Later, when asked the full nature of the medical condition that had prompted Brown's urgent trip to the hospital, Whitney's public relations person insisted that it was the "mind-boggling" heat and humidity that had dehydrated Brown, who had been spending long hours working in the recording studio on the estate. "He hadn't been getting enough fluids and basically he was lightheaded," said the spokeswoman.

Such drama—even if it were not the first time such a crisis had occurred—would be enough to preoccupy any household. However, dramatic events—especially unfortunate ones—always seemed to cluster in Whitney's turbulent life. The same day that Brown made his mysterious visit to Morristown

Hospital, Houston's brother Michael was arrested and charged for alleged possession of cocaine, marijuana, and drug paraphernalia, and being under the influence of drugs. The thirty-nine-year-old had been pulled over by Fort Lee, New Jersey police after he failed to yield to oncoming traffic while exiting a Holiday Inn parking lot. According to reports, when officers searched his vehicle, they found "14 (partially) smoked marijuana cigarettes, a bag of marijuana, and some cocaine." Although Michael was taken into custody by the police, his companion, a teenage Manhattan girl who was a wannabe singer, was released into her parents' safekeeping. Michael was arraigned the next morning—Whitney's thirty-eighth birthday—and released on bail of $3,500.

For months, it was hyped that Whitney would be among the many celebrities who would perform at Michael Jackson's thirtieth-anniversary celebration, to be held over two nights in September at Madison Square Garden in New York City. As preparations continued for the star-studded double event—which would feature a reunion of Jackson and his brothers onstage—Whitney's actual participation remained in question. Several commentators wondered whether, if she really was suffering failing health due to drug usage, she could be up to the occasion. Producer David Gest assured everyone that Whitney would definitely be performing, as would Bobby Brown.

Friday September 7 came, and the Garden was filled with music-industry figures, showbusiness notables, and fans awaiting the start of the tribute. An hour after the scheduled showtime, the Prince of Pop was seated out front (surrounded by Elizabeth Taylor, his parents, and actor Macaulay Culkin) and the proceedings began. The opening offering was a jungle-themed, dance-intensive rendition of an old Jackson song, "Wanna Be Startin' Somethin'," featuring the combined talents of Usher, Maya, and Whitney Houston. When Whitney emerged on stage, there was an audible gasp from the audience at how emaciated—near skeletal—she looked. Her shocking appearance wasn't helped by her abbreviated outfit or her wild hairstyle. After spending less than five minutes in the limelight, Whitney vanished. She did not appear at Jackson's follow-up September 10 tribute concert as originally planned.

The artist's brief, gaunt turn in the spotlight was enough to start a media stampede, with newspaper, magazine and TV stories featuring a ghastly photo of the "new" Whitney next to the "old" beautiful one. For those people who had not believed previous rumors about her supposed drug problems, this unsightly cameo at Madison Square Garden supplied new and convincing evidence.

A few days later, news spread on the Internet and in the press that Houston had tragically died of a drug overdose. It was shocking enough information to distract many from grieving about the September 11, 2001 catastrophe at the World Trade Center. Arista Records quelled rumors about Houston's demise by stating, "Whitney thanks everyone for their concern. . . . We're not sure how this all started, but she is very much alive." Meanwhile, as a patriotic gesture following the terrorist attacks on Manhattan's Twin Towers, Arista rushed out a reissue of Houston's 1991 recording of "The Star Spangled Banner." Net proceeds and royalties were to be divided between the New York Firefighters 9–11 Disaster Relief Fund and the New York Fraternal Order of Police. The "new" release would earn over $1 million.

When Michael Jackson's thirtieth-anniversary show was finally aired on November 13, 2001 on the CBS network, it was much edited down to fit a two-hour format (with a longer version for European release). Also, it was later revealed, the images of a few key participants had been digitally enhanced for the telecast version, including Whitney, who had been doctored so she no longer seemed quite as skeletal as she had on stage.

As Whitney Houston's figure was being electronically revamped for the TV broadcast, the real Whitney visited two exclusive spas, one near Tucson, Arizona and another in Lenox, Massachusetts. It was apparently a compromise alternative to her seeking traditional substance-abuse treatment. The potential of these plush "resorts" to be in any way beneficial was not increased by Whitney and Bobby Brown (who accompanied her) reputedly partying before, during, and after their high-priced sojourns.

Ending her hellish year on a low note, the supermarket publications were now reporting: "Whitney Beaten Up by Her Drug Dealer." By now, the tabloids had published, and other media recounted, so many grim accounts of Houston's supposedly nightmarish drug-addicted life that it was difficult not to conclude that the diva, no matter how resilient she might seem, was nearing the end of a dangerous journey.

☆

"Whitney and I are in preliminary discussions about a new album and have already started listening to songs," announced Arista chief L. A. Reid in February 2002. This was part of Houston's new pact with Arista, signed in 2001, which extended her existing contract with the label. This agreement for several albums was rumored to be worth $100 million to the star. This high sum caused skepticism among industry veterans, as the music business had been suffering a bad downward spiral due to the state of the economy, the availability of "free" music on the Internet, piracy, and so forth. Besides, it was argued, with Whitney's relatively modest sales in recent years compared to her salad days, such an enormous figure seemed unrealistic. When L. A. Reid was asked if he was not troubled about investing so heavily in a talent reputed to have substance-abuse problems, he dismissed the notion by saying, "I'm trying to think of which artist hasn't had drug rumors in their career."

Sporadically, Whitney went into the studios to prepare her new album. She took time off in late May to fly to Nevada to participate in *Divas Las Vegas* at the MGM Grand Hotel Garden Arena. The live show was aired on VH1. This was Whitney's first appearance at the annual charity fundraising event since 1999. As it developed, there was more postmortem coverage of the tensions, apprehensions, and diva-like behavior on Whitney's part during rehearsals than of her actual very brief turn onstage. Her sole contribution was to join with Mary J. Blige for a heated rendition of "Rainy Dayz." After this quick stint, Whitney blew kisses to the audience and departed, not even returning for the show's grand finale.

In recent years, it was usually those around Whitney who had provided comfort and support to the superstar. In May 2002, there was a brief turnaround. Whitney's cousin Dionne Warwick, travelling en route to Los Angeles, was stopped at Miami International Airport by police, who claimed to have found eleven marijuana joints secreted in a lipstick container in her baggage. Whitney could certainly relate to the plight of her sixty-one-year-old cousin.

The next month, while Bobby Brown was accompanying Whitney back to New Jersey aboard her tour bus after recording sessions in Atlanta, he suddenly became ill. His symptoms included a high fever, the shakes, and profuse sweating. Brown was taken to the closest emergency facility, Mary Washington Hospital in Fredericksburg, Virginia, and admitted. He was given antibiotics intravenously to treat a serious infection. When he was released three days later, he said jauntily, looking at Whitney: "No biggie. I had my angel here looking after me." The couple then headed to New Jersey, where Brown continued to take antibiotics for his still-undisclosed infection.

In June 2002, Babyface, who was producing several cuts on Whitney's new album, was asked how things were going with the project. "She's singing better than I've heard her sing in years," he claimed. "Her voice is in tip-top shape and it's back to goose-bump time. When she's in the studio, I'm really excited about how she's going at it. She's going at it hard. She's very focused." There was mention that Whitney was contributing to the songwriting on at least one track for the new album.

As the Browns reached their tenth wedding anniversary on July 17, 2002, the *Boston Globe*'s Renée Graham wrote an article entitled "Life in the Pop Lane; An Imperfect 10: Whitney and Bobby, A Decade Later." Mulling over their matrimonial longevity, she asked, "Who'd'a thunk it?" The reporter said of Brown: "Marriage didn't curb his wild ways; instead Bobby, now 33, seemed to get in even more trouble. Then again, with his singing career all dried up, he had to do something to fill his days." Next, the journalist recited a shopping list of Whitney's recent misadventures: Hawaii, the Oscarcast in 2000, and her frail appearance at the Michael Jackson tribute in September 2001. Graham concluded her intriguing commentary by reflecting on the secret of their marital togetherness: "Whatever it is, it's allowed Mr. and Mrs. Brown to sustain storms both public and private, both real and imagined. If theirs isn't quite the greatest love of all, it's been an enduring one, outrunning . . . every shrill story predicting divorce, death, and devastation. And as off-key as they can sometimes be, Whitney and Bobby, 10 years and counting, are still a duo with a song worth singing."

Bobby Brown had his own distinctive take on his enduring relationship with Whitney. Speaking from the Los Angeles set of *Guns and Roses*, a low-budget Western about a gang of black female gunslingers with Bobby as the male outlaw in their midst, he said of their hot-tempered union: "We love hard and we fight hard." However, he believed their marriage would survive: "You can't break a diamond, and that's what our love is. A diamond." As to persistent gossip about substance abuse and its adverse affects on his wife's health, he scoffed, "We're still together and all the rest of the bull and the madness, it doesn't matter to us."

In contrast, another family member was not feeling well disposed toward Whitney, or so it seemed: her father. In late August 2002, the Newark-based John Houston Entertainment company filed a breach-of-contract suit against the singer. The action—spearheaded by John's partner, Kevin Skinner—claimed that Whitney had hired her dad and Skinner to help her navigate out of the legal difficulties engendered by the Hawaii case, as well as to negotiate her sizable new contract with Arista Records in 2001.

Skinner expanded on the situation in an interview with MTV. "We weren't her managers per se, at least not in name. But we were, in effect. She had no management at that time, and we masterminded the whole situation. All of the parties involved, we selected. And we did whatever it took to get her [finances secure]. It took her five years to run through her money, and it took us five weeks to get it back. But we didn't do it for free." As the squabble accelerated in the media, it remained unclear how much involvement eighty-one-year-old John Houston, now quite ill, actually had in the proceedings. In October, the skirmish escalated further when it was uncovered that Kevin Skinner had filed a police report back in March in East Orange, New Jersey claiming that he had received a death threat allegedly linked directly to Whitney and Bobby.

Reinforcing Whitney's growing belief that everyone was picking on her, in early September she received a summons for violating New Jersey's water-use restrictions. State officials had imposed limits on domestic water use the previous month because of drought conditions on the East Coast. Police had found lawn sprinklers running at Whitney's Mendham Township estate and learned that they had been left on overnight. Although she had not been at her home when the incident occurred, as the owner of the property she was being held responsible.

The long-term pressures of Whitney's personal and professional woes seem to have caught up with her that fall. She and Bobby were seeking rest and relaxation at a modest hotel in Alpharetta, Georgia. They arrived at the inn in their flashy midnight-blue Porsche convertible. When guests became excited by the presence of the celebrity couple, Houston reportedly grew angry and snarled, "Dammit—what's your problem?" She uttered a profanity and then continued her tirade: "Everywhere I go, it's the same thing—everybody look' at me!" Bobby hastily escorted her into the nearest elevator, and over the next few days the duo rarely left the confines of their room.

Of all the times to get into a legal scrape, Bobby had to pick November 7, 2002. What made that day so special was that after much negotiation— including numerous changes of date and locale—Whitney was finally to be interviewed by Diane Sawyer on ABC-TV's *PrimeTime*. The interview was to take place in Whitney's own home. She hoped the prerecorded program (to be aired a few weeks hence) would provide good promotion for her much-delayed and now soon-to-be-released album, *Just Whitney*. Whitney and Bobby Brown had recently moved into a large new home, complete with manicured lawns, in a gated community in Atlanta. With their diverse schedules and the logistics involved, they had scarcely unpacked their belongings and much of the house still remained unfurnished.

Around 2.30 A.M. on November 7, Bobby Brown was driving in his black Cadillac Escalade SUV along Atlanta's Peachtree Road when he was pulled over for speeding. The arresting officer found marijuana in Brown's possession and discovered that he was carrying neither a driver's license nor proof of car insurance. By now, Brown was growing angry. He was handcuffed and taken to jail. During the booking procedure in Fulton County, the outstanding warrant for his 1996 arrest (and his later failure to make a court appearance) in DeKalb County came to light. Therefore, after Bobby posted bail of $1,300, the police transferred him to the neighboring county jail. Shortly after he was booked in, his attorney got him released on bail of $10,000.

As this bad-luck Thursday progressed, the news of Brown's two bookings circulated on the news wires. When he returned home in the early afternoon, the *PrimeTime* team was already setting up the cameras for the interview. Whitney, her staff, and her relatives had spent the day being gracious to the TV crew as final preparations were made. Besides Whitney's concerns about what questions might be forthcoming and how she would respond, she now had to deal with Bobby's latest crisis. Adding to her discomfort, she was also suffering from laryngitis.

The actual question-and-answer session began at about 7 P.M. Whitney was seated on her living-room couch with Doogie Howser, her Yorkshire terrier, next to her. The grilling began.

On the use of drugs

SAWYER: Is it alcohol? Is it marijuana? Is it cocaine? Is it pills?
WHITNEY: It has been at times.
SAWYER: All?
WHITNEY: At times. Uh-hm.
SAWYER: And the . . . if you had to name the devil . . . for you . . .
the biggest devil among them . . .
WHITNEY: That would be me . . . I'm either my best friend or my
worst enemy. And that's how I have to deal with it.

On her health

WHITNEY: I'm not sick, Diane. I am not sick. Let's get that straight. I
am not sick. Okay? I've always been a thin girl. . . .
Whitney is not going to be fat, ever. Okay?

On her former lifestyle

WHITNEY: My business is sex, drugs, rock and roll. You know? My
friends, we have a good time. But as you get older and you
get wiser . . . you stop a lot of the kid stuff. . . . [However] I
think I kind of reverted back as I got older and said, 'Well,
I'm just gonna party.' . . . It was kind of a rebel in me. . . .
[But] you get to a point where you know . . . the party's over.

On the alleged expense of her drug usage

WHITNEY: Come on! . . . [$730,000?] I wish. No. I wish whoever was
making that money off of me would share it with me. No
way. No way. I want to see the receipts. From the drug
dealer that I bought 730,000 dollars' worth of drugs from.
I want to see receipts. Yeah, right.

When Sawyer bluntly inquired whether Houston used crack cocaine,
as rumors insisted, Whitney shot back, "Crack is cheap. I make too much

for me to ever smoke crack. Let's get that straight, OK? I don't do crack. I don't do that. Crack is whack."

The diva went on to say that she considered herself addicted to "making love. . . . [But] I don't like to think of myself as addicted. I like to think. . . . I had a bad habit . . . which can be broken." She claimed that career and family pressures over the years had a lot to do with her lifestyle, and admitted, "I would stay in my room for days . . . for days at a time just trying to get it together . . . to know what my next phase was going to be."

The singer confided she turned an emotional corner in September 2001 when rumors surfaced that she had died of a drug overdose. It was then that, "I changed my mind. I changed my mind. Yeah. . . . It frightened me. I don't want to ever be in the realm of, where I am." She admitted, "I pray every day, Diane. I'm not the strongest every day, but I'm not the weakest, either. And I won't break."

When Bobby Brown came into Sawyer's line of fire, he insisted he used marijuana because he was bipolar and it helped to keep him stable, whereas the prescription drug lithium made him feel catatonic. He said that for medicinal purposes, "I smoke a joint. . . . Every now and then. You know. It's not an everyday thing . . . it keeps me calm. Keeps my spirits well." He also acknowledged that his 1995 statements about having overcome his attraction to alcohol were premature.

Before and after a brief oncamera appearance by Bobbi Kristina, Whitney discussed her father's recent lawsuit ("it hurts"), and Clive Davis's departure from Arista. Of her marriage to Bobby, she declared, "Love is where you find it. It's where you find it. And I found it in him. And he found it in me." Whitney told Sawyer that if she were to apologize for anything in her life, it would be for having missed concerts and disappointed her fans.

In conclusion, Houston professed that she was "on the right path" now. "I know I'm a child of God. And I know he loves me. Jesus loves me. This I know."

The tell-all interview was originally scheduled to air on November 21, but the network rescheduled the event for December 4. Meanwhile, tantalizing teasers from and commentary on the much-anticipated program resounded throughout the media. Diane Sawyer told the TV show *Entertainment Tonight*: "[Whitney] is completely fascinating. This is such an emotional ride. Sometimes she seems angry; sometimes she's tearful, and always it is a no-holds-barred, I-am-going-to-talk-to-you-about-it-all tone."

When the interview finally aired, it drew a whopping 24 million viewers, giving *PrimeTime* the most tremendous ratings. Everyone had an opinion about the show, in which the celebrity seemed frequently distracted and not always grounded in everyday logic. Many commentators felt the self-destructive star had totally derailed her career with her display of apparent arrogance, defensiveness, and a steadfast refusal to openly admit the errors of her past ways (and bad habits).

The website of a rival U.S. TV network observed, "Admitting to taking cocaine, pills and marijuana while your profusely sweating husband admits smoking pot isn't usually the way to promote a comeback. Yet Whitney Houston bravely—and unwisely—went that route in a chat with ABC's Diane Sawyer. The interview with the confrontational, unrepentant Whitney was an instant classic up there with Michael [Jackson] & Lisa Marie [Presley] and Mike Tyson and Robin Givens."

Another perspective on Whitney's notorious hour in the hot seat came from Clive Davis. When asked his reaction to the artist's candid session with Diane Sawyer, he said, "I am not objective enough to respond clearly. . . . Whitney is family to me. She and I know that our bond is still here. I was emotional for her. She was candid in her admissions and it is painful to know what she has gone through. Having laryngitis at the time didn't help the presentation." After a pause, he added, "But I will tell you this. Aretha Franklin aside, Whitney is the greatest female singer on the planet. Period. She's going to reach deep down inside and prevail. Only she can do it for herself, but she can do it. I know she can."

26

Whatchulookinat

"Music is a part of my life I can't forget. I want to make good music. This is what I do. This is what Bobby [Brown] and I both do. We make music, and it keeps the bills paid and the clothes on our children's backs and shoes on their feet, food on the table. This is the main part of what we have to do."

WHITNEY HOUSTON, 1998

It had been a long and often painful struggle bringing *Just Whitney* to completion. There was the necessity of dealing with the staff changes and revamped procedures at Arista Records since L. A. Reid took over the label's reins. Then, it proved to be a harder task than anticipated to find the proper mix of producers and songs; costs mounted as recorded tracks were discarded and others substituted to make Houston's first studio album in four years a truly back-to-basics experience. In addition, there was Whitney's array of personal problems with which to contend. As the disc's announced release date kept being pushed further back into 2002, industry observers wondered if it would ever be finished. When L. A. Reid was asked if he thought Whitney's much-publicized woes and Bobby's ongoing legal troubles would hurt sales for *Just Whitney*, he responded, "It's not my job to worry about the tabloid stuff. My job is to help Whitney make great music."

The first *Just Whitney* cut to receive airplay was "Whatchulookinat," a song cowritten by Whitney. Its bitter lyrics dealt with media gossips and busybodies who are "messing with my reputation" by fabricating stories about the artist. The accusatory number was leaked to radio stations and

Internet music listeners in mid-2002. Despite the initial hype, the song failed to grab the attention of music fans. It stalled at number ninety-six on the Billboard Hot 100 chart. (The song had more success in Europe.) A program director at a Baltimore R&B station explained the cut's lukewarm reception: "A lot of listeners said [this] song sounded dated. Maybe going the disses route wasn't the way to reintroduce herself to the marketplace." Everyone agreed this did not augur well for the album. Ironically, the much-ignored cut was produced by Bobby Brown, whom Houston thanked in the liner notes for being "the best producer in the world."

A week after the notorious *PrimeTime* interview was aired in early December 2002, *Just Whitney* was released into record stores. After the initial core of faithful fans and the curious rushed to purchase the latest Whitney Houston disc, sales tapered off drastically. (To gain additional sales, a limited-edition CD and DVD package was released, containing interviews and music videos as well as the album tracks.) Weighing in at less than forty minutes, the album's lyrics covered self-pity (for example, "Baby, you don't know what I been going through"), kiss-off diatribes, and love. Overall, the album floundered in its choice of numbers, many of which, it was agreed, were presented in a musical idiom that had become passé.

Of the slim pickings, one of the better-liked offerings was "One of Those Days," a smoky reflection on the need to chill out. It was produced and cowritten by Kevin "She'kspere" Briggs, who was also responsible for the album's "Dear John Letter." Missy Elliott returned to produce and cowrite "Things You Say." Babyface, Houston's longtime pal, produced three of the entries, including a gospel-flavored rehash of the 1970s hit ballad "You Light Up My Life." Whitney and Bobby dueted on the unmemorable "My Love," another ode to their "enduring" relationship. The disappointing end results of *Just Whitney* were a far cry from the high goals established at the outset. During its preparation, Whitney had told *Billboard* magazine that this disc would be "a positive, feel-good, very soul-oriented album, something I felt was missing. I hear a lot of things on the radio, but I don't hear any R&B songs with a bold new flavor . . . songs you can sing along to and love the melody. That's what I was looking for."

Many reviews for *Just Whitney* seemed more like direct assaults on the artist's much-dissected personal life. *Time* magazine's Josh Tyrangiel felt the album "has loads of energy. Negative energy." John Caramancia in *Rolling Stone* suggested, "The decline of Whitney Houston's career has run in rough parallel to her marriage to New Edition castoff Bobby Brown—every year, she seems to spend less time on her music." Nekesa Mumbi of the *London Free Press* commented, "Given what's on this disc, it probably won't hold anyone's attention long. . . . The problem isn't with her dynamic voice, which still sparkles, though it sounds a bit raspy at times and doesn't soar as high as it once did. . . . It's the choice of material that demotes Houston from timeless diva to run-of-the-mill R&B songstress. Though her previous songs have been criticized as schmaltzy or pop fluff, they had an appeal that, when combined with Houston's regal voice, made them classics."

There was qualified praise from *Los Angeles Weekly*'s Ernest Hardy: "Dubbed dead before it even hit shelves, *Just Whitney* is nowhere near the disaster that many have claimed. It's easily the second best overall effort of Houston's career (coming in right behind 1998's admittedly sleeker, relatively baggage-free *My Love Is Your Love* . . .). Even more easily, Whitney trumps other recent (and for the most part critically and commercially disappointing) comeback attempts by such R&B stalwarts as Mariah Carey, Toni Braxton, Deborah Cox and TLC. These are truly hard times for divas."

Relatively more enthusiastic was Tom Sinclair of *Entertainment Weekly*. He rated the album a B– because it "has a refreshingly old-school vibe. Whatever her personal problems, our gal sounds plucky and on top of her game. . . . Of course, amid the wheat, there's some chaff, like the cover of the Debby Boone chestnut 'You Light Up My Life' and the treacly keyboards-and-strings big ballad 'Try It on My Own.' Still in her third decade as a diva, Houston remains a formidable role model for [*American*] *Idol* [TV show] wannabes, proving that a great voice goes a long way toward kicking adversity in the butt."

In a downsliding market, which saw many top music artists faltering badly with the public, *Just Whitney* would sell only just over 500,000 copies in the U.S., with many copies soon relegated to the remainder bins. By its third month on release, the album had tumbled down to number 100 in the charts. On the other hand, thanks to several remixes of individual tracks and the impact of the music videos (directed by Kevin Bray) produced in support of the disc, some of the songs won popularity in dance clubs and as singles.

Following the washing of Whitney Houston's dirty linen in public on TV's *PrimeTime*, the ABC network balanced the scales by showcasing, on its *Good Morning America* TV program (December 10, 2002), a Whitney mini-concert held in the plaza of Manhattan's Lincoln Center. The segment had been taped two days earlier on a bitterly cold afternoon. Despite the frigid weather, over 3,000 fans crowded into the plaza to see the Queen of Real Life Soap Opera sing. It was the artist's first live performance in the U.S. in fifteen months. Whitney arrived nearly an hour late for the occasion, blaming her tardiness on midtown traffic. The diva wore an ensemble of skin-tight designer jeans and a white turtleneck sweater, plus a floor-length suede coat. For the occasion, her hair was in curls with red highlights. She sang "One of Those Days" and "Tell Me No" from her new album. When the thirty-five-member choir from Talent Unlimited High School (in New York City) joined her for a gospel rendering of "Do You Hear What I Hear?" there were a few musical missteps. After a couple of faltering verses, Whitney demanded, "Stop! Stop! We're going to start this again." She and the choir took the number from the top and thereafter everything went fine.

The Christmas season is supposed to be a time of peace and joy, but that seemed impossible in Whitney's bizarre world, which had more highs and lows than a daytime TV drama. One of the results of her Diane Sawyer interview was a huge outcry from some viewers who, after seeing the singer's self-indictment, contacted New Jersey social services to register concern about the wellbeing of young Bobbi Kristina in such a seemingly dysfunctional household.

Thereafter, a spokesman for the New Jersey Division of Youth and Family Services announced: "Our policy is that if we get complaints that a parent is using hard drugs, we are required by law to investigate the situation. If we do find that a parent is abusing drugs, we will first ask the parents to cooperate with the department to remedy the problem through drug testing and counseling. . . . If the parents do not cooperate, then the department may petition family court to require the parents to comply. They may also ask the court at that time to move the child away from the parents, placing the child with a relative or in a foster home. . . . If the parents do not show any progress through drug testing or counseling, then the termination of parental rights would be considered. But this is a very extreme step and it is hoped that every avenue is explored before entertaining the possibility." The agency was not permitted by policy to state publicly if an actual investigation of the Houston–Brown home was underway.

☆

In January 2003, Bobby Brown was growing increasingly restless as he awaited the disposition of his legal difficulties in Georgia. Some weeks earlier, he'd been spotted partying with friends in Miami's South Beach club district. Then, on January 13, 2003, he turned up at the televised American Music Awards where he duetted on "Thug Lovin'" with hot rap artist Ja Rule. Their appearance had been heavily promoted, and following his performance Brown granted an interview to the TV tabloid show *Access Hollywood*. Regarding Whitney's revelations on *PrimeTime*, he said, "I guess people took it wrong, but whatever happened is whatever happened. Me and my wife are fine and we just want people to know we live and love each other, so just accept us for what we are. We're entertainers. This is what we do. We got into this business for that." Finally, the urban singer noted for the record: "I'm just Bobby, man. People know me for just being Bobby, and I can't change. I'm going to be me for the rest of my life, and I just hope people . . . you know, keep your words to yourself. If you have anything bad to say, just don't say it at all, because I'm not in the mood."

Meanwhile, back in Georgia, the DeKalb County court system was up in arms that Bobby Brown had first missed his required Monday visit to a court bailiff, and then had left Georgia for the West Coast without official permission. As such, a new DeKalb County warrant was issued. It ordered Brown's arrest because he had breached the stated bail conditions and was now a fugitive from justice. When contacted, Brown's attorney assured irate officials that his client would surrender by the coming Friday. Brown's own cool response to the ruckus was: "When you're an entertainer, you've got to perform sooner or later."

Amid much international hoopla, the wanted man flew back to the East Coast to turn himself in to the Georgia authorities. In court on January 17, he was sentenced to eight days in jail and ordered not to drive for one year. He was also required to perform 240 hours of community service, pay $2,000 in fines and $8,000 in court costs, and to undergo substance-abuse counseling. A further condition required the defendant to remain on probation for two years.

But the high drama did not end there. Early on the morning of

Tuesday, January 21, inmate Brown complained of having severe chest pains and generally not feeling well. Reportedly, when help reached the ailing man, he was shouting, "Oh my God!" and calling out "Whitney, Whitney." Brown was immediately transferred from jail to Grady Memorial Hospital's special prisoner section, which had deputies posted on sentry duty. By the next day, however, Bobby had recovered from his mysterious ailment. Since the Georgia jurisdiction operated on a policy of early release for good behavior, he was now eligible to be discharged from custody. So he did not have to return to jail and was again a free man on Wednesday, January 22. The Fulton County, Georgia charges for his November 2002 escapade still remained unsettled.

While Bobby was creating his latest legal havoc, Whitney was dealing with her father's lawsuit. The situation had taken an even uglier turn when, a day after the *PrimeTime* interview, John Houston appeared on a segment of TV's *Celebrity Justice* (videotaped from his hospital sickbed), imploring his daughter to "pay the money you owe me." Although distraught over the financial matters that had created a huge gulf between them, Whitney visited her seriously ill dad at the New York hospital where he was being treated for a degenerative heart condition and diabetes.

Hardly had the world digested and recovered from the *PrimeTime* interview than new Whitney soundbites were flying around the Internet. This time the outrageous dialogue derived from a January 30, 2003 interview between Whitney and controversial radio talk-show host Wendy Williams. Describing the combative and salty exchange between the diva and the Manhattan shock jock, the *New York Times* reported, "Speaking over the phone—which was probably best, from the point of averting bloodshed—Ms. Williams asked Ms. Houston questions about her husband, Bobby Brown, and his jail time and asked about her drug use. Ms. Houston answered in language best called unrestrained. Imagine two women who don't like each other and find themselves late at night at the same end of the bar." One of the most intriguing segments of the interview was a discussion of the breast implants Whitney had allegedly acquired and whether Bobby was happy with the results. Later, Houston flew off the handle when Williams referred to tabloid articles which claimed the singer had recently cut staff salaries, including that of her mother, as part of an economy drive following John Houston's lawsuit.

The sad news was not unexpected, but it still came as a shock. In the early hours of Sunday morning, February 2, 2003, John Houston, aged eighty-two, died at Manhattan's Columbia Presbyterian Hospital. His wife, Peggy, and his personal nurse were at his side.

As the Houston clan gathered in New York, Whitney, who had been at a magazine cover shoot, flew in from Miami. That Thursday, she attended her father's wake at the Whigham Funeral Home in Newark. She spent much of the day in the funeral home's viewing room saying her traumatic goodbyes to him. The funeral was held on Friday at the St. James Zionist Church on Dr. Martin Luther King Boulevard in Newark. It was snowing hard as family and friends gathered to pay their final respects to Mr. Houston.

To avoid causing a media flurry and also because she could not bring herself to share her grief in public, Whitney did not attend the service. Afterwards, interment took place at the Fairview Cemetery in Westfield, New Jersey. Because John was an armed-services veteran, he was buried with full military honors. A stoic-looking Cissy attended both the service and burial. Whitney's cousin Dionne Warwick was at the service, while close family friend Aretha Franklin had a recording of "Amazing Grace" delivered to the Houstons, along with a personal message of admiration for John as a father.

In the weeks following John Houston's death, the *Star* tabloid revealed that John had given them an interview from his deathbed. The dying man had stated, "Whitney will always be my daughter and I will always love her. . . . I think Whitney would have paid the debt by now if it wasn't for that Bobby Brown. . . . He's driven a wedge between me and my daughter. I never trusted him." While many assumed that the lawsuit would dissolve now that Mr. Houston had passed on, Kevin Skinner, the late man's business partner, insisted that because the claim derived from obligations to the management firm, it would still be pursued.

☆

Following her father's death, Whitney maintained a relatively low profile. But already there were reports in the trade press of possible new film ventures for her. For example, movie producer Lee Daniels, one of those responsible for Halle Berry's *Monster's Ball* (2001), hoped to interest the singer in the lead female role in a project entitled *The Woodsman*, which dealt with pedophilia.

Meanwhile, Bobby Brown wanted to party. His bash to honor his thirty-fourth birthday on February 5 had been postponed due to John Houston's death. But it took place eight days later at the downtown Atlanta nightclub Level 3. Following the event, Brown was interviewed on *Access Hollywood* and he was in an unusually subdued mood. He mentioned sadly that Whitney had not attended the celebration, pointing out, "It's hard to be humans when you are Whitney Houston and Bobby Brown. . . . It's hard when everyone is against us."

By mid-March 2003, everything seemed back to "normal" in the Brown household. *People* magazine snapped the couple lunching at a restaurant in Bal Harbour, Florida. The couple were in a playful mood at their table, evidently still on a high from just spending $140,000 at Cartier on a diamond ring and other expensive trinkets.

In late March, Whitney and Bobby Brown made a surprise appearance at the Haitian Music and Entertainment Awards in Miami. A few days later, on April 3, Whitney flew to Manhattan for the Reverend Al Sharpton's Keepers of the Dream Awards dinner at the Sheraton Hotel. After receiving a standing ovation from the audience, the artist told the crowd, "I'm so full tonight. Today was the first time I've been back [north] since my father died. I sat with my brother today and we just cried." While performing a song from her *Just Whitney* album—which she dedicated to her late father—Whitney began tearing up. After completing the song, she left the stage in a highly emotional state.

In mid-April 2003, the diva filmed a guest-starring role in the Fox-TV series *Boston Public*, to be aired on May 12. Playing herself in the story line, she sang "Try It On My Own" from her recent album.

On May 22, 2003, Whitney participated in VH1's *Divas Duets 2003*, the network's annual bash. Broadcast live from the MGM Grand Hotel Garden Arena in Las Vegas, the concert was hosted by Queen Latifah and featured artists such as Chaka Khan, Lisa Marie Presley, Celine Dion, Mary J. Blige, Shania Twain, and Stevie Wonder. Whitney performed "Try It on My

Own" and duetted on "Something in Common" with Bobby Brown. In the *Los Angeles Times*, Richard Cromelin labeled the latter performance the "evening's major curiosity" and noted, "[Houston] and Brown moved busily in separate orbits during their segment, with absolutely no connection."

Three days after the *Divas* show, Whitney, along with Bobby Brown and their daughter, Bobbi Kristina, flew to Israel. Explaining she was going on a "spiritual retreat," the singer and her family were en route to the city of Dimona, where they planned to visit the Black Hebrews, an African-American sect. When the trio stopped over in Jerusalem, they were greeted by Prime Minister Ariel Sharon. Whitney, dressed exotically all in red, said of Israel: "It's home. It's a friendship I've never had with any other country." During her stay in the Holy Land, the artist kept repeating, "This is my land. . . . This is *my* land!" This much-reported-upon trip led syndicated gossip columnist Liz Smith to wonder, "Can we expect Whitney and Bobby to settle in a kibbutz anytime soon? Probably not, but who knows with these two? Who knew they considered themselves part of the Lost Tribes of Israel?"

Meanwhile, having regained her former sleek, healthy looks, Whitney undertook a cover photo shoot at the Biltmore Hotel in Coral Gables, Florida for the July issue of *Essence* magazine. During this transitional period, she also recorded a selection of holiday songs, tentatively scheduled for release by Arista in October 2003. Obviously, the Whitney Houston of today is keen to regain her showbusiness throne, despite the fierce competition from a host of best-selling newcomers.

In recent years, Whitney Houston's personal demons and controversial—often disastrous—life choices have frequently obscured her amazing talents and overshadowed her instinctive need to perform. This has led one showbusiness observer to comment, "If it turns out that she has finally squandered her talent, it will be sad but perhaps understandable. Such a vast 'gift' is undoubtedly also a curse. Squandering it might be the last act of will available to a very willful lady called Whitney." Frequently cited as part of her pattern of destructive behavior has been her ongoing codependent relationship with the much-troubled Bobby Brown. On the other hand, it should be remembered that this strong-willed diva once instructed a reporter: "Tell 'em that Whitney Houston still loves entertaining as much as she did when she was nineteen. And she probably still will when she's ninety-nine."

In the early years of her fame, Whitney was asked whether her overwhelming success was "fair." The artist, who had suddenly risen from obscurity to superstardom, responded, "There's nothing unfair about working hard and getting what you want. . . . I [have] worked hard and I'm very serious about what I do." As to her magical talent, she stated in one of her more lucid moments that it is and always will be about "carefully chosen and carefully felt songs. I have to feel it, love it, and live it. Music isn't supposed to bring you down; it's supposed to bring you up."

Sadly, in recent years, the public's fixation with Whitney's tumultuous personal life has frequently overshadowed her many achievements and the artistic potential still left untapped in her being. Discussing the artist's recurring troubles, Ernest Hardy wrote in the *Los Angeles Weekly*: "Like Michael Jackson, another diva on the moist side of a meltdown, Whitney Houston has seemingly taken her cues from the old-school handbook: she's very Judy Garland these days. But as with that patron saint of the drugged and resilient, Houston's recent travails have added pathos to her voice, grit to the material she applies it to." Singer Luther Vandross said of his friend: "She's such a survivor. Most women today are simply pretenders to her throne. There is only one Whitney."

Certainly, no one can accurately predict what twists and turns Whitney Houston's hectic professional and personal lives will take in the years ahead. Safe to say, the diva, now in her forties, will often do the unexpected and will probably continue to be quite amazed by people's strong reactions to her often unusual actions. But she has always been unfazed by others' viewpoints, just as, early on, she found strength and security in marching to her own beat: "Listen, I always move. Nothing can stop me from movin'. What didn't kill me made me stronger, sweetie."

For emotional nourishment, Whitney relies strongly on her Christian faith. "Basically I am centered with me and my God. I mean, no matter what I do, no matter what's happening I say, 'God, I am going to take care of it, I can move on.' I have that anchor." Her spiritual conviction is that "If you just anchor yourself with God, you can resist a lot of temptations. Prayer helps a lot." She subscribes to the belief that "tomorrow's not promised. If I'm here, hopefully, I'll still be making good music."

Whatever paths the celebrated singer may follow in the future, they will reflect her own declaration: "I'm Whitney. I am Whitney Houston. I've always had my own style. There's nobody else."

Discography*

Whitney Houston (Arista, 1985)
You Give Good Love/Thinking about You/Someone for Me/Saving All My Love for You/Nobody Loves Me Like You Do/How Will I Know/All at Once/Take Good Care of My Heart/Greatest Love of All/Hold Me

Whitney (Arista, 1987)
I Wanna Dance with Somebody (Who Loves Me)/Just the Lonely Talking Again/Love Will Save the Day/Didn't We Almost Have It All/So Emotional/Where Are You/Love Is a Contact Sport/You're Still My Man/For the Love of You/Where Do Broken Hearts Go/I Know Him So Well

I'm Your Baby Tonight (Arista, 1990)
I'm Your Baby Tonight/My Name Is Not Susan/All the Man That I Need/Lover for Life/Anymore/Miracle/I Belong to You/Who Do You Love/We Didn't Know/After We Make Love/I'm Knockin'

The Bodyguard (Arista, 1992; soundtrack album)
Whitney Houston tracks: I Will Always Love You/I Have Nothing/I'm Every Woman/Run to You/Queen of the Night/Jesus Loves Me
Other tracks: Even If My Heart Would Break/Someday (I'm Coming Back)/It's Gonna Be a Lovely Day/(What's So Funny 'Bout) Peace, Love and Understanding/Theme from *The Bodyguard*/Trust in Me

---

* Compilation albums featuring multiple artists and releases of remixed Whitney recordings are generally not included in this listing.

Waiting to Exhale (Arista, 1995; soundtrack album)
Whitney Houston tracks: Exhale (Shoop, Shoop)/Why Does It Hurt So Bad/Count on Me
Other tracks: Let It Flow/It Hurts Like Hell/Sittin' Up in My Room/This Is How It Works/Not Gon' Cry/My Funny Valentine/And I Gave My Love to You/All Night Long/Wey U/My Love, Sweet Love/Kissing You/Love Will Be Waiting at Home/How Could You Call Her Baby

The Preacher's Wife (Arista 1996; soundtrack album)
Whitney Houston tracks: I Believe in You and Me/Step by Step/Joy/Hold on, Help Is on the Way/I Go to the Rock/I Love the Lord/Somebody Bigger Than You and I/You Were Loved/My Heart Is Calling/I Believe in You and Me/Step by Step/Who Would Imagine a King/He's All over Me/Joy to the World
Other track: The Lord Is My Shepherd

The Prince of Egypt (DreamWorks, 1998; soundtrack album)
Whitney Houston and Mariah Carey track: When You Believe
Other tracks: Deliver Us/The Reprimand/Follow Tzipporah/All I Ever Wanted (with Queen's Reprise)/Goodbye Brother/Through Heaven's Eyes/The Burning Bush/Playing with the Big Boys/Cry/Rally/The Plagues/Death of the First Born/When You Believe/Red Sea/Through Heaven's Eyes/River Lullaby/Humanity/I Will Get There

My Love Is Your Love (Arista, 1998)
It's Not Right But It's Okay/Heartbreak Hotel/My Love Is Your Love/When You Believe/If I Told You That/In My Business/I Learned from the Best/Oh Yes/Get It Back/Until You Come Back/I Bow Out/You'll Never Stand Alone

Whitney Houston: The Greatest Hits (Arista, 2000)
Disc 1—Cool Down: You Give Good Love/Saving All My Love For You/Greatest Love of All/All at Once/If You Say My Eyes Are Beautiful/Didn't We Almost Have It All/Where Do Broken Hearts Go/All the Man That I Need/Run to You/I Have Nothing/I Will Always Love You/Exhale (Shoop, Shoop)/Why Does It Hurt So Bad/I Believe in You and Me/Heartbreak Hotel/My Love Is Your Love/Same Script, Different Cast/Could I Have This Kiss Forever

Disc 2—Throw Down: Fine/If I Told You That/It's Not Right But It's Okay/My Love Is Your Love/Heartbreak Hotel/I Learned from the Best/Step by Step/I'm Every Woman/Queen of the Night/I Will Always Love You/Love Will Save the Day/I'm Your Baby Tonight/So Emotional/I Wanna Dance with Somebody (Who Loves Me)/How Will I Know/Greatest Love of All/One Moment in Time/The Star Spangled Banner

Just Whitney (Arista, 2002)
One of Those Days/Tell Me No/Things You Say/My Love/Love That Man/Try It on My Own/Dear John Letter/Unashamed/You Light Up My Life/Whatchulookinat

Filmography

The Bodyguard (Warner Bros., 1992). Color, 130 minutes. R-rated.
Producers: Kevin Costner, Lawrence Kasdan, and Jim Wilson. Director: Mick Jackson. Story/screenplay: Lawrence Kasdan. Production designer: Jeffrey Beecroft. Art director: William Ladd Skinner. Set decorator: Lisa Dean. Costumes: Susan Nininger. Music: Alan Silvestri. Choreographer: Sean Cheesman. Supervising sound editors: Julia Evershade and George Simpson. Camera: Andrew Dunn. Editors: Donn Cambern and Richard A. Harris.
Cast: Kevin Costner (Frank Farmer), Whitney Houston (Rachel Marron), Gary Kemp (Sy Spector), Bill Cobbs (Bill Devaney), Ralph Waite (Herb Farmer), Tomas Arana (Greg Portman), Michele Lamar Richards (Nicki Marron), Mike Starr (Tony Scipelli), Christopher Birt (Henry), DeVaughn Nixon (Fletcher Marron), Gerry Bamman (Ray Court), Joe Urla (Minella), Tony Pierce (Dan), Charles Keating (Klingman), Robert Wuhl (Oscar show host), Debbie Reynolds (herself), Richard Schiff (Skip Thomas), Chris Connelly (emcee at Oscar show arrivals), David Foster (Oscar show conductor). John Tesh (*Entertainment Tonight* host) [uncredited], Mark Thomason (killer with mask) [uncredited].

Waiting to Exhale (Twentieth Century-Fox, 1995). Color, 127 minutes. R-rated.
Executive producers: Ronald Bass and Terry McMillan. Producers: Deborah Schindler and Ezra Swerdlow. Director: Forest Whitaker. Based on the novel by Terry McMillan. Screenplay: Terry McMillan and Ronald Bass. Production designer: David Gregman. Art director: Marc Fishichella. Set decorator: Michael W. Foxworthy. Costumes: Judy L. Ruskin. Music: Kenneth "Babyface" Edmonds. Sound supervisor: Tim Chau. Camera: Toyomichi Kurita. Editor: Richard Chew.

Cast: Whitney Houston (Savannah Jackson), Angela Bassett (Bernadine Harris), Loretta Devine (Gloria Matthews), Lela Rochon (Robin Stokes), Gregory Hines (Marvin King), Dennis Haysbert (Kenneth Dawkins), Mykelti Williamson (Troy), Michael Beach (John Harris Sr.), Leon (Russell), Wendell Pierce (Michael Davenport), Donald Adeosun Faison (Tarik Matthews), Jeffrey D. Sams (Lionel), Jazz Raycole (Onika Harris), Brandon Hammond (John Harris Jr.), Kenya Moore (Denise), Lamont Johnson (Joseph), Wren T. Brown (minister), Starletta DuPois (Savannah's mother), Delaina Mitchell (Michelle—Tarik's girlfriend), Ezra Swerdlow (Bill), Wally Bujack (judge), Giancarlo Esposito (David Matthews) [uncredited], Wanda-Lee Evans (Jane Millhouse) [uncredited], Kelly Preston (Kathleen) [uncredited], Wesley Snipes (James Wheeler) [uncredited].

The Preacher's Wife (Touchstone, 1996). Color, 124 minutes. PG-rated. Executive producers: Elliot Abbott and Robert Greenhut. Producer: Samuel Goldwyn Jr. Co-producers: Timothy M. Bourne, Debra Martin Chase, Amy Lemisch. Associate producer: Bonnie Hlinomaz. Director: Penny Marshall. Based on the novel *The Bishop's Wife* by Robert Nathan. Prior screenplay: Robert E. Sherwood and Leonardo Bercovici. Screenplay: Nat Mauldin and Allan Scott. Production designer: Bill Groom. Art director: Dennis Bradford. Set decorator: George DeTitta. Costumes: Cynthia Flynt. Music: Hans Zimmer. Supervising sound editor: Dennis Drummond. Camera: Miroslav Ondricek. Editors: George Bowers and Stephen A. Rotter.
Cast: Denzel Washington (Dudley), Whitney Houston (Julia Biggs), Courtney B. Vance (Reverend Henry Biggs), Gregory Hines (Joe Hamilton), Jenifer Lewis (Marguerite Coleman), Loretta Devine (Beverly), Justin Pierre Edmund (narrator/Jeremiah Biggs), Lionel Richie (Britsloe), Paul Bates (Saul Jeffrey), Lex Monson (Osbert), Darvel Davis Jr. (Hakim), William James Stiggers Jr. (Billy Eldridge), Marcella Lowery (Anna Eldridge), Cissy Houston (Mrs. Havergal), Aaron A. McConnaughey, Shyheim Franklin, Tarai Hicks, and Kennan Scott (teens), Jernard Burks (pizza man), Lizan Mitchell (judge), Charlotte d'Ambroise (Debbie Paige), Delores Mitchell (Mary Halford), Mervyn Warren (pianist), Roy Haynes (drummer), George Coleman (sax player), Ted Dunbar (guitar player), Jamil Nasser (bass player).

Rodgers and Hammerstein's Cinderella (ABC-TV, November 2, 1997). Color, 88 minutes. G-rated.

Executive producers: Debra Martin Chase, David R. Ginsburg, Whitney Houston, Neil Meron, and Craig Zadan. Producers: Mike Moder and Chris Montan. Associate producer: Robyn Crawford. Director: Robert Iscove. Book and lyrics: Oscar Hammerstein II. Teleplay: Robert L. Freedman. Production designer: Randy Ser. Set decorator: Julie Kaye Fanton. Costumes: Ellen Mirojnick. Music: Richard Rodgers. Additional music: Martin Erskine and Danny Troob. Music stager/choreographer: Rob Marshall. Supervising sound editor: Albert Gasser. Camera: Ralf Bode. Editors: Casey O. Rohrs and Tanya Swerling.

Cast: Whitney Houston (fairy godmother), Bernadette Peters (Cinderella's stepmother), Jason Alexander (Lionel), Whoopi Goldberg (Queen Constantina), Victor Garber (King Maximillian), Veanne Cox (Calliope), Natalie Desselle (Minerva), Paolo Montalban (the Prince), Brandy (Cinderella), Michael Haynes (the coachman), Scott Fowler, Nathan Prevost, Travis Payne, Jennifer Lee Keyes, Melanie Gage, Stacey Harper, Sergio Trujillo, and Melissa Hurley (dancers).

Bibliography

Books

Ammons, Kevin, with Bacon, Nancy. *Good Girl, Bad Girl: An Insider's Biography of Whitney Houston*. Secaucus, N.J.: Birch Lane, 1996.

Bego, Mark. *Aretha Franklin: The Queen of Soul*. New York: St. Martin's, 1989.

———. *Whitney!* New York: PaperJacks, 1986.

Bona, Damien. *Inside Oscar 2*. New York: Ballantine, 2002.

Bowman, Jeffery. *Diva: The Totally Unauthorized Biography of Whitney Houston*. New York: RoseBooks/HarperCollins, 1995.

Brode, Douglas. *Denzel Washington: His Films and Career*. Secaucus, N.J.: Birch Lane, 1997.

Bronson, Fred. *The Billboard Book of Number One Hits* (4th edn.) New York: Billboard, 1997.

Brooks, Tim, and Marsh, Earle. *The Complete Directory to Prime Time Network and Cable TV Shows: 1946–Present* (7th edn.). New York: Ballantine, 1999.

Busnar, Gene. *The Picture Life of Whitney Houston*. New York: Franklin Watts, 1988.

Cader, Michael (ed.). *Saturday Night Live: The First Twenty Years*. Boston: Cader/Houghton Mifflin, 1994.

Carruth, Gorton. *What Happened When: A Chronology of Life & Events in America*. New York: Penguin, 1991.

Cox, Ted. *Whitney Houston: Pop Superstar*. Broomall, Pa.: Chelsea House, 1997.

Crown, Lawrence. *Penny Marshall*. Los Angeles: Renaissance, 1999.

Daniels, Clifton (ed.-in-chief). *Chronicle of the 20th Century*. Mount Kisco, N.Y.: Chronicle, 1987.

Dickerson, James. *Women on Top: The Quiet Revolution That's Rocking the American Music Industry*. New York: Billboard, 1998.

Dougan, Andy. *Untouchable: A Biography of Robert De Niro*. New York: Thunder's Mouth, 1996.

Ellis, Brett Easton. *American Psycho*. New York: Vintage, 1991.

Erlewine, Michael *et al.* (eds.). *All.Music Guide to Rock* (2nd edn.). San Francisco: Miller Freeman, 1997.

Greenberg, Keith Elliot. *Whitney Houston*. Minneapolis, Minn.: Lerner, 1988.

Houston, Cissy, with Jonathan Singer. 1998. *How Sweet the Sound: My Life With God and Gospel.* New York: Doubleday, 1998.

Keith, Todd. *Kevin Costner.* London, U.K.: Ikon/Print, 1991.

Mabunda, L. Mpho, and Shirelle Phelps (eds.). *Contemporary Black Biography.* Detroit, Mich.: Gale Research, 1996.

McMillan, Terry. *Waiting to Exhale.* New York: Pocket, 1995.

Nathan, David. *The Soulful Divas.* New York: Billboard, 1999.

O'Dair, Barbara (ed.). *Trouble Girls: The Rolling Stone Book of Women in Rock.* New York: Random House, 1997.

O'Neil, Thomas. *The Emmys* (3rd edn.). New York: Perigee, 2000.

_____. *The Grammys* (2nd edn.). New York: Perigee, 1999.

_____. *Movie Awards.* New York: Perigee, 2001.

Parish, James Robert. *Hollywood Bad Boys.* Chicago: Contemporary, 2002.

_____. *Hollywood Divas.* Chicago: Contemporary, 2002.

_____. *Today's Black Hollywood.* New York: Kensington, 1995.

_____, and Hill, George H. *Black Action Pictures from Hollywood.* Jefferson, N.C.: McFarland, 1989.

_____, and Pitts, Michael R. *Hollywood Songsters* (2nd edn.). New York: Routledge, 2002.

_____, and Stanke, Don E. *Hollywood Baby Boomers.* New York: Garland, 1992.

_____, and Taylor, Allan. *The Encyclopedia of Ethnic Groups in Hollywood.* New York: Facts on File, 2002.

Patrick, Diane. *Terry McMillan.* New York: Thomas Dunne/St. Martin's, 1999.

Romanowski, Patricia, and George-Warren, Holly (eds.). *The New Rolling Stone Encyclopedia of Rock & Roll.* New York: Fireside, 1995.

Rosen, Craig. *The Billboard Book of Number One Albums.* New York: Billboard, 1996.

Ruuth, Marianne. *Eddie.* Los Angeles: Holloway House, 1985.

Sanello, Frank. *Eddie Murphy: The Life and Times of a Comic on the Edge.* Secaucus, N.J.: Birch Lane, 1997.

Savage, Jeff. *Whitney Houston.* Parsippany, N.J.: Dillon, 1998.

Seal, Richard. *Whitney Houston: One Moment in Time.* London, U.K.: Britannia, 1994.

Shore, Michael. *Music Video: A Consumer Guide.* New York: Ballantine, 1987.

Speace, Geri. *Newsmakers: The People Behind Today's Headlines.* Detroit, Mich.: Gale Research, 1999.

Terrace, Vincent. *Television Specials: 3,201 Entertainment Spectaculars, 1939–1993.* Jefferson, N.C.: McFarland, 1995.

Wallner, Rosemary, *Whitney Houston: Singer, Actress, Superstar.* Edina, Minn.: Abdo & Daughters, 1994.

Westergaard, Barbara. *New Jersey: A Guide to the State* (2nd edn.). New Brunswick, N.J.: Rutgers University Press, 1998.

Whitburn, Joel. *The Billboard Book of Top 40 Hits.* New York: Billboard, 2000.

_____. *Billboard Top 1000 Singles: 1955–2000.* Milwaukee, Wisc.: Hal Leonard, 2001.

_____. *Top Adult Contemporary: 1961–2001.* New York: Billboard, 2002.

Publications

Among those used were:
Atlanta Journal Constitution, Billboard, Biography, BRE, Boston Globe, Boxoffice, Calgary Sun (Ontario, Canada), *Chicago Sun-Times, Chicago Tribune, Current Biography, Daily Variety, Detroit Free Press, Ebony, Empire, Entertainment Today, Entertainment Weekly, Essence, Film Threat, Globe, Good Housekeeping, Harper's Bazaar, Hollywood Reporter, In Style, Jane, Jet, L.A. Weekly, Las Vegas Review Journal, Los Angeles Daily News, Los Angeles Sentinel, Los Angeles Times, Minneapolis Star Tribune, Movie Collectors World, Movieline, National Enquirer, New York, New York Amsterdam News, New York Daily News, New York Observer, New York Post, New York Times, Newark Star-Ledger, News of the World, Newsday, Newsweek, Out, People, Playboy, Premiere, Q, Record* (Bergen County, N.J.), *Redbook, St. Louis Post-Dispatch, San Francisco Chronicle, San Francisco Examiner, Savoy, Sight & Sound, Sister 2 Sister, Star, Sun Reporter, Time, The Times* (U.K.), *Total Film, TV Guide, Us Weekly, USA Today, Vanity Fair, Washington Post, Weekly Journal, Windsor Star* (Canada), *You.*

Television

Among the television biographies, documentaries, news programs, and specials used were:
Access Hollywood (Syndicated), *Barbara Walters Specials* (ABC), *Driven* (VH1), *Entertainment Tonight* (Syndicated), *Extra: The Entertainment Magazine* (Syndicated), *Good Morning America* (ABC), *PrimeTime* (ABC), *Today* (NBC), *True Hollywood Story* (E! Entertainment Television), *Whitney Houston: The True Story* (Channel 4, U.K.).

Websites

Among the English-language websites used were:

All Music Guide	www.allmusic.com
AllWhitney.com	whfan.free.fr
Billboard magazine	www.billboard.com
Classic Whitney	www.classicwhitney.com
E! Entertainment TV Online	www.eonline.com
Electronic Library	www.elibrary.com
Inside of Whitney	www.inside-whitney.com
Internet Movie Database	www.pro.imdb.com
MTV	www.mtv.com
Nippy Online	www.nippyonline.com
People magazine	www.people.com
Rolling Stone magazine	www.rollingstone.com
VH1	www.vh1.com
Whitney – A Divine Voice	www.whitney-voice.com
Whitney & Bobby News	www.geocities.com/marie_eve_whbbfan/info.htm

Whitney Houston Platinum Club   www.whitneyhouston.com
Whitney Houston Worship Fan Page www.whitney-fan.com
Yahoo! News   news.yahoo.com

About the Author

JAMES ROBERT PARISH, a former entertainment reporter, publicist, and book series editor, is the author of many published major biographies and reference books on the entertainment industry, including *The Hollywood Book of Love, Hollywood Divas, Jet Li, Hollywood Bad Boys, The Encyclopedia of Ethnic Groups in Hollywood, The Hollywood Book of Death, Gus Van Sant, Jason Biggs, Whoopi Goldberg, Rosie O'Donnell's Story, The Unofficial "Murder, She Wrote" Casebook, Today's Black Hollywood, Let's Talk! America's Favorite TV Talk Show Hosts, The Great Cop Pictures, Ghosts and Angels in Hollywood Films, Black Action Pictures, Hollywood's Great Love Teams,* and *The RKO Gals.* Mr. Parish is frequently interviewed on cable and network TV for documentaries on the performing arts. The author lives in Studio City, California.

Index